MW00862274

In-Memory Analytics with Apache Arrow

Perform fast and efficient data analytics on both flat and hierarchical structured data

Matthew Topol

BIRMINGHAM—MUMBAI

In-Memory Analytics with Apache Arrow

Copyright © 2022 Packt Publishing

Publishing Product Manager: Devika Battike
Senior Editor: Tazeen Shaikh
Content Development Editor: Shreya Moharir
Technical Editor: Devanshi Ayare
Copy Editor: Safis Editing
Project Coordinator: Aparna Nair
Proofreader: Safis Editing
Indexer: Sejal Dsilva
Production Designer: Shyam Sundar Korumilli
Marketing Coordinator: Nivedita Singh

First published: June 2022

Production reference: 2230622

Published by Packt Publishing Ltd.
Livery Place
35 Livery Street
Birmingham
B3 2PB, UK.

ISBN 978-1-80107-103-1

www.packt.com

For Kat, Haley, and Juno, who managed to tolerate me the entire time I was writing this.

Also, for Logan, my most consistent fuzzy coding companion.

Foreword

Since launching as an open source project in 2016, Apache Arrow has rapidly become the de facto standard for interoperability and accelerated in-memory processing for tabular data. We have broadened support to a dozen programming languages while expanding substantially beyond the project's initial goal of defining a standardized columnar data format to create a true multilanguage developer toolbox for creating high-performance data applications.

While Arrow has helped greatly with improving interoperability and performance in heterogeneous systems (such as across programming languages or different kinds of execution engines), it is also increasingly being chosen as the foundation for building new data processing systems and databases. With Dremio as the first true "Arrow-native" system, we hope that many more production systems will become "Arrow-compatible" or "Arrow-native" over the coming years.

Part of Arrow's success and the rapid growth of its developer community comes from the passion and time investment of its early adopters and most prolific core contributors. Matt Topol has been a driving force in the Go libraries for Arrow, and with this new book, he has made a significant contribution to making the whole project a lot more accessible to newcomers. The book goes in depth into the details of how different pieces of Arrow work while highlighting the many different building blocks that could be employed by an Arrow user to accelerate or simplify their application.

As the first true "Arrow book" since the project's founding, I'm happy to see it written and recommend it to new users of Arrow as well as existing users who are looking to deepen their knowledge by learning from an expert like Matt.

– Wes McKinney

CTO and co-founder, Voltron Data

Co-creator and PMC for Apache Arrow

Acknowledgments

Writing a book has been a unique experience and wouldn't have happened without specific individuals. I want to thank the team at Packt that I've been working with, including Shreya, Tazeen, and Kirti; your patience and assistance have been amazing. Thanks so much for reaching out to me in the first place to write this book! I also want to acknowledge my various colleagues who, at various points, read and gave me feedback on early versions of chapters as I was just starting: Steve, Jen, Greg, Frankie, and William. Aside from being great co-workers, you're all also great friends and shared my excitement for writing a book.

A very special thanks goes out to my friends, Hope and Stan. I only decided to go for it and write this because of the encouragement from both of you. You both, at different points in writing, were excellent sounding boards to bounce ideas off of when it came to titles and the non-technical aspects, such as my bio. Thanks for being my family!

Thanks also go out to the product team at Dremio for reviewing this book and helping to flesh out some rough edges. You guys rock! Thank you for supporting this book!

Finally, thanks go to my parents. You both beamed with pride every time I gave you an update on the book's progress. I can't wait to see when you read this part, Dad! (Let's be honest, Mom's not going to read this book. Too technical!) Thanks for being there for me through everything, you two are the best.

Contributors

About the author

Matthew Topol is an Apache Arrow contributor and a principal software architect at FactSet Research Systems, Inc. Since joining FactSet in 2009, Matt has worked in both infrastructure and application development, led development teams, and architected large-scale distributed systems for processing analytics on financial data. In his spare time, Matt likes to bash his head against a keyboard, develop and run delightfully demented games of fantasy for his victims—er—friends, and share his knowledge with anyone interested enough to listen.

About the reviewers

An Apache Arrow and Dremio contributor, and co-founder of Bit Quill Technologies, **James Duong** has worked with databases for over 15 years, from query engines to protocols. He's worked with databases such as Dremio, SQL Server, Redshift, and Hive. At Simba Technologies, James built connectors for sources and architected the Simba engine SDK connector framework. Bit Quill Technologies builds backend software in the data and cloud space. Bit Quill has built a name for itself as a producer of high-quality software, a collaborative approach to design and development, and a love for good tech and happy people.

I would like to thank my wife and children for their ongoing support and encouragement to be active in the OSS community.

Jason Hughes is a Director of Product Management at Dremio, where he heads the tech advocacy team. He has held multiple roles previously at Dremio, including Senior Solution Architect and Tech lead for Solution Architects. Prior to Dremio, he spent time in multiple roles at Teradata, including the lead for Presto and Teradata QueryGrid for the Americas. Before this, he developed, deployed, and managed a custom CRM system for multiple auto dealerships, whereby looking at the challenges first-hand, he developed a passion for the capability of analytics. He is passionate about making people successful and self-sufficient. When he's not working, he's usually taking his dog to the dog park, playing hockey, or cooking (when he feels like it).

Table of Contents

3
Data Science with Apache Arrow

Section 2: Interoperability with Arrow: pandas, Parquet, Flight, and Datasets

4
Format and Memory Handling

5

Crossing the Language Barrier with the Arrow C Data API

6

Leveraging the Arrow Compute APIs

7

Using the Arrow Datasets API

8

Exploring Apache Arrow Flight RPC

Section 3: Real-World Examples, Use Cases, and Future Development

9

Powered by Apache Arrow

10

How to Leave Your Mark on Arrow

11

Future Development and Plans

Index

Other Books You May Enjoy

Preface

To quote a famous blue hedgehog, *Gotta Go Fast!* When it comes to data, speed is important. It doesn't matter if you're collecting or analyzing data or developing utilities for others to do so, performance and efficiency are going to be huge factors in your technology choices, not just in the efficiency of the software itself, but also in development time. You need the right tools and the right technology, or you're dead in the water.

The **Apache Arrow** ecosystem is developer-centric, and this book is no different. Get started with understanding what Arrow is and how it works, then learn how to utilize it in your projects. You'll find code examples, explanations, and diagrams here, all with the express purpose of helping you learn. You'll integrate your data sources with Python DataFrame libraries such as pandas or NumPy and utilize **Arrow Flight** to create efficient data services.

With real-world datasets, you'll learn how to leverage Apache Arrow with Apache Spark and other technologies. Apache Arrow's format is language-independent and organized so that analytical operations are performed extremely quickly on modern CPU and GPU hardware. Join the industry adoption of this open source data format and save yourself valuable development time creating high-performant, memory-efficient, analytical workflows.

This book has been a labor of love to share knowledge. I hope you learn a lot from it! I sure did when writing it.

Who this book is for

This book is for developers, data analysts, and data scientists looking to explore the capabilities of Apache Arrow from the ground up. This book will also be useful for any engineers who are working on building utilities for data analytics, query engines, or otherwise working with tabular data, regardless of the language they are programming in.

What this book covers

Chapter 1, Getting Started with Apache Arrow, introduces you to the basic concepts underpinning Apache Arrow. It introduces and explains the Arrow format and the data types it supports, along with how they are represented in memory. Afterward, you'll set up your development environment and run some simple code examples showing the basic operation of Arrow libraries.

Chapter 2, Working with Key Arrow Specifications, continues your introduction to Apache Arrow by explaining how to read both local and remote data files using different formats. You'll learn how to integrate Arrow with the Python pandas library and how to utilize the zero-copy aspects of Arrow to share memory for performance.

Chapter 3, Data Science with Apache Arrow, wraps up our initial overview by providing specific examples to enhance data science workflows. This will include practical examples of using Arrow with Apache Spark and Jupyter, along with using Arrow-formatted data to create a chart. This will be followed by a brief discussion on **Open Database Connectivity** (**ODBC**) and an end-to-end demonstration of ingesting Arrow-formatted data into an Elasticsearch index and then querying it.

Chapter 4, Format and Memory Handling, discusses the relationships between Apache Arrow and Parquet, Feather, Protocol Buffers, JSON, and CSV data, along with when and why to use these different formats. Following this, the Arrow IPC format is introduced and described, along with an explanation of using memory mapping to further improve performance.

Chapter 5, Crossing the Language Barrier with the Arrow C Data API, introduces the titular C Data API for efficiently passing Apache Arrow data between different language runtimes. This chapter will cover the struct definitions utilized for this interface along with describing use cases that make it beneficial.

Chapter 6, Leveraging the Arrow Compute APIs, describes how to utilize the Arrow Compute APIs in both C++ and Python. You'll learn when and why you should use the Compute APIs to perform analytics rather than implement something yourself.

Chapter 7, Using the Arrow Datasets API, demonstrates querying, filtering, and otherwise interacting with multi-file datasets that can potentially be across multiple sources. Partitioned datasets are also covered, along with utilizing the Arrow Compute API to perform streaming filtering and other operations on the data.

Chapter 8, Exploring Apache Arrow Flight RPC, examines the Flight RPC protocol and its benefits. You will be walked through building a simple Flight server and client in multiple languages to produce and consume tabular data.

Chapter 9, Powered By Apache Arrow, provides a few examples of current real-world usage of Arrow, such as Dremio and Spice.ai.

Chapter 10, How to Leave Your Mark on Arrow, provides a brief introduction to contributing to open source in general, but specifically, how to contribute to the Arrow project itself. You will be walked through finding starter issues and setting up your first pull request to make a contribution, and what to expect when doing so. To that end, this chapter also contains various instructions on locally building the Arrow C++, Python, and Go libraries to test your contribution.

Chapter 11, Future Development and Plans, wraps up the book by examining the features that are still in heavy development at the time of writing. FlightSQL, DataFusion, and Substrait are all briefly explained and covered here with what to look forward to and, potentially, contribute to. Finally, there are some parting words and a challenge from me to you.

To get the most out of this book

It is assumed that you have a basic understanding of writing code in at least one of C++, Python, or Go to benefit from and use the code snippets. You should know how to compile and run code in the desired language. Some familiarity with the basic concepts of data analysis will help you to get the most out of this book. Beyond this, concepts such as tabular data and installing software on your machine are assumed to be understood.

Software/hardware covered in the book	Operating system requirements
An internet-connected computer	
Git	Windows, macOS, or Linux
C++ compiler capable of C++11 or higher	Windows, macOS, or Linux
Python 3.7 or higher	Windows, macOS, or Linux
Conda (optional)	Windows, macOS, or Linux
vcpkg (optional)	Windows
MSYS2 (optional)	Windows
CMake 3.5 or higher	Windows, macOS, or Linux
make or ninja	macOS or Linux
Docker	Windows, macOS, or Linux
Go 1.16 or higher	Windows, macOS, or Linux

The sample data is in the book's GitHub repository. You'll need to use **Git Large File Storage** (**LFS**) or a browser to download the large data files. There are also a couple of large sample data files in a publicly accessible AWS S3 bucket. The book will provide a link to download the files when necessary. Code examples are provided in C++, Python, and Go.

If you are using the digital version of this book, we advise you to type the code yourself or access the code from the book's GitHub repository (a link is available in the next section). Doing so will help you avoid any potential errors related to the copying and pasting of code.

Take your time, enjoy, and experiment in all kinds of ways, and please, have fun with the exercises.

Download the example code files

You can download the example code files for this book from GitHub at `https://github.com/PacktPublishing/In-Memory-Analytics-with-Apache-Arrow-`. If there's an update to the code, it will be updated in the GitHub repository.

We also have other code bundles from our rich catalog of books and videos available at `https://github.com/PacktPublishing/`. Check them out!

Download the color images

We also provide a PDF file that has color images of the screenshots and diagrams used in this book. You can download it here: `https://static.packt-cdn.com/downloads/9781801071031_ColorImages.pdf`.

Conventions used

There are a number of text conventions used throughout this book.

`Code in text`: Indicates code words in text, database table names, folder names, filenames, file extensions, pathnames, dummy URLs, user input, and Twitter handles. Here is an example: "When we call `ListFlights`, it returns a stream that we can then use to retrieve each one of our `FlightInfo` objects."

A block of code is set as follows:

```
...
    // add these imports
    "fmt"
    "github.com/apache/arrow/go/v8/arrow/arrio"
...
```

When we wish to draw your attention to a particular part of a code block, the relevant lines or items are set in bold:

```
...
flights = list(client.list_flights(b'2009'))
data = client.do_get(flights[0].endpoints[0].ticket)
print(data.read_all())
```

Any command-line input or output is written as follows:

```
$ pip install pyodbc
```

Bold: Indicates a new term, an important word, or words that you see onscreen. For instance, words in menus or dialog boxes appear in **bold**. Here is an example: "After clicking the button, you'll have a window pop open; click the **Save** button in the bottom-right corner."

> **Tips or Important Notes**
> Appear like this.

Get in touch

Feedback from our readers is always welcome.

General feedback: If you have questions about any aspect of this book, email us at customercare@packtpub.com and mention the book title in the subject of your message.

Errata: Although we have taken every care to ensure the accuracy of our content, mistakes do happen. If you have found a mistake in this book, we would be grateful if you would report this to us. Please visit www.packtpub.com/support/errata and fill in the form.

Piracy: If you come across any illegal copies of our works in any form on the internet, we would be grateful if you would provide us with the location address or website name. Please contact us at copyright@packt.com with a link to the material.

If you are interested in becoming an author: If there is a topic that you have expertise in and you are interested in either writing or contributing to a book, please visit authors.packtpub.com.

Share Your Thoughts

Once you've read *In-Memory Analytics with Apache Arrow*, we'd love to hear your thoughts! Scan the QR code below to go straight to the Amazon review page for this book and share your feedback.

https://packt.link/r/1-801-07103-9

Your review is important to us and the tech community and will help us make sure we're delivering excellent quality content.

Section 1: Overview of What Arrow Is, its Capabilities, Benefits, and Goals

This section is an introduction to Apache Arrow as a format specification, the benefits it claims, and the goals it's trying to achieve, along with a high-level overview of basic use cases and examples.

This section comprises the following chapters:

- *Chapter 1, Getting Started with Apache Arrow*
- *Chapter 2, Working with Key Arrow Specifications*
- *Chapter 3, Data Science with Apache Arrow*

1
Getting Started with Apache Arrow

Regardless of whether you are a data scientist/engineer, a **machine learning** (**ML**) specialist, or a software engineer trying to build something to perform data analytics, you've probably heard or read about something called **Apache Arrow** and either looked for more information or wondered what it was. Hopefully, this book can serve as a springboard both in understanding what Apache Arrow is and isn't, and also as a reference book to be continuously utilized in order to supercharge your analytical capabilities.

For now, let's just start off by explaining what Apache Arrow is and what you will use it for. Following that, we will walk through the Arrow specifications, set up a development environment where you can play around with the Apache Arrow libraries, and walk through a few simple exercises to get a feel for how to use them.

In this chapter, we're going to cover the following topics:

- Understanding the Arrow format and specifications
- Why does Arrow use a columnar in-memory format?
- Learning the terminology and the physical memory layout
- Arrow format versioning and stability
- Setting up your shooting range

Technical requirements

For the portion of the chapter describing how to set up a development environment for working with the Arrow libraries, you'll need the following:

- Your preferred **Integrated Development Environment** (**IDE**): For example, VSCode, Sublime, Emacs, and Vim

- Plugins for your desired language (optional but highly recommended)

- Interpreter or toolchain for your desired language(s):

  - Python 3+: `pip` and `venv` and/or `pipenv`

  - Go 1.16+

  - C++ Compiler (capable of compiling C++11 or newer)

Understanding the Arrow format and specifications

According to the Apache Arrow documentation [1]:

> *Apache Arrow is a development platform for in-memory analytics.*
> *It contains a set of technologies that enable big data systems to process and*
> *move data fast. It specifies a standardized language-independent columnar*
> *memory format for flat and hierarchical data, organized for efficient*
> *analytic operations on modern hardware.*

Well, that's a lot of technical jargon! Let's start from the top. Apache Arrow (just *Arrow* for brevity) is an open source project from the Apache Software Foundation that is released under the Apache License, Version 2.0 [2]. It was co-created by Dremio and Wes McKinney, the creator of pandas, and first released in 2016. To simplify, Arrow is a collection of libraries and specifications that make it easy to build high-performance software utilities for processing and transporting large datasets. It consists of a collection of libraries related to in-memory data processing, including specifications for memory layouts and protocols for sharing and efficiently transporting data between systems and processes. When we're talking about *in-memory data processing*, we are talking exclusively about the processing of data in RAM and eliminating slow data accesses wherever possible to improve performance. This is where Arrow excels and provides libraries to support this with utilities for streaming and transportation in order to speed up data access.

When working with data, there are two primary situations to consider, and each has different needs: the **in-memory format** and the **on-disk format**. When data is stored on disk, the biggest concerns are the size of the data and the **input/output (I/O)** cost to read it into the main memory before you can operate on it. As a result, formats for data on disk tend to be focused much more on increasing I/O throughput, such as compressing the data to make it smaller and faster to read into memory. One example of this might be the Apache Parquet format, which is a columnar on-disk file format. Instead of being an on-disk format, Arrow's focus is the in-memory format case, which targets CPU efficiency as the goal, with numerous tactics such as cache locality and vectorization of computation.

The primary goal of Arrow is to essentially become the *lingua franca* of data analytics and processing, the *One Framework to Rule Them All*, so to speak. Different databases, programming languages, and libraries tend to implement and use their own separate internal formats for managing data, which means that any time you are moving data between these components for different uses, you're paying a cost to serialize and deserialize that data every time. Not only that, but lots of time and resources get spent reimplementing common algorithms and processing in those different data formats over and over. If instead, we can standardize on an efficient, feature-rich internal data format that can be widely adopted and used, this excess computation and development time is no longer necessary. *Figure 1.1* shows a simplified diagram of multiple systems, each with its own data format, having to be copied and/or converted in order for the different components to work with each other:

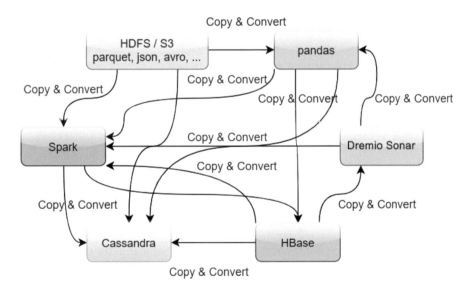

Figure 1.1 – Copy and convert components

In many cases, the serialization and deserialization can end up taking nearly 90% of the processing time in such a system rather than being able to spend that CPU on the analytics. Alternatively, if every component is using Arrow's in-memory format, you end up with a system as in *Figure 1.2*, where the data can be transferred between components at little-to-no cost. All of the components can either share memory directly or send the data *as-is* without having to convert between different formats.

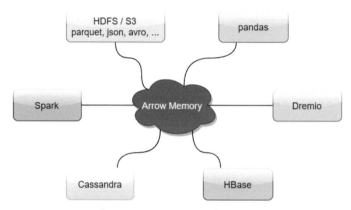

Figure 1.2 – Sharing Arrow memory between components

At this point, there's no need for the different components and systems to implement custom connectors or re-implement common algorithms and utilities. The same libraries and connectors can be utilized, even across programming languages and process barriers, by sharing memory directly to refer to the same data rather than copying multiple times between them.

Most data processing systems now use distributed processing by breaking the data up into chunks and sending those chunks across the network to various workers, so even if we can share memory across processes on a box, there's still the cost to send it across the network. This brings us to the final piece of the puzzle: the format of raw Arrow data on the wire is the same as it is in memory. You can directly reference the memory buffers used for the network protocols without having to deserialize that data before you can use it, or reference the memory buffers you were operating on to send it across the network without having to serialize it first. Just a bit of metadata sent along with the raw data buffers and interfaces that perform zero-copies can be created in order to achieve performance benefits, by reducing memory usage and improving CPU throughput.

Let's quickly recap the features of the Arrow format we were just describing before moving on:

- Using the same high-performance internal format across components allows much more code reuse in libraries instead of reimplementing common workflows.

- The Arrow libraries provide mechanisms to directly share memory buffers to reduce copying between processes by using the same internal representation regardless of the language. This is what is being referred to whenever you see the term **zero-copy**.

- The wire format is the same as the in-memory format to eliminate serialization and deserialization costs when sending data across networks between components of a system.

Now, you might be thinking *well this sounds too good to be true!* and of course, being skeptical of promises like this is always a good idea. The community around Arrow has done a ton of work over the years to bring these ideas and concepts to fruition. The project itself provides and distributes libraries in a variety of different programming languages so that projects that want to incorporate and/or support the Arrow format don't need to implement it themselves. Above and beyond the interaction with Arrow-formatted data, the libraries provide a significant amount of utility in assisting with common processes such as data access and I/O-related optimizations. As a result, the Arrow libraries can be useful for projects, even if they don't actually utilize the Arrow format themselves.

Here's just a quick sample of use cases where using Arrow as the internal/intermediate data format can be very beneficial:

- SQL execution engines (such as Dremio Sonar, Apache Drill, or Impala)

- Data analysis utilities and pipelines (such as pandas or Spark)

- Streaming and message queue systems (such as Apache Kafka or Storm)

- Storage systems and formats (such as Apache Parquet, Cassandra, and Kudu)

As for how Arrow can help you, it depends on which piece of the data puzzle you personally work with. The following are a few different roles that work with data and show how using Arrow could potentially be beneficial; it's by no means a complete list though:

- If you're a *data scientist*:

  - You can utilize Arrow via pandas and NumPy integration to significantly improve the performance of your data manipulations.

  - If the tools you use integrate Arrow support, you can gain significant speed-ups to your queries and computations by using Arrow directly yourself to reduce copies and/or serialization costs.

- If you are a *data engineer* specializing in **extract, transform, and load** (ETL):

  - The higher adoption of Arrow as an internal and externally-facing format can make it easier to integrate with many different utilities.

- By using Arrow, data can be shared between processes and tools with shared memory increasing the tools available to you for building pipelines, regardless of the language you're operating in. You could take data from Python and use it in Spark and then pass it directly to the **Java Virtual Machine** (**JVM**) without paying the cost of copying between them.

- If you are a *software engineer* or *ML specialist* building computation tools and utilities for data analysis:

  - Arrow as an internal format can be used to improve your memory usage and performance by reducing serialization and deserialization between components.

  - Understanding how to best utilize the data transfer protocols can improve the ability to parallelize queries and access your data, wherever it might be.

  - Because Arrow can be used for any sort of tabular data, it can be integrated into many different areas of data analysis and computation pipelines, and is versatile enough to be beneficial as an internal and data transfer format, regardless of the shape of your data.

Now that you know what Arrow is, let's dig into its design and how it delivers on the aforementioned promises of high-performance analytics, zero-copy sharing, and network communication without serialization costs. First, you'll see why a column-oriented memory representation was chosen for Arrow's internal format. Afterward, in later chapters, we'll cover specific integration points, explicit examples, and transfer protocols.

Why does Arrow use a columnar in-memory format?

Most traditional data processing of tabular data will have its own custom data structures for representing and managing those datasets in memory while processing them, such as query engines and data services, for example. Of course, if there are custom data structures, this means it requires developing custom serialization protocols between file formats, network protocols, libraries, and any other interface you could think of. I can vouch from experience that the result is a huge amount of developer time and CPU cycles being wasted dealing with these various serialization schemes, rather than being able to spend it all on the analytical workloads. One goal of the Arrow project is for fewer systems to have to create their own data structures and utilize Arrow as their internal format. Doing so would allow those components to expose Arrow directly as a wire format and benefit from not having to pay a serialization or deserialization cost to pass the data around.

There is often a lot of debate surrounding whether a database should be row-oriented or column-oriented, but this primarily refers to the on-disk format of the underlying storage files. Arrow's data format is different from most cases discussed so far since it uses a columnar organization of data structures in memory directly. If you're not familiar with **columnar** as a term, let's take a look at what exactly it means. First, imagine the following table of data:

	ARCHER	LOCATION	YEAR
ROW 1	Legolas	Mirkwood	1954
ROW 2	Oliver	Star City	1941
ROW 3	Merida	Scotland	2012
ROW 4	Lara	London	1996
ROW 5	Artemis	Greece	-600

Figure 1.3 – Sample data table

Traditionally, if you were to read this table into memory, you'd likely have some structure to represent a row and then read the data in one row at a time. Maybe something like `struct { string archer; string location; int year }`. The result is that you have the memory grouped closely together for each row, which is great if you always want to read all the columns for every row. But, if this were a much bigger table, and you just wanted to find out the minimum and maximum years or any other column-wise analytics such as the unique locations, you would have to read the whole table into memory and then jump around in memory, skipping the fields you didn't care about so that you could read the value for each row of one column.

Most operating systems, while reading data into main memory and CPU caches, will attempt to make predictions about what memory it is going to need next. In our example table of archers, consider how many memory pages of data would have to be accessible and traversed to get a list of unique locations if the data were organized in row or column orientations:

		Traditional Memory Buffer			Arrow Columnar Memory Buffer
Row 1	Legolas Mirkwood 1954		archer	Legolas Oliver Merida Lara Artemis	
Row 2	Oliver Star City 1941		location	Mirkwood Star City Scotland London Greece	
Row 3	Merida Scotland 2012		year	1954 1941 2012 1996 -600	
Row 4	Lara London 1996				
Row 5	Artemis Greece -600				

Figure 1.4 – Row versus columnar memory buffers

A columnar format keeps the data organized by column instead of by row, as shown in the preceding figure. As a result, operations such as grouping, filtering, or aggregations based on column values become much more efficient to perform since the entire column is already contiguous in memory. Considering memory pages again, it's plain to see that for a large table, there would be significantly more pages that need to be traversed to get a list of unique locations from a row-oriented buffer than a columnar one. Fewer page faults and more cache hits mean increased performance and a happier CPU. Computational routines and query engines tend to operate on subsets of the columns for a dataset rather than needing every column for a given computation, making it significantly more efficient to operate on columnar data.

If you look closely at the construction of the column-oriented data buffer on the right side of *Figure 1.4*, you can see how it benefits the queries I mentioned earlier. If we wanted all the archers that are in Europe, we can easily scan through *just the location column* and discover which rows are the ones we want, and then spin through *just the archer block* and grab only the rows that correspond to the row indexes we found. This will come into play again when we start looking at the physical memory layout of Arrow arrays; since the data is column-oriented, it makes it easier for the CPU to predict instructions to execute and maintains this *memory locality* between instructions.

By keeping the column data contiguous in memory, it enables vectorization of the computations. Most modern processors have **single instruction, multiple data (SIMD)** instructions available that can be taken advantage of for speeding up computations and require having the data in a contiguous block of memory to operate on it. This concept can be found heavily utilized by graphics cards, and in fact, Arrow provides libraries to take advantage of **Graphics Processing Units (GPUs)** precisely because of this. Consider the example where you might want to multiply every element of a list by a static value, such as performing a currency conversion on a column of prices with an exchange rate:

Figure 1.5   SIMD/vectorized versus non-vectorized

From the figure, you can see the following:

- The left side of the figure shows that an ordinary CPU performing the computation in a non-vectorized fashion requires loading each value into a register, multiplying it with the exchange rate, and then saving the result back into RAM.

- On the right side of the figure, we see that vectorized computation, such as using SIMD, performs the same operation on multiple different inputs at the same time, enabling a single load to multiply and save to get the result for the entire group of prices. Being able to vectorize a computation has various constraints; often, one of those constraints is requiring the data being operated on to be in a contiguous chunk of memory, which is why columnar data is much easier to do this with.

> **SIMD versus Multithreading**
>
> If you're not familiar with SIMD, you may wonder how it differs from another parallelization technique: multithreading. Multithreading operates at a higher conceptual level than SIMD. Each thread has its own set of registers and memory space representing its execution context. These contexts could be spread across separate CPU cores or possibly interleaved by a single CPU core switching whenever it needs to wait for I/O. SIMD is a processor-level concept that refers to the specific instructions being executed. Put simply, multithreading is multitasking and SIMD is doing less work to achieve the same result.

Another benefit of utilizing column-oriented data comes into play when considering compression techniques. At some point, your data will become large enough that sending it across the network could become a bottleneck, purely due to size and bandwidth. With the data being grouped together in columns that are all the same type as contiguous memory, we end up with significantly better compression ratios than we would get with the same data in a row-oriented configuration, simply because data of the same type is easier to compress together than data of different types.

Learning the terminology and physical memory layout

As mentioned before, the **Arrow columnar format** specification includes definitions of the in-memory data structures, metadata serialization, and protocols for data transportation. The format itself has a few key promises, as follows:

- Data adjacency for sequential access
- O(1) (constant time) random access
- SIMD and vectorization friendly
- Relocatable, allowing for zero-copy access in shared-memory

To ensure we're all on the same page, here's a quick glossary of terms that are used throughout the format specification and the rest of the book:

- **Array**: A list of values with a known length of the same type.
- **Slot**: The value in an array identified by a specific index.
- **Buffer/contiguous memory region**: A single contiguous block of memory with a given length.

- **Physical layout**: The underlying memory layout for an array without accounting for the interpretation of the logical value. For example, a 32-bit signed integer array and a 32-bit floating-point array are both laid out as contiguous chunks of memory where each value is made up of four contiguous bytes in the buffer.

- **Parent/child arrays**: Terms used for the relationship between physical arrays when describing the structure of a nested type. For example, a struct parent array has a child array for each of its fields.

- **Primitive type**: A type that has no child types and so consists of a single array, such as fixed-bit-width arrays (for example, `int32`) or variable-size types (for example, string arrays).

- **Nested type**: A type that depends on one or more other child types. Nested types are only equal if their child types are also equal (for example, `List<T>` and `List<U>` are equal if `T` and `U` are equal).

- **Logical type**: A particular type of interpreting the values in an array that is implemented using a specific physical layout. For example, the decimal logical type stores values as 16 bytes per value in a fixed-size binary layout. Similarly, a timestamp logical type stores values using a 64-bit fixed-size layout.

Now that we've got the fancy words out of the way, let's have a look at how we actually lay out these arrays in memory. An array or vector is defined by the following information:

- A logical data type (typically identified by an `enum` value and metadata)

- A group of buffers

- A length as a 64-bit signed integer

- A null count as a 64-bit signed integer

- Optionally, a dictionary for dictionary-encoded arrays (more on these later in the chapter)

To define a nested array type, there would additionally be one or more sets of this information that would then be the **child arrays**. Arrow defines a series of **logical types** and each one has a well-defined physical layout in the specification. For the most part, the physical layout just affects the sequence of buffers that make up the raw data. Since there is a null count in the metadata, it comes as a given that any value in an array may be considered to be null data rather than having a value, regardless of the type. Apart from the *union* data type, all the arrays have a validity bitmap as one of their buffers, which can optionally be left out if there are no nulls in the array. As might be expected, 1 in the corresponding bit means it is a valid value in that index, and 0 means it's null.

Quick summary of physical layouts, or TL;DR

When working with Arrow formatted data, it's important to understand how it is physically laid out in memory. Understanding the physical layouts can provide ideas for efficiently constructing (or deconstructing) Arrow data when developing applications. Here's a quick summary:

Layout Type	Buffer 0	Buffer 1	Buffer 2	Children
Primitive	Bitmap	Data		No
Variable Binary	Bitmap	Offsets	Data	No
List	Bitmap	Offsets		1
Fixed-Size List	Bitmap			1
Struct	Bitmap			1 per field
Sparse Union	Type IDs			1 per type
Dense Union	Type IDs	Offsets		1 per type
Null				No
Dictionary Encoded	Bitmap	Data (Indices)		Dictionary (not considered a child)

Figure 1.6 – Table of physical layouts

The following is a walkthrough of the physical memory layouts that are used by the Arrow format. This is primarily useful for either implementing the Arrow specification yourself (or contributing to the libraries) or if you simply want to know what's going on under the hood and how it all works.

Primitive fixed-length value arrays

Let's look at an example of a 32-bit integer array that looks like this: [1, null, 2, 4, 8]. What would the physical layout look like in memory based on the information so far (*Figure 1.7*)? Something to keep in mind is that all of the buffers should be padded to a multiple of 64 bytes for alignment, which matches the largest SIMD instructions available on widely deployed x86 architecture processors (Intel AVX-512), and that the values for null slots are marked *UNF* or *undefined*. Implementations are free to zero out the data in null slots if they desire, and many do. But, since the format specification does not define anything, the data in a null slot could technically be anything.

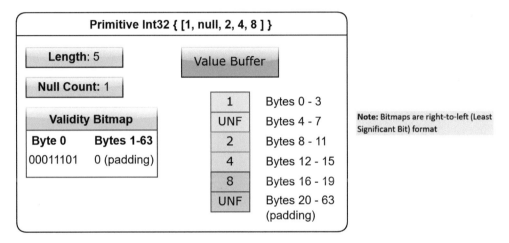

Figure 1.7 – Layout of primitive int32 array

This same conceptual layout is the case for any fixed-size primitive type, with the only exception being that the validity buffer can be left out entirely if there are no nulls in the array. For any data type that is physically represented as simple fixed-bit-width values, such as integers, floating-point values, fixed-size binary arrays, or even timestamps, it will use this layout in memory. The padding for the buffers in the subsequent diagrams will be left out just to avoid cluttering them.

Variable-length binary arrays

Things get slightly trickier when dealing with variable-length value arrays, generally used for variable size binary or string data. In this layout, every value can consist of 0 or more bytes and, in addition to the data buffer, there will also be an **offsets** buffer. Using an offsets buffer allows the entirety of the data of the array to be held in a single contiguous memory buffer. The only lookup cost for finding the value of a given index is to look up the indexes in the offsets buffer to find the correct slice of the data. The offsets buffer will always contain `length + 1` signed integers (either 32-bit or 64-bit, based on the logical type being used) that indicate the starting position of each corresponding slot of the array. Consider the array of two strings: `[ "Water", "Rising" ]`.

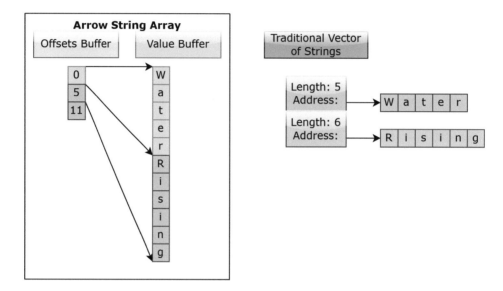

Figure 1.8 – Arrow string versus traditional string vector

This differs from a lot of standard ways of representing a list of strings in memory in most library models. Generally, a string is represented as a pointer to a memory location and an integer for the length, so a vector of strings is really a vector of these pointers and lengths (*Figure 1.8*). For many use cases, this is very efficient since, typically, a single memory address is going to be much smaller than the size of the string data, so passing around this address and length is efficient for referencing individual strings.

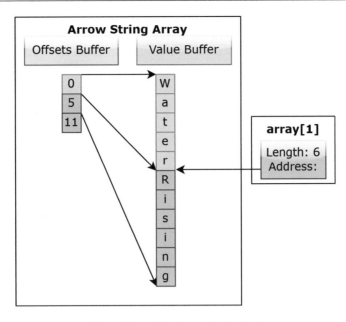

Figure 1.9 – Viewing string index 1

If your goal is operating on a large number of strings though, it's much more efficient to have a single buffer to scan through in memory. As you operate on each string, you can maintain the **memory locality** we mentioned before, keeping the memory we need to look at physically close to the next chunk of memory we're likely going to need. This way, we spend less time jumping around different pages of memory and can spend more CPU cycles performing the computations. It's also extremely efficient to get a single string, as you can simply take a view of the buffer by using the address indicated by the offset to create a string object without copying the data.

List and fixed-size list arrays

What about nested formats? Well, they work in a similar way to the variable-length binary format. First up is the **variable-size list** layout. It's defined by two buffers, a validity bitmap and an offsets buffer, along with a child array. The difference between this and the variable-length binary format is that instead of the offsets referencing a buffer, they are instead indexes into the child array (which could itself potentially be a nested type). The common denotation of list types is to specify them as List<T>, where T is any type at all. When using 64-bit offsets instead of 32-bit, it is denoted as LargeList<T>. Let's represent the following List<Int8> array: [[12, -7, 25], null, [0, -127, 127, 50], []].

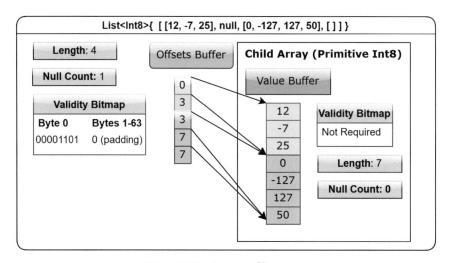

Figure 1.10 – Layout of list array

The first thing to notice in the preceding diagram is that the offsets buffer has exactly one more element than the List array it belongs to since there are *four* elements to our List<Int8> array and we have *five* elements in the offsets buffer. Each value in the offsets buffer represents the starting slot of the corresponding list index *i*. Looking closer at the offsets buffer, we notice that 3 and 7 are repeating, indicating that those lists are either null or empty (have a length of 0). To discover the length of a list at a given slot, you simply take the difference between the offset for that slot and the offset after it: $offsets[i + 1] - offset[i] = len(list[i])$, and the same holds true for the previous variable-length binary format; the number of bytes for a given slot is the difference in the offsets. Knowing this, what is the length of the list at index *2* of *Figure 1.10*? $offsets[3] - offsets[2] = 7 - 3 = 4$ (*remember, 0-based indexes!*). With this, we can tell that the list at index *3* is empty because the bitmap has a 1, but the length is 0 (*7 – 7*). This also explains why we need that extra element in the offsets buffer! We need it to be able to calculate the length of the last element in the array.

Given that example, what would a `List<List<Int8>>` array look like? I'll leave that as an exercise for you to figure out.

There's also a `FixedSizeList<T>[N]` type, which works nearly the same as the variable-sized list, except there's no need for an offsets buffer. The child array of a fixed-size list type is the values array, complete with its own validity buffer. The value in slot j of a fixed-size list array is stored in an N-long slice of the values array, starting at offset $j * N$. *Figure 1.11* shows what this looks like:

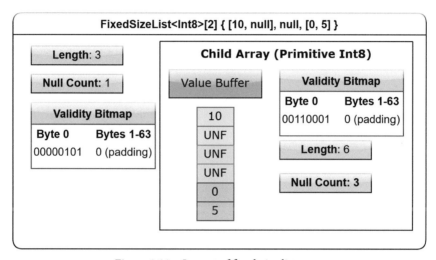

Figure 1.11 – Layout of fixed-size list array

What's the benefit of `FixedSizeList` versus `List`? Look back at the two diagrams again! Determining the values for a given slot of `FixedSizeList` doesn't require any lookups into a separate offsets buffer, making it more efficient if you know that your lists will always be a specific size. As a result, you also save space by not needing the extra memory for an offsets buffer at all!

> **Important Note**
>
> One thing to keep in mind is the semantic difference between a `null` value and an empty list. Using JSON notation, the difference is equivalent to the difference between `null` and `[]`. The meaning of such a difference would be up to a particular application to decide, but it's important to note that a `null` list is not identical to an empty list, even though the only difference in the physical representation is the bit in the validity bitmap.

Phew! That was a lot. We're almost done!

Struct arrays

The next type on our tour of the Arrow format is the **struct** type's layout. A struct is a nested type that has an *ordered* sequence of fields that can all have their own distinct types. It's semantically very similar to a simple object with attributes that you might find in a variety of programming languages. Each field must have its own UTF-8 encoded name, and these field names are part of the metadata for defining a struct type. Instead of having any physical storage allocated for its values, a struct array has one child array for each of its fields. All of these children arrays are independent and don't need to be adjacent to each other in memory; remember our goal is column- (or field-) oriented, not row-oriented. A struct array must, however, have a validity bitmap if it contains one or more `null` struct values. It can still contain a validity bitmap if there are no `null` values, it's just optional in that case.

Let's use the example of a struct with the following structure: `Struct<name: VarBinary, age: Int32>`. An array of this type would have two child arrays, one `VarBinary` array (a variable-sized binary layout), and one 4-byte primitive value array having a logical type of `Int32`. With this definition, we can map out a representation of the array: `[{"joe", 1}, {null, 2}, null, {"mark", 4}]`.

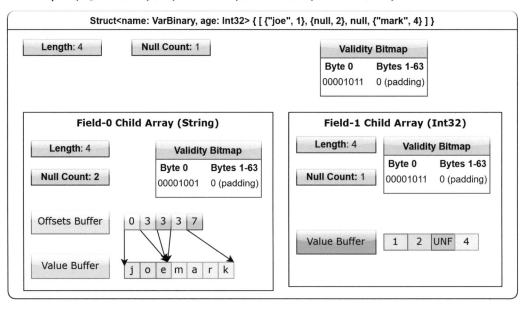

Figure 1.12 – Layout of struct array

When an entire slot of the struct array is set to null, the null is represented in the parent's validity bitmap, which is different from a particular value in a child array being null. In *Figure 1.12*, the child arrays each have a slot for the null struct in which they could have any value at all, but would be *hidden* by the struct array's validity bitmap marking the corresponding struct slot as null and taking priority over the children.

Union arrays – sparse and dense

For the case when a single column could have multiple types, there exists the `Union` type array. Whereas the struct array is an ordered sequence of fields, a union type is an ordered sequence of *types*. The value in each slot of the array could be of any of these types, which are named like struct fields and included in the metadata of the type. Unlike other layouts, the union type *does not have its own validity bitmap*. Instead, each slot's validity is determined by the children, which are composed to create the union array itself. There are two distinct union layouts that can be used when creating an array: **dense** and **sparse**, each optimized for a different use case.

A *dense* union represents a mixed-type array with 5 bytes of overhead for each value, and contains the following structures:

- One child array for each type
- A *types* buffer: A buffer of 8-bit signed integers, with each value representing the type ID for the corresponding slot, indicating which child vector to read from for that slot
- An *offsets* buffer: A buffer of signed 32-bit integers, indicating the offset into the corresponding child's array for the type in each slot

The dense union allows for the common use case of a union of structs with non-overlapping fields: Union<s1: Struct1, s2: Struct2, s3: Struct3......>. Here's an example of the layout for a union of type Union<f: float, i: int32> with the values [{f=1.2}, null, {f=3.4}, {i=5}]:

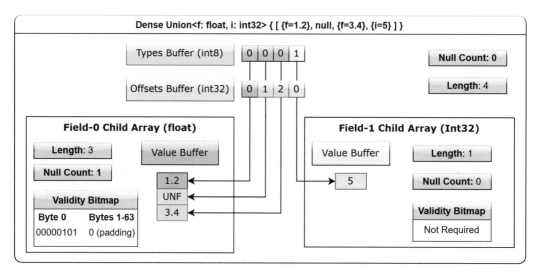

Figure 1.13 – Layout of dense union array

A *sparse* union has the same structure as the dense, except without an offsets array, as each child array is equal in length to the union itself. *Figure 1.14* shows the same union array from *Figure 1.13* as a sparse union array. There's no offsets buffer; both children are the same length of 4 as opposed to being different lengths:

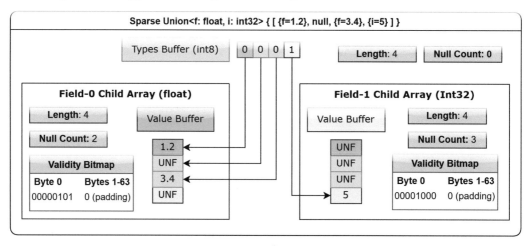

Figure 1.14 – Layout of sparse union array

Even though a sparse union takes up significantly more space compared to a dense union, it has some advantages for specific use cases. In particular, a sparse union is much more easily used with vectorized expression evaluation in many cases, and a group of equal length arrays can be interpreted as a union by only having to define the types buffer. When interpreting a sparse union, only the slot in a child indicated by the types array is considered; the rest of the *unselected* values are ignored and could be anything.

Dictionary-encoded arrays

Next, we arrive at the layout for dictionary-encoded arrays. If you have data that has many repeated values, then significant space can potentially be saved by using dictionary encoding to represent the data values as integers referencing indexes into a dictionary that usually consists of unique values. Since a dictionary is an optional property on any array, any array can be dictionary-encoded. The layout of a dictionary-encoded array is that of a primitive integer array of non-negative integers, which each represent the index in the dictionary. The dictionary itself is a separate array with its own respective layout of the appropriate type.

For example, let's say you have the following array: ["foo", "bar", "foo", "bar", null, "baz"]. Without dictionary encoding, we'd have an array that looks like this:

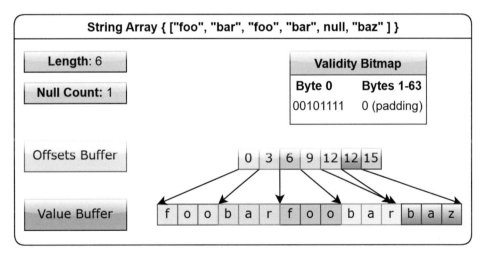

Figure 1.15 – String array without dictionary encoding

If we add dictionary encoding, we just need to get the unique values and create an array of indexes that references a dictionary array. The common case is to use int32, but any integral type would work:

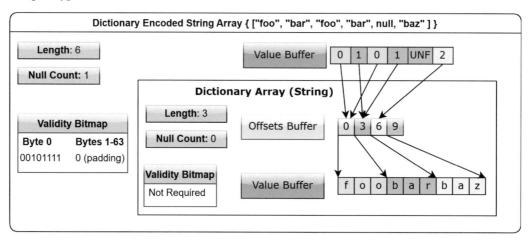

Figure 1.16 – Dictionary-encoded string array

For this trivial example, it's not particularly enticing, but it's very clear how, in the case of an array with a lot of repeated values, this could be a significant memory usage improvement. You can even perform operations directly on a dictionary array, updating the dictionary if needed or even swapping out the dictionary and replacing it.

As written in the specification, a dictionary is allowed to contain duplicates and even null values. However, the null count of a dictionary-encoded array is dictated by the validity bitmap of the indices, regardless of any nulls that might be in the dictionary itself.

Null arrays

Finally, there is only one more layout, but it's simple: a **null** array. A null array is an optimized layout for an array of all null values, with the type set to null; the only thing it contains is a length, no validity bitmap, and no data buffer.

How to speak Arrow

We've mentioned a few of the logical types already when describing the physical layouts, but let's get a full description of the current available logical types, as of Arrow release version 7.0.0, for your reading pleasure. In general, the logical types are what is referred to as the *data type* of an array in the libraries rather than the physical layouts. These types are what you will generally see when working with Arrow arrays in code:

- `Null` logical type: Null physical type
- `Boolean`: Primitive array with data represented as a bitmap
- **Primitive integer types**: Primitive, fixed-size array layout:
  - `Int8`, `Uint8`, `Int16`, `Uint16`, `Int32`, `Uint32`, `Int64`, and `Uint64`
- **Floating-point types**: Primitive fixed-size array layout:
  - `Float16`, `Float32` (float), and `Float64` (double)
- **VarBinary types**: Variable length binary physical layout:
  - `Binary` and `String` (UTF-8)
  - `LargeBinary` and `LargeString` (variable length binary with 64-bit offsets)
- `Decimal128` and `Decimal256`: 128-bit and 256-bit fixed-size primitive arrays with metadata to specify the precision and scale of the values
- **Fixed-size binary**: Fixed-size binary physical layout
- **Temporal types**: Primitive fixed-size array physical layout
  - **Date types**: Dates with no time information:
    - `Date32`: 32-bit integers representing the number of days since the Unix epoch (1970-01-01)
    - `Date64`: 64-bit integers representing milliseconds since the Unix epoch (1970-01-01)

- **Time types**: Time information with no date attached:

  - `Time32`: 32-bit integers representing elapsed time since midnight as seconds or milliseconds. A unit specified by metadata.

  - `Time64`: 64-bit integers representing elapsed time since midnight as microseconds or nanoseconds. A unit specified by metadata.

- `Timestamp`: 64-bit integer representing the time since the Unix epoch, not including leap seconds. Metadata defines the unit (seconds, milliseconds, microseconds, or nanoseconds) and, optionally, a time zone as a string.

- **Interval types**: An absolute length of time in terms of calendar artifacts:

  - `YearMonth`: Number of elapsed whole months as a 32-bit signed integer.

  - `DayTime`: Number of elapsed days and milliseconds as two consecutive 4-byte signed integers (8-bytes total per value).

  - `MonthDayNano`: Elapsed months, days, and nanoseconds stored as contiguous 16-byte blocks. Months and days as two 32-bit integers and nanoseconds since midnight as a 64-bit integer.

  - `Duration`: An absolute length of time not related to calendars as a 64-bit integer and a unit specified by metadata indicating seconds, milliseconds, microseconds, or nanoseconds.

- `List` and `FixedSizeList`: Their respective physical layouts:

- `LargeList`: A list type with 64-bit offsets

- `Struct`, `DenseUnion`, and `SparseUnion` types: Their respective physical layouts

- `Map`: A logical type that is physically represented as `List<entries: Struct<key: K, value: V>>`, where K and V are the respective types of the keys and values in the map:

- Metadata is included indicating whether or not the keys are sorted.

Whenever speaking about the types of an array from an application or semantic standpoint, we will always be using the types indicated in the preceding list to describe them. As you can see, the logical types make it very easy to represent both flat and hierarchical types of data. Now that we've covered the physical memory layouts, let's have a quick word about the versioning and stability of the Arrow format and libraries.

Arrow format versioning and stability

In order to ensure confidence that updating the version of the Arrow library in use won't break applications and the long-term stability of the Arrow project, there are *two versions* used to describe each release of the project: The **format version** and the **library version**. Different library implementations and releases can have different versions, but will always be implementing a specific format version. From version 1.0.0 onward, **semantic versioning** is used with releases.

Provided the *major version* of the format is the same between two libraries, any new library is backward-compatible with any older library with regards to being able to read data and metadata produced by an older library. Increases in the *minor version* of the format, such as an increase from version 1.0.0 to version 1.1.0, indicate new features that were added. As long as these new features are not used (such as new logical types or physical layouts), older libraries will be able to read data and metadata produced by newer versions of the libraries.

As far as the long-term stability of the format and libraries, only increases in the major version of the format would indicate any issue with the previous guarantees about compatibility. The Arrow project says that they *do not expect this to be a frequent occurrence*, rather it would be an exceptional event, in which case such a release would exercise caution for deployment. As a result of these compatibility guarantees, it ends up being safe and simple to ensure backward and forward compatibility when using the Arrow libraries and format.

Would you download a library? Of course!

As mentioned before, the Arrow project contains a variety of libraries for multiple programming languages. These official libraries enable anyone to work with Arrow data without having to implement the Arrow format themselves, regardless of the platform and programming language they are utilizing. There are two primary types of libraries that exist so far: ones that are distinct implementations of the Arrow specification, and ones that are built on other implementations. As of the time of writing this book, there are currently implementations for Arrow in C++ [3], C# [4], Go [5], Java [6], JavaScript [7], Julia [8], and Rust [9], which are all distinct implementations.

On top of those, there are libraries for C (Glib) [10], MATLAB [11], Python [12], R [13], and Ruby[14], which are all built on top of the C++ library, which happens to have the most active development. As you might expect, the various implementations all have different stages as far as what features and aspects of the specification are implemented, and the documentation helpfully provides an implementation matrix showing what features are implemented in which libraries. The implementation matrix [15] is then updated as these aspects of the specification and features are implemented in a given library.

With so many different implementations, you might be concerned about interoperability between them. As a result, the various library versions are integration tested via automated **continuous integration** (**CI**) jobs in order to ensure this interoperability among them. Depending on the language and development, these libraries are tested on a very large variety of platforms, including but not limited to the following:

- x86/x86-64

- arm64

- s390x (IBM Mainframes)

- macOS

- Windows 32 and 64 bit

- Debian/Ubuntu/Red Hat/CentOS

These libraries are deployed with their various respective package managing methods to attempt to make it as easy as possible to acquire and download the libraries. As a result, there's been significant adoption of Arrow, whether you're a data scientist using pandas, numpy, or Dask, or you're performing calculations and analytics using Apache Spark or AirFlow. And, if you're looking to get the libraries so you can try them out for yourself, the Apache Software Foundation hosts various ways to download and acquire the libraries.

Some of the channels where the libraries are made available are as follows:

- Conda (https://conda-forge.github.io/) for Linux, Windows, and macOS

- Homebrew (https://brew.sh/) for macOS

- MSYS2 for cross-platform Windows development

- vcpkg (`https://github.com/Microsoft/vcpkg`) for MSVC++

- R packages on CRAN (`https://cran.r-project.org/`)

- Julia packages in the general registry (`https://github.com/JuliaRegistries/General`)

- Ruby packages with RubyGems (`https://rubygems.org/`)

- C# packages with NuGet (`https://www.nuget.org/packages/Apache.Arrow/`)

- APT and Yum repositories for various Debian, Ubuntu, Red Hat, and CentOS distributions

- Java Artifacts on Maven Central

- Pip wheels for Python

When developing something that will utilize the Arrow libraries, keep the terms that were mentioned a few pages ago in mind, as most of the libraries utilize similar terminology and naming for describing their **Application Programming Interfaces** (**APIs**).

Setting up your shooting range

By now, you should have a pretty solid understanding of what Arrow is, the basics of how it's laid out in memory, and the basic terminology. So now, let's set up a development environment where you can test out and play with Arrow. For the purposes of this book, I'm going to primarily focus on the three libraries that I'm most familiar with: the C++ library, the Python library, and the Go library. While the basic concepts will apply to all of the implementations, the precise APIs may differ between them so, armed with the knowledge gained so far, you should be able to make sense of the documentation for your preferred language, even without precise examples for that language being printed here.

For each of C++, Python, and Go, after the instructions for installing the Arrow library, I'll go through a few exercises to get you acquainted with the basics of using the Arrow library in that language.

Using pyarrow For Python

With *data science* being a primary target of Arrow, it's no surprise that the Python library tends to be the most commonly used and interacted with by developers. Let's start with a quick introduction to setting up and using the **pyarrow** library for development.

Most modern IDEs provide plugins with exceptional Python support so you can fire up your preferred Python development IDE. I highly recommend using one of the methods for creating virtual environments with Python, such as pipenv, venv, or virtualenv, for setting up your environment. After creating that virtual environment, in most cases, installing pyarrow is as simple as using pip to install it:

```
$ pipenv install pyarrow # this or
$ python3 -m venv arrow_playground && pip3 install pyarrow #
this
```

It's also possible that, depending on your settings and platform, pip may attempt to build pyarrow locally. You can use the --prefer-binary or --only-binary arguments to tell pip to install the pre-build binary package rather than build from source:

```
$ pip3 install pyarrow --only-binary pyarrow
```

Alternately to using pip, Conda [16] is a common toolset utilized by data scientists and engineers, and the Arrow project provides binary Conda packages on conda-forge [17] for Linux, macOS, and Windows for Python 3.6+. You can install it with Conda and conda-forge as follows:

```
$ conda install pyarrow=6.0.* -c conda-forge
```

Understanding the basics of pyarrow

With the package installed, first let's confirm that the package installed successfully by opening up the Python interpreter and trying to import the package:

```
>>> import pyarrow as pa
>>> arr = pa.array([1,2,3,4])
>>> arr
<pyarrow.lib.Int64Array object at 0x0000019C4EC153A8>
```

```
[
    1,
    2,
    3,
    4
]
```

The important piece here to note is the highlighted lines where we import the library and create a simple array, letting the library determine the type for us, which it decides on using Int64 as the logical type.

Now that we've got a working installation of the pyarrow library, we can create a small example script to generate some random data and create a **record batch**:

```
import pyarrow as pa
import numpy as np
NROWS = 8192
NCOLS = 16
data = [pa.array(np.random.randn(NROWS)) for i in range(NCOLS)]
cols = ['c' + str(i) for i in range(NCOLS)]
rb = pa.RecordBatch.from_arrays(data, cols)
print(rb.schema)
print(rb.num_rows)
```

Going through this trivial example, this is what happens:

1. First, the numpy library is used to generate a bunch of data to use for our arrays. Calling pa.array(values), where values is a list of values for the array, will construct an array with the library inferring the logical type to use.

2. Next, a list of strings in the style of 'c0', 'c1', 'c2'... is created as names for the columns.

3. Finally, the highlighted line is where we construct a record batch from this random data, and then the subsequent two lines print out the schema and the number of rows.

We have got a new term here, *record batch*! A record batch is a common concept used when interacting with Arrow that we'll see show up in many places and refers to a group of equal length arrays and a schema. Often, a record batch will be a subset of rows of a larger dataset with the same schema. Record batches are a useful unit of parallelization for operating on data, as we'll see more in-depth in later chapters. That said, a record batch is actually very similar to a struct array when you think about it. Each field in a struct array can correspond to a column of the record batch. Let's use our archer example from earlier:

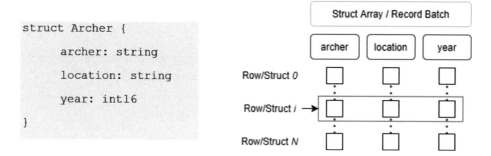

Figure 1.17 – Archer struct array

Since we're talking about a struct array, it will use the struct physical layout: an array with one child array for each field of our struct. This means that to refer to the entire struct at index *i*, you simply get the value at index *i* from each of the child arrays in the same way that if you were looking at a record batch; you do the same thing to get the semantic row at index *i* (*Figure 1.17*).

When constructing such an array, there are a couple of ways to think about how it would look in code. You could build up your struct array by building all three children simultaneously in a row-based fashion, or you could build up the individual child arrays completely separately and then just semantically group them together as a struct array with the column names. This shows another benefit of using columnar-based in-memory handling of this type of structure: each column could potentially be built in parallel and then brought back together at the end without the need for any extraneous copies. Parallelizing in a row-oriented fashion would typically be done by grouping batches of these records together and operating on the batches in parallel, which can still be done with the column-oriented approach, providing extra avenues of parallelization that wouldn't have existed in a row-oriented solution.

Building a struct array

The following steps describe how to construct a struct array from your data using a Python dictionary, but the data itself could come from anywhere, such as a JSON or CSV file:

1. First, let's create a dictionary of our archers from previously to represent our data:

    ```
    archer_list = [{
         'archer': 'Legolas',
         'location': 'Mirkwood',
         'year': 1954,
    }, {
         'archer': 'Oliver',
         'location': 'Star City',
         'year': 1941,
    }, ......]
    ```

    The rest of the values in this list are just the values from all the way back in *Figure 1.3*!

2. Then, we define a data type for our struct array:

    ```
    archer_type = pa.struct([('archer', pa.utf8()),
                             ('location', pa.utf8()),
                             ('year', pa.int16())])
    ```

3. Now, we can construct the struct array itself:

    ```
    archers = pa.array(archer_list, type=archer_type)
    print(archers.type)
    print(archers)
    ```

Data Types

See the usage of pa.utf8() and pa.int16()? These usages are creating data type instances with the data types API. Specifying a list would be pa.list_(t1), where t1 is some other type, just as we're doing here with pa.struct; check the documentation [18] for the full listing.

The output is as follows (assuming you pulled the data from *Figure 1.3* as I said):

```
struct<archer: string, location: string, year: int16>
-- is_valid: all not null
-- child 0 type: string
  [
    "Legolas",
    "Oliver",
    "Merida",
    "Lara",
    "Artemis"
  ]
-- child 1 type: string
  [
    "Mirkwood",
    "Star City",
    "Scotland",
    "London",
    "Greece"
  ]
-- child 2 type: int16
  [
    1954,
    1941,
    2012,
    1996,
    -600
  ]
```

Do you recognize the similarity between the printed struct data and our earlier example of columnar data?

Using record batches and zero-copy manipulation

Often, after ingesting some data, there is still a need to further clean or reorganize it before running whatever processing or analytics you need to do. Being able to rearrange and move around the structure of your data like this with Arrow without having to make copies also results in some significant performance improvements over other approaches. To exemplify how we can optimize memory usage when utilizing Arrow, we can take the arrays from the struct array we created and easily flatten them into a record batch without any copies being made. Let's take the struct array of archers and flatten it into a record batch:

```python
# archers is the struct array created earlier, flatten()
returns
# the fields of the struct array as a python list of array
objects
# remember 'pa' is from import pyarrow as pa
rb = pa.RecordBatch.from_arrays(archers.flatten(),
                                ['archer', 'location', 'year'])
print(rb)
print(rb.num_rows) # prints 5
print(rb.num_columns) # prints 3
```

Since our struct array was 3 fields and had a length of 5, our record batch will have five rows and three columns. Record batches require having a **schema** defined, which is similar to defining a struct type; it's a list of fields, each with a name, a logical type, and metadata. The highlighted print statement in the preceding code to print out the record batch will just print the schema of the record batch:

```
pyarrow.RecordBatch
archer: string
location: string
year: int16
```

The record batch we created holds references to the exact same arrays we created for the struct array, not copies, which makes this a very efficient operation, even for very large data sets. Cleaning, restructuring, and manipulating raw data into a more understandable or easier to work with format is a common task for data scientists and engineers. One of the strengths of using Arrow is that this can be done efficiently and without making copies of the data.

Another common situation when working with data is when you only need a particular slice of your dataset to work on, rather than the entire thing. As before, the library provides a `slice` function for slicing record batches or arrays without copying memory. Think back to the structure of the arrays; because any array has a length, null count, and sequence of buffers, the buffers that are used for a given array can be slices of the buffers from a larger array. This allows working with subsets of data without having to copy it around.

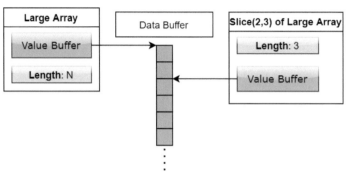

Figure 1.18 – Making a slice

A slice of a record batch is just slicing each of the constituent arrays which make it up; the same goes for any array of a nested type. Using our previous example, we use the following:

```
slice = rb.slice(1,3) # (start, length)
print(slice.num_rows) # prints 3 not 5
print(rb.column(0)[0]) # <pyarrow.StringScalar: 'Legolas'>
print(slice.column(0)[0]) # <pyarrow.StringScalar: 'Oliver'>
```

There's also a shortcut syntax for slicing an array, which should be comfortable for Python developers since it matches the same syntax for slicing a Python list:

```
archerslice = archers[1:3] # slice of length 2 viewing indexes
1
# and 2 from the struct array, so it slices all three arrays
```

One thing that *does* make a copy though is to convert Arrow arrays back to native Python objects for use with any other Python code that isn't using Arrow. Just like I mentioned back at the beginning of this chapter, shifting between different formats instead of the libraries all using the same one has costs to copy and convert the data:

```
print(rb.to_pydict()) # prints dictionary {column:
list<values>}
```

```
print(archers.to_pylist()) # prints the same list of
                              dictionaries
                         # we started with
```

Both of the preceding calls, to_pylist and to_pydict, perform copies of the data in order to put them into native Python object formats and should be used sparingly with large datasets.

Handling none values

The last thing to mention is the handling of null values. The None Python object is always converted to an Arrow null element when converting to an array, and vice versa when converting back to native Python objects.

An exercise for you

To get a feel for what real usage of the library might look like, here's an exercise to try out. You can find the solution along with the full code for any examples in the book in a GitHub repository located at https://github.com/PacktPublishing/In-Memory-Analytics-with-Apache-Arrow-:

- Take a (row-wise) list of objects with the following structure and convert them to a column-oriented record batch:

    ```
    { id: int, cost: double, cost_components: list<double> }
    ```

    An example might be { "id": 4, "cost": 241.21, "cost_components": [100.00, 140.10, 1.11] } for a single object.

- Now that you've converted the row-based data in the list to a column-oriented Arrow record batch, do the reverse and convert the record batch back into the row-oriented list representation.

Now, let's take a look at the C++ library.

C++ for the 1337 coders

Due to the nature of C++, the setup potentially isn't as straightforward as Python or Go. There are a few different routes you can use to install the development headers and libraries, along with the necessary dependencies depending on your desired platform.

Technical requirements for using C++

Before we can develop, you need to first install the Arrow library on your system. The process is obviously going to differ based on the operating system you're using:

- If you are using Windows, you will need one of the following, along with either Visual Studio, C++, or **Mingw gcc/g++** as your compiler:

  - Conda: Replace 7.0.0 with the version you wish to install:

    ```
    conda install arrow-cpp=7.0.0 -c conda-forge
    ```

  - MSYS2 [19]: After installing MSYS2, you can use pacman to install the libraries:

    - For 64-bit:

      ```
      pacman -S --noconfirm mingw-w64-x86_64-arrow
      ```

    - For 32-bit:

      ```
      pacman -S --noconfirm mingw-w64-i686-arrow
      ```

  - vcpkg: This is kept up to date by Microsoft team members and community contributors:

    ```
    git clone https://github.com/Microsoft/vcpkg.git
    cd vcpkg
    ./bootstrap-vcpkg.sh
    ./vcpkg integrate install
    ./vcpkg install arrow
    ```

  Build it from source yourself: https://arrow.apache.org/docs/developers/cpp/windows.html.

  Whichever way you decide to install the libraries, you need to add the path to where it installs the libraries to your environment path in order for them to be found at runtime.

- If using macOS and you don't want to build it yourself from source, you can use Homebrew [20] to install the library:

  ```
  brew install apache-arrow
  ```

- If using Linux and you don't want to build it from source:

  Packages for Debian GNU/Linux, Ubuntu, CentOS, Red Hat Enterprise Linux, and Amazon Linux are provided via APT and Yum repositories.

Rather than cover all of the instructions here, all of the installation instructions for the C++ library can be found at https://arrow.apache.org/install/. Only libarrow-dev is needed for the exercises in this chapter.

Once you've got your environment all set up and configured, let's take a look at the code. When compiling it, the easiest route is to use pkg-config if it's available on your system, otherwise, make sure you've added the correct include path and link against the Arrow library with the appropriate options (-I<path to arrow headers> -L<path to arrow libraries> -larrow).

Just like with the Python examples, let's start with a very simple example to walk through the API of the library.

Understanding the basics of the C++ library

Let's do the same first example in C++ that we did in Python:

```cpp
#include <arrow/api.h>
#include <arrow/array.h>
#include <iostream>

int main(int argc, char** argv) {
    std::vector<int64_t> data{1,2,3,4};
    auto arr = std::make_shared<arrow::Int64Array>(data.size(),
arrow::Buffer::Wrap(data));
    std::cout << arr->ToString() << std::endl;
}
```

Just like the Python example previously, this outputs the following:

```
[
  1,
  2,
  3,
  4,
]
```

Let's break down the highlighted line in the source code and explain what we did.

After creating `std::vector` of `int64_ts` to use as an example, we initialize
`std::shared_ptr` to `Int64Array` by specifying the array length, or the number of
values, and then wrapping the raw contiguous memory of the vector in a buffer for the
array to use as its value buffer. It's important to note that using `Buffer::Wrap` does not
copy the data, instead we're just referencing the memory that is used for the vector and
using that same block of memory for the array. Finally, we use the `ToString` method of
our array to create a string representation that we then output. Pretty straightforward, but
also very useful in terms of getting used to the library and confirming your environment
is set up properly.

When working with the C++ library, the Builder Pattern is commonly used for efficient
construction of arrays. We can do the same random data example in C++ that we did
earlier using Python, although it's a bit more verbose. Instead of `numpy`, we can just use
the `std` library's normal distribution generator:

```
#include <random>
// later on
std::random_device rd{};
std::mt19937 gen{rd()};
std::normal_distribution<> d{5, 2};
```

Once we've done this setup, we can use `d(gen)` to produce random 64-bit float (or
double) values. All that's left is to feed them into a builder and generate the arrays and
a schema since, in order to create a record batch, you need to provide a schema.

First, we create our builder:

```
#include <arrow/builder.h>
auto pool = arrow::default_memory_pool();
arrow::DoubleBuilder builder{arrow::float64(), pool};
```

Just like how in Python we had `pa.utf8()` and `pa.int16()`, `arrow::float64()`
returns a `DataType` object that is used to denote the logical type to use for this array.
There's also the usage of the `default_memory_pool()` function, which returns the
current global memory pool that this instance of Arrow has. The memory pool will get
cleaned up at the process exit, and different pools can be created if needed, but in the
majority of cases, just using the default one will be sufficient.

Now that we have our random number generator and our builder, let's create those arrays with random data:

```cpp
#include <arrow/record_batch.h>
// previous code sections go here
constexpr auto ncols = 16;
constexpr auto nrows = 8192;
arrow::ArrayVector columns(ncols);
arrow::FieldVector fields;
for (int i = 0; i < ncols; ++i) {
    for (int j = 0; j < nrows; ++j) {
        builder.Append(d(gen));
    }
    auto status = builder.Finish(&columns[i]);
    if (!status.ok()) {
        std::cerr << status.message() << std::endl;
      // handle the error
    }
      fields.push_back(arrow::field("c" + std::to_string(i),
                        arrow::float64()));
}
auto rb = arrow::RecordBatch::Make(arrow::schema(fields),
            columns[0]->length(), columns);
std::cout << rb->ToString() << std::endl;
```

The most important lines are highlighted showing the population of the arrays and the record batch creation. Calling `Builder::Finish` also resets the builder so that it can be re-used to build more arrays of the same type. We also use a vector of **fields** to construct a schema that we use to create the record batch. After this, we can perform whatever operations we wish on the record batch, such as rearranging, flattening, or unflattening columns, performing aggregations or calculations on the data, or maybe just calling `ToString` to write out the data to the terminal.

Building a struct array, again

When building nested type arrays in C++, it's a little more complex when working with the builders. We can do the same struct example for our archers that we did in Python! If you remember, a struct array is essentially just a collection of children arrays that are the same size and a validity bitmap. This means that one way to build a struct array would be to simply build each constituent array as previously, and construct the struct array using them:

1. Let's first mention `include` and some `using` statements for convenience, along with our initial data:

    ```
    #include <arrow/api.h>
    using arrow::field;
    using arrow::utf8;
    using arrow::int16;
    // vectors of archer data to start with
    std::vector<std::string> archers{"Legolas", "Oliver",
    "Merida", "Lara", "Artemis"};
    std::vector<std::string> locations{"Mirkwood", "Star
    City", "Scotland", "London", "Greece"};
    std::vector<int16_t> years{1954, 1941, 2012, 1996, -600};
    ```

2. Now, we construct the constituent Arrow arrays that will make up our final struct array:

    ```
    arrow::ArrayVector children;
    children.resize(3);
    arrow::StringBuilder str_bldr;
    str_bldr.AppendValues(archers);
    str_bldr.Finish(&children[0]); // resets the builder
    str_bldr.AppendValues(locations); // re-use it!
    str_bldr.Finish(&children[1]);
    arrow::Int16Builder year_bldr;
    year_bldr.AppendValues(years);
    year_bldr.Finish(&children[2]);
    ```

3. Finally, with our children arrays constructed, we can define the struct array:

```
arrow::StructArray arr{arrow::struct_({
    field("archer", utf8()),
    field("location", utf8()),
    field("year", int16())}),
    children[0]->length(), children};
std::cout << arr.ToString() << std::endl;
```

You can see the similarities to the Python version. We create our struct array by creating the struct type and defining the fields and types for each field, and then just hand it references to the child arrays that it needs. Being able to do this makes building up or splitting apart struct arrays extremely efficient and easy to do, regardless of the complexity of the types. Also, remember that it's not copying the data; the resulting StructArray just references the children arrays instead.

Rather, if you have your data and want to build out the struct array from scratch, we can use StructBuilder. It's very similar to our previous builder example, except the builders for the individual fields are owned by StructBuilder itself and we can build them all up together at one time. This is pretty straightforward and easy if there are no null structs since the validity bitmap can be left out, but if there are any nulls, we need to make sure that the builder is aware of them in order to build the bitmap (see *Figure 1.12* for a reminder of the layout of a struct array in memory):

1. First, we create our data type:

```
using arrow::field;
std::shared_ptr<arrow::DataType> st_type =
    arrow::struct_({field("archer", arrow::utf8()),
                    field("location", arrow::utf8()),
                    field("year", arrow::int16())});
```

2. Now, we create our builder:

```
std::unique_ptr<arrow::ArrayBuilder> tmp;
// returns a status, handle the error case
arrow::MakeBuilder(arrow::default_memory_pool(),
                   st_type, &tmp);
std::shared_ptr<arrow::StructBuilder> builder;
builder.reset(
static_cast<arrow::StructBuilder*>(tmp.release()));
```

Some notes to keep in mind with the highlighted lines are as follows:

- By using the MakeBuilder call as seen in the highlighted line, the builders for our fields will be automatically created for us. It will use the data type that is passed in to determine the correct builder type to construct.

- Then, in the second highlighted line, we cast our pointer to ArrayBuilder to a StructBuilder pointer.

3. Now we can append the data we need to, and since we know the types of the fields, we can just use the same technique of casting pointers in order to be able to use the field builders. Since they are all owned by the struct builder itself, we can just use raw pointers:

```cpp
using namespace arrow;
StringBuilder* archer_builder =
    static_cast< StringBuilder*>(builder->field_
builder(0));
StringBuilder* location_builder =
    static_cast<StringBuilder*>(builder->field_
builder(1));
Int16Builder* year_builder =
    static_cast<Int16Builder*>(builder->field_
builder(2));
```

4. Finally, now that we've got our individual builders, we can append whatever values we need to them as long as we make sure that when we call Finish on the struct builder, all of the field builders *must* have the same number of values. If there are any null structs, you can call the Append, AppendNull, or AppendValues functions on the struct builder to indicate which indexes are valid and which are null. Just as with the field builders, this must either be left out entirely (if there are no nulls) or equal to the same number of values in each of the fields.

5. And, of course, the last step, just like before, is to call Finish on the struct builder:

```cpp
std::shared_ptr<arrow::Array> out;
builder->Finish(&out);
std::cout << out->ToString() << std::endl;
```

Now that we've covered building arrays in C++, here's an exercise for you to try out!

An exercise for you

Try doing the same exercise from the Python section but with C++, converting `std::vector<row>` to an Arrow record batch where `row` is defined as the following:

```cpp
struct row {
    int64_t id;
    double cost;
    std::vector<double> cost_components;
};
```

Then, write a function to convert the record batch back into the row-oriented representation of `std::vector<row>`.

Go Arrow go!

The Golang Arrow library is the one I've been most directly involved in the development of and is also very easy to install and use, just like the `pyarrow` library. Most IDEs will have a plugin for developing in Go, so you can set up your preferred IDE and environment for writing code, and then the following commands will set you up with downloading the Arrow library for import:

```
$ mkdir arrow_chapter1 && cd arrow_chapter1
$ go mod init arrow_chapter1
$ go get -u github.com/apache/arrow/go/v7/arrow@v7
```

> **Tip**
> If you're not familiar with Go, the *Tour of Go* is an excellent introduction to the language and can be found here: `https://tour.golang.org/`.

By this point, I think you can guess what our first example is going to be; just create a file with the `.go` extension in the directory you created:

```go
package main
import (
    "fmt"

    "github.com/apache/arrow/go/v7/arrow/array"
    "github.com/apache/arrow/go/v7/arrow/memory"
)
```

```go
func main() {
    bldr := array.NewInt64Builder(memory.DefaultAllocator)
    defer bldr.Release()
    bldr.AppendValues([]int64{1, 2, 3, 4}, nil)
    arr := bldr.NewArray()
    defer arr.Release()
    fmt.Println(arr)
}
```

Just as we started with the C++ and Python libraries, this is a minimal Go file that creates an Int64 array with the values [1, 2, 3, 4] and prints it out to the terminal. The builder pattern that we saw in the C++ library is also the same pattern that the Go library utilizes; the big difference between them is the highlighted lines. You can run the example with the go run command:

```
$ go run .
[1, 2, 3, 4]
```

Because Go is a garbage-collected language, there's less direct control over exactly when a value is cleaned up or memory is deallocated. While in C++ we have shared_ptr and unique_ptr objects, there is not an equivalent construct in Go. To allow that more granular control, the library adds function calls for Retain and Release on most of the constructs such as arrays. These present a way to perform reference counting on your values using Retain to ensure that the underlying data stays alive, particularly when passing through channels or other cases where internal memory might get undesirably garbage-collected, and Release to free up the internal references to the memory so it can get garbage-collected earlier than the array object itself. If you're unfamiliar with it, the **defer** keyword marks a function to be called just before the enclosing function, not necessarily the scope, ends. Calls that are deferred will execute in the reverse order that they appear in code, similar to C++ destructors.

Let's create the same second example, populating arrays with random data and creating a record batch:

1. We can import the standard rand library for generating our random values. Technically, it generates a pseudo-random value between 0 and 1.0 (not including 1) that we could combine with some math to increase the range of values, but for the purposes of this example, that's not necessary:

    ```go
    import (

            "math/rand"
    ```

```
...
"github.com/apache/arrow/go/v7/arrow"
...
)
```

2. Next, we just create our builder that we can use and re-use to append values to, just like before:

```
fltBldr := array.NewFloat64Builder(memory.
DefaultAllocator)
defer fltBldr.Release()
```

The usage of memory.DefaultAllocator is equivalent to the call of arrow::default_memory_pool in the C++ library, referring to a default allocator that is initialized for the process. Alternately, you could call memory.NewGoAllocator or otherwise.

3. As in the C++ example, we need a list of column arrays and a list of fields to build a schema from, so let's create the slices:

```
const ncols = 16
columns := make([]arrow.Array, ncols)
fields  := make([]arrow.Field, ncols)
```

4. Then, we can add our random data to the builder and create our columns:

```
const nrows = 8192
for i := range columns {
        for j := 0; j < nrows; j++ {
        fltBldr.Append(rand.Float64())
    }
    columns[i] = fltBlder.NewArray()
    defer columns[i].Release()
    fields[i] = arrow.Field{
                Name: "c" + strconv.Itoa(i),
                Type: arrow.PrimitiveTypes.Float64}
}
```

As with the other two libraries, we need to specify the type for our field.

5. Finally, we create our record batch and print it out:

```
record := array.NewRecord(arrow.NewSchema(fields, nil),
                          columns, -1)
defer record.Release()
fmt.Println(record)
```

When creating the new record, we have to create a schema from the list of fields. The `nil` that is passed in there represents that we're not providing any schema-level metadata for this record. Schemas can contain metadata at the top level and each individual field can also contain metadata.

The `-1` value that we pass is the numRows argument that also existed in the other libraries. We could have used `columns[0].Len()` to know the length, but by passing `-1`, we can have the number of rows lazily determined by the record itself rather than us having to pass it in.

We can see all the same conceptual trappings across different libraries:

- Record batches are made up of a group of same length arrays with a schema.

- A schema is a list of fields, where each field contains a name, type, and some metadata.

- A single array knows its type and has the raw data, but a name and metadata must be tied to a `Field` object.

I bet you can guess the next example we're going to code up!

Building a struct array, yet again!

Building nested type arrays in Go is closer to the way it is done in the C++ library than in the Python library, but there are still similar steps of creating your struct type, populating each of the constituent arrays, and then finalizing it.

First, we create our type:

```
archerType := arrow.StructOf(
    arrow.Field{Name: "archer", Type: arrow.BinaryTypes.String},
    arrow.Field{Name: "location", Type: arrow.BinaryTypes.String},
    arrow.Field{Name: "year", Type: arrow.PrimitiveTypes.Int16})
```

Just like before, there's two ways to go about it:

- Build each constituent array separately and then join references to them together into a single struct array:

```
mem := memory.DefaultAllocator
namesBldr := array.NewStringBuilder(mem)
defer namesBldr.Release()
locationsBldr := array.NewStringBuilder(mem)
defer locationsBldr.Release()
yearsBldr := array.NewInt16Builder(mem)
defer yearsBldr.Release()
// populate the builders and create the arrays named
names,
// locations, and years
data := array.NewData(archerType, names.Len(),
                      []*memory.Buffer{nil},
                      []arrow.ArrayData{names.Data(),
                      locations.Data(), years.Data()},
                      0, 0)
defer data.Release()
archers := array.NewStructData(data)
defer archers.Release()
fmt.Println(archers)
```

Breaking down the highlighted line, which is something new, in both the C++ and Go libraries, there is the concept of ArrayData, which is contained within each array. It contains the pieces mentioned before that make up the array: the type, the buffers, the length, the null count, any children arrays, and the optional dictionary. In the highlighted line, we create a new Data object, which has its own reference count, and initialize it with the struct type we created, the length of our struct, and a slice made up of the pointers to the Data objects of each of the field arrays. Remember, struct arrays only have one buffer, a null bitmap, which can be left out if there are no nulls, so we pass a nil buffer as []*memory.Buffer{nil}.

- The other option is to use a struct builder directly and build up all of the constituent arrays simultaneously. If you don't already have the arrays from something else, this is the easier and more efficient option:

```
// archerType is the struct type from before, and lets
// assume the data is in a slice of archer structs
// named archerList
bldr := array.NewStructBuilder(memory.DefaultAllocator,
                                archerType)
defer bldr.Release()
f1b := bldr.FieldBuilder(0).(*array.StringBuilder)
f2b := bldr.FieldBuilder(1).(*array.StringBuilder)
f3b := bldr.FieldBuilder(2).(*array.Int16Builder)
for _, ar := range archerList {
    bldr.Append(true)
    f1b.Append(ar.archer)
    f2b.Append(ar.location)
    f3b.Append(ar.year)
}
archers := bldr.NewStructArray()
defer archers.Release()
fmt.Println(archers)
```

Just like in the C++ example before, the field builders are owned by the struct builder itself, so we just assert the types of the appropriate builder so we can call Append on them.

In the last highlighted line, we call Append on the struct builder itself so the builder keeps track that it is a non-null struct we are adding. We could pass false there to tell the builder to add a null struct, or we can call the AppendNull function to do the same.

An exercise for you (yes, it's the same one)

Try using the Arrow library for Go to write a function that takes a row-oriented slice of structs and converts them into an Arrow record batch, and vice versa. Use the following type definition:

```
type datarow struct {
    id          int64
    cost        float64
```

```
       costComponents []float64
}
```

You should probably be pretty good at this by now if you did this exercise in the Python and C++ libraries already!

Summary

The goal of this chapter was to explain what Apache Arrow is, get you acquainted with the format, and have you use it in some simple use cases. This knowledge forms the baseline of everything else for us to talk about in the rest of the book!

Just as a reminder, you can check the GitHub repository (`https://github.com/ PacktPublishing/In-Memory-Analytics-with-Apache-Arrow-`) for the solutions to the exercises presented here and for the full code samples to make sure you understand the concepts!

The previous examples and exercises are all fairly trivial and are meant to help reinforce the concepts introduced about the format and the specification while helping you get familiar with using Arrow in code.

In *Chapter 2, Working with Key Arrow Specifications*, we will introduce how to read your data into the Arrow format, whether it's on your local disk, **Hadoop Distributed File System** (**HDFS**), **S3**, or elsewhere, and integrate Arrow into some of the various processes and utilities you might already use with your data, such as the `pandas` integration. We will also discover how to pass your data around between services and processes while keeping it in the Arrow format for performance.

Ready? Onward and upward!

References

Here's a list of the URL references we made in this chapter since there were quite a lot!

1. Apache Arrow documentation: `https://arrow.apache.org/docs/`
2. Apache License 2.0: `https://apache.org/licenses/LICENSE-2.0`
3. C++ Apache Arrow documentation: `https://arrow.apache.org/docs/ cpp/`
4. C# documentation for Arrow: `https://github.com/apache/arrow/blob/ master/csharp/README.md`

5. Golang documentation for Arrow: `https://pkg.go.dev/github.com/apache/arrow/go/v7/arrow`

6. Java documentation for Arrow: `https://arrow.apache.org/docs/java/`

7. JavaScript documentation for Arrow: `https://arrow.apache.org/docs/js/`

8. Julia documentation for Arrow: `https://arrow.juliadata.org/stable/`

9. Rust documentation for Arrow: `https://docs.rs/crate/arrow/`

10. Glib documentation for Arrow: `https://arrow.apache.org/docs/c_glib/`

11. MATLAB documentation for Arrow: `https://github.com/apache/arrow/blob/master/matlab/README.md`

12. Python documentation for Arrow: `https://arrow.apache.org/docs/python/`

13. R documentation for Arrow: `https://arrow.apache.org/docs/r/`

14. Ruby documentation for Arrow: `https://github.com/apache/arrow/blob/master/ruby/README.md`

15. Implementation matrix for Arrow features across languages: `https://arrow.apache.org/docs/status.html`

16. Documentation for using Conda: `https://docs.conda.io/projects/conda/en/latest/index.html`

17. Home page for Conda-Forge: `https://conda-forge.org`

18. Data type documentation for PyArrow: `https://arrow.apache.org/docs/python/api/datatypes.html#api-types`

19. Installation guide for MSYS2: `https://www.msys2.org/#installation`

20. Home page for Brew.sh: `https://brew.sh/`

2
Working with Key Arrow Specifications

Utilities to perform analytics and computations are only useful if you have **data** to perform them on. That data can live in many different places and formats, both local and remote to the machine being used to analyze it. The Arrow libraries provide a bunch of functionalities that we'll cover for reading data from and interacting with multiple different formats in multiple different locations. Now that you have a solid understanding of what Arrow is and how to manipulate arrays, in this chapter, you will learn how to get data into the Arrow format and communicate it between different processes.

In this chapter, we're going to cover the following topics:

- Importing data from multiple formats, including CSV, Apache Parquet, and pandas DataFrames

- Interactions between Arrow and pandas data

- Utilizing shared memory for near zero-cost data sharing

Technical requirements

Throughout this chapter, I'll be providing various code samples while using the Python, C++, and Golang Arrow libraries and the public *NYC Taxi Trip Duration* dataset.

To run the practical examples in this chapter, you will need the following:

- A computer that's connected to the internet

- Your preferred IDE (VS Code, Sublime, Emacs, Vim, and so on)

- Python 3+ with the `pyarrow` and `pandas` modules installed

- Go 1.16+

- A C++ compiler (capable of compiling C++11 or newer) with the Arrow libraries installed

- The `sample_data` folder from this book's GitHub repository: `https://github.com/PacktPublishing/In-Memory-Analytics-with-Apache-Arrow-`

Let's get started!

Playing with data, wherever it might be!

Modern data science, machine learning, and other data manipulation techniques frequently require data to be merged from multiple locations to perform tasks. Often, this data isn't locally accessible but rather is stored in some form of cloud storage. Most of the implementations of the Arrow libraries provide native support for local filesystem access, AWS **Simple Storage Service (S3)**, and **Hadoop Distributed File System (HDFS)**. In addition to the natively supported systems, filesystem interfaces are generally implemented or used in language-specific cases to make it easy to add support for other filesystems.

Once you're able to access the platform your files are located on (whether that is local, in the cloud, or otherwise), you need to make sure that the data is in a format that is supported by the Arrow libraries for importing. Check the documentation for the Arrow library of your preferred language to see what data formats are supported. The abstractions provided by the Arrow libraries make it very easy to create a single process for manipulating data that will work regardless of the location or format of that data, and then write it out to different formats wherever you'd like. The following diagram only shows a few data formats that are supported by most Arrow libraries, but remember, just because a format isn't listed doesn't necessarily mean it's not supported:

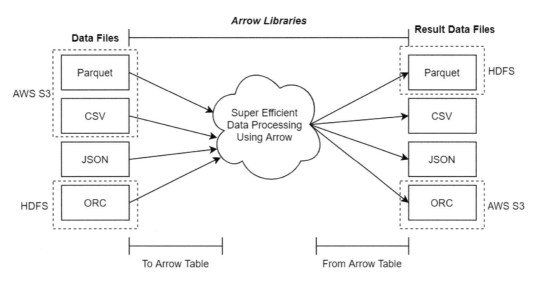

Figure 2.1 – Using Arrow libraries with data files

In the preceding diagram, the dotted outlines point out how the data files may exist in one location before they are processed (such as in S3 or an HDFS cluster); the result of this processing can be written out to an entirely different storage location and format.

To provide optimized and consistent usage of the library functions, and for ease of implementation, many Arrow libraries define specific interfaces for filesystem usage. The exact nature of these interfaces will differ from language to language, but all of them are used to abstract away the particulars of the filesystem when it's interacting with imported data files. Before we jump into working with data files directly, we need to introduce a couple of important Arrow concepts. We covered Arrow arrays and record batches in *Chapter 1*, *Getting Started with Apache Arrow*, so let's introduce **chunked arrays** and **tables**.

Working with Arrow tables

To quickly review, a **record batch** is a collection of equal length Arrow arrays along with a schema describing the columns in terms of names, types, and metadata. Often, when reading in and manipulating data, we get that data in chunks and then want to assemble it to treat it as a single large table, as shown in the following diagram:

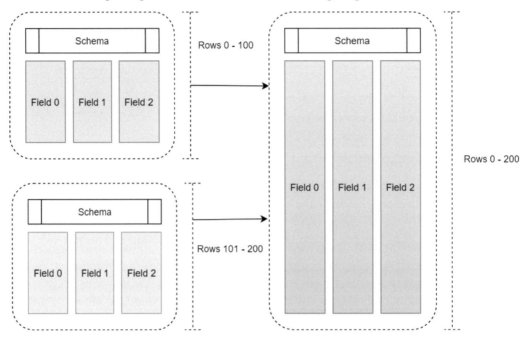

Figure 2.2 – Multiple record batches

One way to do this would be to simply allocate enough space to hold the full table and then copy the columns of each record batch into the allocated space. That way, we end up with the finished table as a single cohesive record batch in memory. There are two big problems with this method that prevent it from being scalable:

- It's potentially very expensive to both allocate an entirely new large chunk of memory for each column and copy all the data over.

- What if we get another record batch of data? We would have to do this again to accommodate the – now larger – table each time we get more data.

This is where the concept of chunked arrays comes to the rescue, as shown in the following diagram:

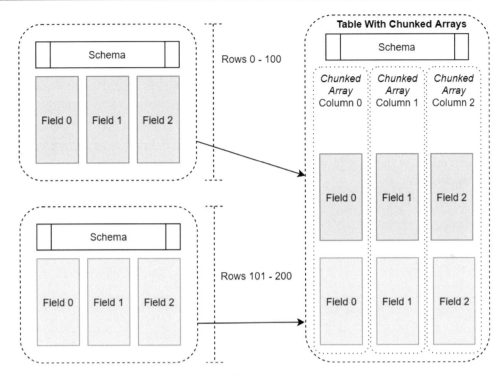

Figure 2.3 – Table with chunked arrays

A **chunked array** is just a thin wrapper around a group of Arrow arrays of the same data type. This way, we can incrementally build up an array, or even a whole table, efficiently without constantly having to allocate larger and larger chunks of memory and copying data. In the same manner, an Arrow **table** holds one or more chunked arrays and a schema, very similar to how a record batch holds regular Arrow arrays and a schema. The table allows us to conceptually treat all the data as if it were a single contiguous table of data, without having to pay the costs to frequently reallocate and copy the data.

Of course, there are trade-offs to this: we lose some of our memory locality by no longer having the arrays as fully contiguous buffers. You want these chunks to be as large as possible to get as much benefit from the locality when processing the data as possible, which means it's a balancing act. You need to balance the cost of the allocations and copies against the cost of processing non-contiguous data. Thankfully, most of this complexity is handled by the Arrow libraries themselves under the hood in the I/O interfaces when reading in data to process. But understanding these concepts is key to getting the best performance possible for your dataset and operations.

With that out of the way, let's start reading and writing some files!

In the interests of brevity, we're just going to focus on Python and C++ in this section. But fear not! Golang will pop up in other examples as we go. In the next section, we're going to look at how to utilize the available filesystem interfaces to import data from the different supported file formats. First up is Python!

Accessing data files with pyarrow

The Python Arrow library defines a base class interface and then provides a few concrete implementations of that interface for different locations to access files, as shown in the following diagram:

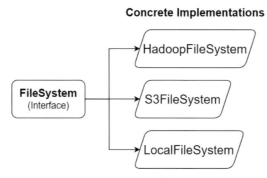

Figure 2.4 – Python Arrow filesystem interfaces

The abstract interface, `FileSystem`, provides utilities both for input and output streams and for directory operations. Abstracting out the underlying implementation of the filesystem interactions provides a single interface that simplifies the view of the underlying data storage. Regardless of the system, the paths will always be separated by forward slashes (/), leave out the special path components such as . and .., and only expose basic metadata about the files, such as their size and last modification time. When constructing a `FileSystem` object, you can either construct the type you need explicitly or allow inference from the URI, like so:

- **Local Filesystem**: The constructor for `LocalFileSystem` takes a single optional argument, use_mmap. It defaults to being `false`, but if set to `true`, it will memory map files when opening them. The implications of memory mapping the file will be covered in *Chapter 4, Format and Memory Handling*, in the *Learning memory cartography* section. Let's construct the object:

```
>>> from pyarrow import fs
>>> local = fs.LocalFileSystem() # create local file
system instance
>>> f, p = fs.FileSystem.from_uri('file:///home/mtopol/')
```

```
>>> f
<pyarrow._fs.LocalFileSystem object at 0x0000021FAF8F6570>
>>> p
'/home/mtopol/'
```

Standard Windows paths, such as `C:\Users\mtopol\...`, will not work due to the colon present in them. Instead, you can specify such a path as a URI with forward slashes: `file:///c/Users/mtopol/`....

- **AWS S3**: The constructor for `S3FileSystem` allows you to specify your credentials, if necessary, through multiple arguments in addition to other connection properties such as the region or endpoint overrides. Alternatively, the constructor will also inspect the standard S3 credential configurations, such as environment variables like `AWS_ACCESS_KEY_ID` or the `~/.aws/config` file:

```
>>> from pyarrow import fs
>>> s3 = fs.S3FileSystem(region='us-east-1') # explicit
create
>>> s3, path = fs.FileSystem.from_uri('s3://my-bucket/')
>>> s3
<pyarrow._s3fs.S3FileSystem object at 0x0000021FAF7F99F0>
>>> path
'my-bucket'
```

- **HDFS**: Using HDFS gets a little tricky as it requires having the **Java Native Interface** (**JNI**) libraries on your path so that they can be loaded. JNI is a framework that allows Java code running in the **Java Virtual Machine** (**JVM**) to call, and get called by, applications and libraries native to the platform it is running on. I won't cover installing HDFS here, but the important pieces necessary for being able to use it with `pyarrow` are `libjvm.so` and `libhdfs.so`. Both of these must be in `$LD_LIBRARY_PATH` (just `$PATH` on Windows and `$DYLD_FALLBACK_LIBRARY_PATH` on newer macOS releases) so that they can be loaded at runtime. Provided these libraries are accessible at runtime, you can communicate with an HDFS cluster with `pyarrow`:

```
>>> from pyarrow import fs
>>> hdfs = fs.HadoopFileSystem(host='namenode', port=8020)
>>> hdfs, path = fs.FileSystem.from_uri('hdfs://
namenode:8020/tmp')
>>> hdfs
```

```
<pyarrow._hdfs.HadoopFileSystem object at 0x7f7a70960bf0>
>>> path
'/tmp'
```

pyarrow will attempt to connect to the HDFS namenode upon construction and will fail if it's not successful. The runtime lookup of the Hadoop libraries depends on a couple different environment variables. If the library isn't in your LD_LIBRARY_PATH, you can use the following environment variables to configure how it is looked up.

If you have a full Hadoop installation, you should have HADOOP_HOME defined, which usually has lib/native/libhdfs.so. JAVA_HOME should be defined to point to your Java SDK installation. If libhdfs.so is installed somewhere other than $HADOOP_HOME/lib/native, you can specify the explicit location with the ARROW_LIBHDFS_DIR environment variable.

Many of the I/O-related functions in pyarrow allow a caller to either specify a URI, inferring the filesystem, or have an explicit argument that allows you to specify the FileSystem instance that will be used. Once you have initialized your desired filesystem instance, the interface can be utilized for many standard filesystem operations, regardless of the underlying implementation. Here's a subset of the abstracted functions to get you started:

- create_dir: Create directories or subdirectories
- delete_dir: Delete a directory and its contents recursively
- delete_dir_contents: Delete a directory's contents recursively
- copy_file, delete_file: Copy or delete a specific file by path
- open_input_file: Open a file for random access reading
- open_input_stream: Open a file for only sequential reading
- open_append_stream: Open an output stream for appending data
- open_output_stream: Open an output stream for sequential writing

In addition to manipulating files and directories, you can also use the abstraction to inspect and list the contents of files and directories. Opening files or streams produces what's referred to as a **file-like object**, which can be used with any functions that work with such objects, regardless of the underlying storage or location.

At this point, you should have a firm grasp of how to open and refer to data files using the Python Arrow library. Now, we can start looking at the different data formats that are natively implemented and how to process them into memory as Arrow arrays and tables.

Working with CSV files in pyarrow

One of the most ubiquitous file formats to be used with data is a delimited text file such as a **comma-separated values** or **CSV** file. In addition to commas, they are also often used as tab or pipe delimited files. Because the raw text of a CSV file doesn't have well-defined types, the Arrow library makes attempts to guess the types and provides a multitude of options for parsing and converting the data into or out of Arrow data when reading or writing. More information about how type inference is performed can be found in the Arrow documentation: `https://arrow.apache.org/docs/python/csv.html#incremental-reading`.

The default options for reading in CSV files are generally pretty good at inferring the data types, so reading simple files is easy. We can see this by using the `train.csv` sample data file, which is a subset of the commonly used NYC Taxi Trip dataset:

```
>>> import pyarrow as pa
>>> import pyarrow.csv
>>> table = pa.csv.read_csv('sample_data/train.csv')
>>> table.schema
vendor_id: string
pickup_at: timestamp[ns]
dropoff_at: timestamp[ns]
passenger_count: int64
trip_distance: double
pickup_longitude: double
pickup_latitude: double
rate_code_id: int64
store_and_fwd_flag: string
dropoff_longitude: double
dropoff_latitude: double
payment_type: string
fare_amount: double
extra: double
```

```
mta_tax: double
tip_amount: double
tolls_amount: double
total_amount: double
```

The first thing to note is that we pass a string directly into the `read_csv` function. Like many of the Python Arrow file reading functions, it can take either of the following as its argument:

- **string**: A filename or a path to a file. The filesystem will be inferred if necessary.

- **file-like object**: This could be the object that's returned from the built-in `open` function or any of the functions on a `FileSystem` that returns a readable object, such as `open_input_stream`.

The first line of the file contains the column headers, which are automatically used as the names of the columns for the generated Arrow table. After that, we can see that the library recognizes the timestamp columns from the values, even determining the precision to be in seconds as opposed to milliseconds or nanoseconds. Finally, you can see the numeric columns versus string columns, which determines the columns being doubles instead of integer columns.

Reading in a CSV file returns an object of the `pyarrow.Table` type that contains a list of `pyarrow.lib.ChunkedArray` objects. This follows the pattern mentioned earlier regarding tables and chunked arrays. When you're reading in the file, it can be parallelized by reading groups of rows at a time and then building the chunked columns without having to copy data around. The following diagram shows a parallelized file read:

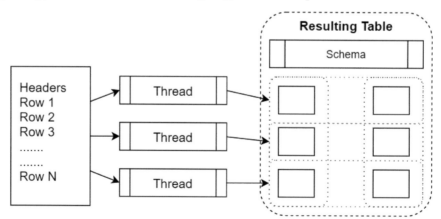

Figure 2.5 – Parallelized file read

Here, we can see threads parallelizing the reads from a file. Each thread reads in a group of rows into array chunks. These are then added to the columns of the table as a zero-copy operation once the Arrow arrays have been created. We can examine the columns of the finished table in the Python interpreter to see this in action:

```
>>> table.column(0).num_chunks
192
>>> table.column(0).chunks
[<pyarrow.lib.StringArray object at 0x000001B2C5EB9FA8>
[
  "VTS",
  "VTS",
  "VTS",
  "VTS",
  "VTS",
  "VTS",
  "VTS",
  ...
  "CMT",
  "VTS",
  "VTS",
  "VTS",
  "VTS",
  "CMT",
  "VTS",
  "VTS",
  "VTS"
], <pyarrow.lib.StringArray object at 0x000001B2C5EBB048>
[......
```

In addition to the input stream or filename, the CSV reading functions have three types of options that can be passed in – ReadOptions, ParseOptions, and ConvertOptions. Each of these has a set of options to control the different aspects of reading the file and creating the Arrow table object, as follows:

- ReadOptions: This allows you to configure whether you should use threads for reading, the block size to read in at a time, and how to generate the column names for the table either by reading from the file, providing them directly, or auto-generating them:

```
# if the extension is a recognized compressed format
extension
# the data will automatically be decompressed during
reading
table = pa.csv.read_csv('file.csv.gz', read_options=pa.
csv.ReadOptions(
        encoding='utf8', # encoding type of the file
        column_names=['col1', 'col2', 'col3'],
        block_size=4096, # number of bytes to process at
a time
)
```

- ParseOptions: This controls the delimiter to use when you're figuring out the columns, quote and escape characters, and how to handle newlines:

```
table = pa.csv.read_csv(input_file, parse_options=pa.csv.
ParseOptions(
        delimiter='|', # for a pipe delimited file
        escape_char='\\', # allow backslash to escape values
    )
```

- ConvertOptions: This provides various options for how to convert the data into Arrow array data, including specifying what strings should be considered null values, which strings should be considered true or false for Boolean values, and various other options for how to parse strings into Arrow data types:

```
table = pa.csv.read_csv('tips.csv', convert_options=pa.
csv.ConvertOptions(
        column_types={
                'total_bill': pa.decimal128(precision=10,
scale=2),
                'tip': pa.decimal128(precision=10, scale=2),
```

```
        },
        # only read these columns from the file, in this
order
        # leaving out any other columns
        include_columns=['tip', 'total_bill', 'timestamp'],
)
```

In addition to all the functionality for reading CSV files, there is a `write_csv` function for writing a CSV file from a record batch or table. Just as with the `read` function, it takes a filename or path or a file-like object that it can write to as an argument. There are only two available options for manipulating the write – include the initial header line with the names of the columns or include the batch size to use when writing out rows. Here's a simple example of a function that can read in a CSV file and write a subset of columns out to a new file:

```
def create_subset_csv(input, output, column_names):
    table = pa.csv.read_csv(input,
                            convert_options=pa.csv.
ConvertOptions(
                                include_columns=column_
names))
    pa.csv.write_csv(table, output,
                        write_options=pa.csv.WriteOptions(
                                include_
header=True))
```

In some situations, you may want to write data out to a CSV file incrementally as you generate or retrieve the data. When you're doing this, you don't want to keep the entire table in memory at once if you can avoid it. Here, you can use `pyarrow.csv.CSVWriter` to write data incrementally:

```
schema = pa.schema([("col", pa.int64())])
with pa.csv.CSVWriter("output.csv", schema=schema) as
writer:
    for chunk in range(10):
        datachunk = range(chunk*10, (chunk+1)*10)
        table = pa.Table.from_arrays([pa.
array(datachunk)],
                                    schema=schema)
        writer.write(table)
```

The next data format we're going to cover is another very common one: **JSON** data.

Working with JSON files in pyarrow

The expected format for JSON data files is that they are line delimited files where each line is a JSON object containing a single row of data. The process of reading JSON files is nearly identical to reading in CSV files! The following is a sample JSON data file:

```
{"a": 1, "b": 2.0, "c": 1}
{"a": 3, "b": 3.0, "c": 2}
{"a": 5, "b": 4.0, "c": 3}
{"a": 7, "b": 5.0, "c": 4}
```

Reading this file into a table is simple:

```
>>> import pyarrow as pa
>>> import pyarrow.json
>>> table = pa.json.read_json(filename)
>>> table.to_pydict()
{'a': [1, 3, 5, 7], 'b': [2.0, 3.0, 4.0, 5.0], 'c': [1, 2, 3, 4]}
```

Just like reading in a CSV file, there are ReadOptions and ParseOptions available that allow you to configure the behavior for creating the Arrow data. You can do this by specifying an explicit schema and defining how to handle unexpected fields. Currently, there is no corresponding write_json function.

Working with ORC files in pyarrow

Unlike the JSON and CSV formats, the **Apache Optimized Row Columnar (ORC)** format isn't as popular unless you already work with the Hadoop data ecosystem. Apache ORC is a row-column format that was originally developed by Hortonworks for storing data in a compressed format so that it can be processed by Apache Hive and other Hadoop utilities. It stores data in a column-oriented format in conjunction with file indexes and splits the file into stripes to facilitate predicate pushdown and optimized reads.

Since the ORC file format is used frequently for data storage and querying, the pyarrow library provides an interface for reading ORC files directly into an Arrow table, aptly named pyarrow.orc.ORCFile. Like Arrow, ORC files have a schema, and the columns are specifically typed, allowing them to be easily converted. This is because no ambiguity exists like when you're trying to infer data types from a JSON or CSV file.

> **Note**
>
> The `orc` module in `pyarrow` is not currently included in the Windows build
> of the Python package wheels. If you're on Windows, you'll have to build it
> yourself from the source.

Let's adjust our previous examples so that it reads an ORC file rather than a CSV or
JSON file:

1. To read an ORC file into one or more Arrow tables, first, create an `ORCFile`
    instance:

    ```
    >>> import pyarrow as pa
    >>> import pyarrow.orc
    >>> of = pa.orc.ORCFile('train.orc')
    >>> of.nrows
    1458644
    >>> of.schema
    vendor_id: string
    pickup_at: timestamp[ns]
    dropoff_at: timestamp[ns]
    passenger_count: int64
    trip_distance: double
    pickup_longitude: double
    pickup_latitude: double
    rate_code_id: int64
    store_and_fwd_flag: string
    dropoff_longitude: double
    dropoff_latitude: double
    payment_type: string
    fare_amount: double
    extra: double
    mta_tax: double
    tip_amount: double
    tolls_amount: double
    total_amount: double
    ```

    As with CSV and JSON files, the argument for creating an `ORCFile` can be a file
    path or a file-like object.

2. With the object, you can now read either a single stripe or the entire file into an Arrow table, including reading only a subset of the columns if desired:

```
>>> tbl = of.read(columns=['vendor_id', 'passenger_
count', 'rate_code_id']) # leave this out or use None to
get all cols
>>> tbl
pyarrow.Table
vendor_id: string
passenger_count: int64
rate_code_id: int64
---
id: [["VTS","VTS","VTS","VTS","VTS",…]]
passenger_count: [[1,1,2,1,1,1,1,1,1,2,...,5,5,1,1,1,3,5,
4,1,1]]
trip_duration: [[1,1,1,1,1,…,1,1,1,1,1,1,1]]
```

Along with reading an ORC file, we can also write to an ORC file using `pyarrow.orc.write_table`. The arguments for this `write_table` method are the table to write and the location of the file to write. The last file format that we're going to cover with the `pyarrow` library is Apache Parquet.

Working with Apache Parquet files in pyarrow

If you're not familiar with it, Parquet is similar to ORC as both are column-oriented, on-disk storage formats with compression. Both also contain various kinds of metadata to make querying directly from the files more efficient. Think of them as two different flavors of column-based storage with different trade-offs made in their designs.

> **Note**
> With all these columnar-based storage formats, you may be wondering why Arrow exists and when to use which format and for what reasons. Well, don't worry! We'll dig into answering these questions, along with other format comparison questions, later in *Chapter 4, Format and Memory Handling*.

At this point, you've probably picked up the pattern in the library design here and can guess what it may look like to read a Parquet file into an Arrow table. Go ahead – sketch out what you think the Python code may look like; I'll wait.

Got something? Okay then, let's take a look:

```
>>> import pyarrow.parquet as pq
>>> table = pq.read_table('train.parquet')
```

Yup. That's it. Of course, there are plenty of options available to customize and fine-tune how the Parquet file is read. Some of the available options are as follows:

- Specifying a list of columns to read so that you only read the portions of the file that contain the data for those columns
- Controlling the buffer size and whether to pre-buffer data from the file into memory to optimize your I/O
- A `filesystem` option that can be passed in so that any file path that's used will be looked up and opened with the provided `FileSystem` object instead of the local on-disk system
- Filter options to push down predicates to filter rows out

With Python covered, let's see how the C++ library covers the same functionality and connections.

Accessing data files with Arrow in C++

Because the Python interface is built on top of the C++ library, the interface is very similar to the `pyarrow` library's `fs` module. You can use the filesystem module of the C++ library by including `arrow/filesystem/api.h` in your code, which will pull in the three main filesystem handlers in the `arrow::fs` namespace – `LocalFileSystem`, `S3FileSystem`, and `HadoopFileSystem` – the same three concrete implementations that exist in the Python library. All three provide your basic functionality for creating, copying, moving, and reading files in their respective physical locations, neatly abstracting away the complexity for easy usage. Of course, just like the `from_uri` function in the Python module, we have `arrow::fs::FileSystemFromUri` and `arrow::fs::FileSystemFromUriOrPath`, which will construct the filesystem instance from the **URI** provided or, in the latter case, a local file path.

Now, let's look at some examples that use these facilities to work with the various data formats. We will start with CSV files.

Working with CSV data files using Arrow in C++

By default, the Arrow library is going to read all the columns from the CSV file. As expected, however, a variety of options can be used to control how the file is processed. Here are just a few of those options, but I encourage you to check the documentation for the full list of options:

- By default, the column names will be read from the first row of the CSV file; otherwise, `arrow::csv::ReadOptions::column_names` can be used to set the column names. If set, the first row of the file will be read as data instead.

- `arrow::csv::ConvertOptions::include_columns` can be used to specify which columns to read and leave out other columns. Unless `ConvertOptions::include_missing_columns` is set to `true`, an error will be returned if any of the desired columns is missing; otherwise, they will just come back as columns full of null values.

- The CSV reader will infer data types of columns by default, but data types can be specified via the optional `arrow::csv::ConvertOptions::column_types` map.

- `arrow::csv::ParseOptions` contains various fields that can be used to customize how the text is parsed into values, such as indicating `true` and `false` values, the column delimiter, and so on.

Now, let's look at a code example:

1. First, we need our includes:

```
#include <arrow/io/api.h> // for opening the file
#include <arrow/csv/api.h>// the CSV functions and objects
#include <arrow/table.h>  // because we're reading the data
                          // in as a table
#include <iostream> // to output to the terminal
```

2. Then, we must open the file. For simplicity, we'll use a local file for now:

```
auto maybe_input = arrow::io::ReadableFile::Open("train.
csv");
if (!maybe_input.ok()) {
    // Handle file open errors via maybe_input.status()
}
std::shared_ptr<arrow::io::InputStream> input = *maybe_
input;
```

3. Next, we must get our options objects squared away. I'm going to use the default options here, but you should try playing with different combinations of options with different examples:

```
auto io_context = arrow::io::default_io_context();


auto read_options = arrow::csv::ReadOptions::Defaults();
auto parse_options = arrow::csv::ParseOptions::Defaults();
auto convert_options =
arrow::csv::ConvertOptions::Defaults();
```

4. Now that everything is in order, all we have to do is create our table reader and get the data:

```
auto maybe_reader = arrow::csv::TableReader::Make(io_
context,
    input, read_options, parse_options, convert_options);


if (!maybe_reader.ok()) {
    // Handle any instantiation errors from the TableReader
}
std::shared_ptr<arrow::csv::TableReader> reader = *maybe_
reader;


// Read the table of data from the file
auto maybe_table = reader->Read();
if (!maybe_table.ok()) {
    // handle any errors such as CSV syntax errors
    // or failed type conversion errors, etc.
}
std::shared_ptr<arrow::Table> table = *maybe_table;
```

You may have noticed a pattern where the functions return arrow::Result objects, templated on the values we want. This is so that it's easy to check for any errors during processing and handle them, rather than just failing or crashing at runtime. We use the ok method to check for success. After that, we can handle an error by getting an arrow::Status object via the status method to get the error code and/or message.

5. Now that we have read the whole file into memory (because that's what the default options and `TableReader` do – you may not want that for very large files), we can just print it out:

```
std::cout << table->ToString() << std::endl;
```

The complete code example can be found in this book's GitHub repository as `csv_reader.cc` in the `chapter2` directory. When you're compiling this, make sure that you link against the libraries correctly. By doing this, you should get output that looks nearly identical to when we did the same thing in Python with `pyarrow`. Just like we did previously, the data is read into chunked arrays for the table so that it can be parallelized during the read operation. Before moving on to the next section, try playing with the options to get different table results and control what you read into memory.

Writing a CSV file is similarly fairly simple to do. As with reading, you can write an entire table in one shot or you can write incrementally. The full code for the following snippet can be found in the `csv_writer.cc` file of the `chapter2` directory in this book's GitHub repository:

```
arrow::Table table = …;
// Write a table in one shot
bool append = false; // set to true to append to an existing
file
auto maybe_output =
    arrow::io::FileOutputStream::Open("train.csv", append);
if (!maybe_output.ok()) {
    // do something with the error here
}
auto output = *maybe_output;
auto write_options = arrow::csv::WriteOptions::Defaults();
auto status = arrow::csv::WriteCSV(*table, write_options,
output.get());
if (!status.ok()) {
    // handle any errors and print status.message()
}
```

Currently, the options for writing are as follows:

- Whether to write the header line with the column names.

- A batch size to control the number of rows written at a time, which impacts performance.

- Passing in `arrow::io::IOContext` for writing instead of using the default one. Using your `IOContext` object allows you to control the memory pool (for allocating any buffers if a zero-copy read is not possible), the executor (for scheduling asynchronous read tasks), and an external ID (for distinguishing executor tasks associated with this specific `IOContext` object).

If you're going to write data incrementally to a CSV file, you must create a `CSVWriter` and incrementally write **record batches** to the file.

> **Remember?**
>
> A record batch is a group of rows, represented in a column-oriented form in memory.

Here is an example of how you would write the same data incrementally:

1. For this example, we'll create `arrow::RecordBatchReader` from the table. However, the reader could come from anywhere, such as other data sources or a computation pipeline:

   ```
   arrow::TableBatchReader table_reader{*table};
   ```

   You can create the output stream, just as we did in the previous example, to write an entire table in one shot.

2. This time, instead of just calling the `WriteCSV` function, we'll create a `CSVWriter` object and cast it to `arrow::ipc::RecordBatchWriter`:

   ```
   auto maybe_writer = arrow::csv::MakeCSVWriter(output,
       table_reader.schema(), write_options);
   if (!maybe_writer.ok()) {
       // handle any instantiation errors for the writer
   }
   std::shared_ptr<arrow::ipc::RecordBatchWriter> writer =
   *maybe_writer;
   ```

   You'll likely need to add an `include` directive to your file to include `<arrow/ipc/api.h>` and have the definition for `RecordBatchWriter`.

3. Now, we can just loop over our record batches and write them out. Because we're using `TableBatchReader` for this, no copying needs to be done. Each record batch is just a view over a slice of the columns in the table, not a copy of the data:

   ```
   std::shared_ptr<arrow::RecordBatch> batch;
   auto status = table_reader.ReadNext(&batch);
   ```

```
// batch will be null when we are done
while (status.ok() && batch) {
    status = writer->WriteRecordBatch(*batch);
    if (!status.ok()) { break; }
    status = table_reader.ReadNext(&batch);
}
if (!status.ok()) {
    // handle write error or reader error
}
```

4. Finally, we must close the writer and the file and handle any errors:

```
if (!writer->Close().ok()) {
    // handle close errors
}
if (!output->Close().ok()) {
    // handle file close errors
}
```

Hopefully, by now, you have started to see some patterns forming in the design of the library and its functionality. Play around with different patterns of writing and reading the data so that you can get used to the interfaces being used since the C++ library isn't quite as straightforward as the Python one.

Now, let's learn how to read JSON data with C++.

Working with JSON data files using Arrow in C++

The expected format of the JSON file is the same as that with the Python library – line-separated JSON objects where each object in the input file is a single row in the resulting Arrow table. Semantically, reading in a JSON data file works the same way as with Python, providing options to control how data is converted or letting the library infer the types. Working with a JSON file in C++ is very similar to working with a CSV file, as we just did.

The differences between reading a JSON file and CSV file are as follows:

*   You include `<arrow/json/api.h>` instead of `<arrow/csv/api.h>`.

*   You call `arrow::json::TableReader::Make` instead of `arrow::csv::TableReader::Make`. The JSON reader takes a `MemoryPool*` instead of an `IOContext`, but otherwise works similarly.

Now that we've dealt with the text-based, human-readable file formats in C++, let's move on to the binary formats! Continuing in the same order as we did for Python, let's try reading an ORC file with the C++ library next.

Working with ORC data files using Arrow in C++

The addition of direct ORC support for Arrow is relatively new compared to the other format. As a result, the support isn't as fully featured. Support for ORC is provided by the official Apache ORC library, unsurprisingly named `liborc`. If the Arrow library is compiled from the source, there is an option to control whether to build the ORC support. However, the officially deployed Arrow packages should all have the ORC adapters built into them, depending on the official ORC libraries.

Unlike the CSV or JSON readers, at the time of writing, the ORC reader does not support streams, only instances of `arrow:io::RandomAccessFile`. Luckily for us, opening a file from a filesystem produces such a type, so it doesn't change anything in the basic pattern that we've been using. Remember, while the examples here are using the local filesystem, you can always instantiate a connection to S3 or an HDFS cluster using their respective filesystem abstractions and open a file from them in the same fashion. Let's get started:

1. After we've opened our file, just like we did previously, we need to create our `ORCFileReader`:

```
#include <arrow/adapters/orc/adapter.h>
// instead of explicitly handling the error, we'll just
throw
// an exception if opening the file fails using
ValueOrDie
std::shared_ptr<arrow::io::RandomAccessFile> file =
    arrow::io::ReadableFile::Open("train.orc").
ValueOrDie();
arrow::MemoryPool* pool = arrow::default_memory_pool();
auto reader =
arrow::adapters::orc::ORCFileReader::Open(file,
    pool).ValueOrDie();
```

2. There are a bunch of different functions available, such as reading particular stripes, seeking specific row numbers, and retrieving the number of stripes or rows. For now, though, we're just going to read the whole file into a table:

```
std::shared_ptr<arrow::Table> data = reader->Read()
        .ValueOrDie();
```

Finally, we can write an ORC file in much the same way:

```
std::shared_ptr<arrow::io::OutputStream> output =
    arrow::io::FileOutputStream::Open("train.orc")
    .ValueOrDie();
auto writer
=     arrow::adapters::orc::ORCFileWriter::Open(output.
get()).ValueOrDie();
status = writer->Write(*data);
if (!status.ok()) {
    // handle write errors
}
status = writer->Close();
if (!status.ok()) {
    // handle close errors
}
```

Because ORC has a defined schema with type support, the conversion between Arrow and ORC is much more well-defined. The schema can be read directly out of an ORC file and converted into an Arrow schema. Reading only specific stripes can be done to optimize the read pattern. With Arrow being an open source project, more features for using ORC files with Arrow will get built out as the community needs them or as people contribute them.

Let's move on to the last directly supported file format – Parquet files.

Working with Parquet data files using Arrow in C++

The Parquet C++ project was incorporated into the Apache Arrow project some time ago, and as a result, it contains a lot of features and has fleshed-out integration with the Arrow C++ utilities and classes. I'm not going to go into all the features of Parquet here, but they are worth looking into and many of them will get covered or mentioned in later chapters. I bet you can guess what I will cover, though.

That's right – let's slurp a Parquet file into an Arrow table in memory. We will follow the same pattern that was used for the ORC file reader – just using the Parquet Arrow reader instead. Similarly, we need an `arrow::io::RandomAccessFile` instance for the input because the metadata for reading a Parquet file is in a footer at the end of the file that describes what locations in the file to read from for a given column's data. Let's get started:

1. The `include` directive we're going to use is going to change too, so after we've created our input file instance, we can create the Parquet reader:

```
#include <parquet/arrow/reader.h>
std::unique_ptr<parquet::arrow::FileReader> arrow_reader;
// use parquet::arrow::FileReaderBuilder if you need more
// fine-grained options
arrow::Status st = parquet::arrow::OpenFile(input, pool,
                                                  &arrow_
reader);
if (!st.ok()) {
    // handle errors
}
```

2. There is a multitude of different functions that can be used to control reading only specific row groups, getting a record batch reader, reading only specific columns, and so on. You can even get access to the underlying raw `ParquetFileReader` object if you so desire. By default, only one thread will be used when reading, but you can enable multiple threads to get used to when you're reading multiple columns. Let's just go through the simplest case here:

```
std::shared_ptr<arrow::Table> table;
st = arrow_reader->ReadTable(&table);
if (!st.ok()) {
    // handle errors from reading
}
```

3. Writing a Parquet file from an Arrow table of data works precisely how you'd expect it to by now:

```
#include <parquet/arrow/writer.h>
PARQUET_ASSIGN_OR_THROW(auto outfile,
    arrow::io::FileOutputStream::Open("train.parquet"));
int64_t chunk_size = 1024; // number of rows per row
```

```
group
PARQUET_THROW_NOT_OK(parquet::arrow::WriteTable(
    table, arrow::default_memory_pool(),
    outfile, chunk_size));
```

The Parquet library provides a few helper macros for handling errors. In this case, we'll just let them throw exceptions if anything fails.

Since the Golang library follows the patterns of the C++ library in most ways, I'm not going to cover it here in its entirety. What I will mention, though, is that rather than providing direct utilities and abstractions for interfacing with HDFS and S3, the Go library is implemented in terms of the interfaces in the standard `io` module. This makes it extremely easy to plug in any desired data sources, so long as there is a library that provides the necessary functions to meet the interface.

Here are my recommendations for libraries for HDFS and S3. The following links are import paths for Go, not URLs to be used in a browser. This is important for using the correct version of the libraries, indicated by the `/v2` suffix of the first link:

- `github.com/colinmarc/hdfs/v2`: This is a native `golang` client for HDFS for implementing interfaces from the `stdlib` OS package, where it can provide an idiomatic interface to HDFS.

- `github.com/aws/aws-sdk-go-v2/service/s3`: AWS provides its own native Go library for interfacing with all the various AWS services, which is the optimal way to interact with S3 at the time of writing.

After reading in the data from our data files, what do we do next? We clean it, manipulate it, perform statistical analysis on it, or whatever we want. For most modern data scientists, this means you need to make this data accessible to the various libraries and tools you're comfortable with and used to. Of those tools and libraries, one of the most commonly used has to be the `pandas` Python library. The next thing we're going to cover is how Arrow integrates with `pandas` DataFrames and accelerates workflows by using them together.

pandas firing Arrow

If you've done any data analysis in Python, you've likely at least heard of the `pandas` library. It is an open source, BSD-licensed library for performing data analysis in Python and one of the most popular tools used by data scientists and engineers to do their jobs. Given the ubiquity of its use, it only makes sense that Arrow's Python library has integration for converting to and from `pandas` DataFrames quickly and efficiently. This section is going to dive into the specifics and the gotchas for using Arrow with `pandas`, and how you can speed up your workflows by using them together.

Before we start, though, make sure you've installed `pandas` locally so that you can follow along. Of course, you also need to have `pyarrow` installed, but you already did that in the previous chapter, right? Let's take a look:

- If you're using conda, `pandas` is part of the Anaconda (`https://docs.continuum.io/anaconda/`) distribution and can easily be installed like other packages:

  conda install pandas

- If you prefer to use `pip`, you can just install it normally via PyPI:

  pip3 install pandas

It's not all sunshine and roses however as it's not currently possible to convert every single column type unmodified. The first thing we need to look at is how the types compare and shape up between Arrow and pandas.

Putting pandas in your quiver

The standard building block of pandas is the DataFrame, which is equivalent to an Arrow table. In both cases, we are describing a group of named columns that all have equal lengths. In the simplest case, there are handy `to_pandas` and `from_pandas` functions on several Arrow types. For example, converting between an Arrow table and a DataFrame is very easy:

```
>>> import pyarrow as pa
>>> import pandas as pd
>>> df = pd.DataFrame({"a": [1,2,3]})
>>> table = pa.Table.from_pandas(df) # convert to arrow
>>> df_new = table.to_pandas() # convert back to pandas
```

There are also a lot of options that exist to control the conversions, such as whether to use threads and manage the memory usage or data types. The pandas objects may also have an `index` member variable that can contain row labels for the data instead of just using a 0-based row index. When you're converting from a DataFrame, the `from_pandas` functions have an option named `preserve_index` that is used to control whether to store the index data and how to store it. Generally, the index data will be tracked as schema metadata in the resulting Arrow table. The options are as follows:

- `None`: This is the default value of the `preserve_index` option. `RangeIndex` typed data is only stored as metadata, while other index types are stored as actual columns in the created table.

- `False`: Does not store any index information at all.

- `True`: Forces all index data to be serialized as columns in the table. This is because storing a `RangeIndex` can cause issues in limited scenarios, such as storing multiple DataFrames in a single Parquet file.

Arrow tables support both flat and nested columns, as we've seen. However, a DataFrame only supports flat columns. This and other differences in how the data types are handled means that sometimes, a full conversion isn't possible. One of the primary difficulties with this conversion is that pandas does not support nullable columns of arbitrary types, while Arrow does. All Arrow arrays can potentially contain null values, regardless of their type. In addition, the datetime handling in pandas always uses nanoseconds as the unit of time. The following table shows the mappings between the data types:

pandas -> Arrow		Arrow -> pandas	
pandas (source)	Arrow (destination)	Arrow (source)	pandas (destination)
bool	BOOL	BOOL	bool
int or uint {8,16,32,64}	int or uint {8,16,32,64}	BOOL with nulls	object with values True, False, None
float32	FLOAT	int or uint {8,16,32,64}	int or uint {8,16,32,64}
float64	DOUBLE	int or uint {8,16,32,64} with nulls	float64
str/unicode	STRING	FLOAT	float32
pandas.Categorical	DICTIONARY	DOUBLE	float64
pandas.Timestamp	TIMESTAMP(unit=ns)	STRING	str
datetime.date	DATE	DICTIONARY	pandas.Categorical
datetime.time	TIME64	TIMESTAMP(unit=*)	Pandas.Timestamp(numpy.datetime64[ns])
		DATE	object with datetime.date objects

Figure 2.6 – Mapping of pandas types to Arrow types

Only some data types in pandas support handling missing data or null values. A specific case of this is that the default integer types do not support nulls and will get cast to float when converting from Arrow if there are any nulls in the array. If there are no nulls, then the column remains the `integer` type it had before conversion, as shown in the following snippet:

```
>>> arr = pa.array([1, 2, 3])
>>> arr
<pyarrow.lib.Int64Array object at 0x000002348DCD02E8>
[
  1,
  2,
  3
]
>>> arr.to_pandas()
0   1
1   2
2   3
dtype: int64
>>> arr = pa.array([1, 2, None])
>>> arr.to_pandas()
0   1.0
1   2.0
2   NaN
dtype: float64
```

When you're working with date and time types there are a few caveats that need to be kept in mind regarding knowing what data type to expect, as follows:

- Most of the time, dates in pandas are handled using the `numpy.datetime64 [ns]` type, but sometimes, dates are represented using arrays of Python's built-in `datetime.date` object. Both will convert into the Arrow `date32` type by default:

  - If you want to use `date64`, you must specify it explicitly:

    ```
    >>> from datetime import date
    >>> s = pd.Series([date(1987, 8, 4), None, date(2000, 1, 1)])
    >>> arr = pa.array(s)
    ```

```
>>> arr.type
DataType(date32[day])
>>> arr = pa.array(s, type='date64')
>>> arr.type
DataType(date64[ms])
```

- Converting back into pandas will get you `datetime.date` objects. Use the `date_as_object=False` argument to get NumPy's `datetime64` type:

```
>>> arr.to_pandas()
0    1987-08-04
1    None
2    2000-01-01
dtype: object
>>> s2 = pd.Series(arr.to_pandas(date_as_object=False))
>>> s2.dtype
dtype('<M8[ns]')
```

- Python's built-in `datetime.time` objects will be converted into Arrow's `time64` type and vice versa.

- The timestamp type that's used by pandas is NumPy's `datetime64[ns]` type, which is converted into an Arrow timestamp using nanoseconds as the unit.

- If you're using a time zone, it will be preserved via metadata when converting. Also, notice that the underlying values are converted into UTC in Arrow, with the time zone in the data type's metadata:

```
>>> df = pd.DataFrame({'datetime': pd.date_range('2020-
01-01T00:00:00-04:00', freq='H', periods=3)})
>>> df
                    datetime
0 2020-01-01 00:00:00-04:00
1 2020-01-01 01:00:00-04:00
2 2020-01-01 02:00:00-04:00
>>> table = pa.Table.from_pandas(df)
>>> table
pyarrow.Table
datetime: timestamp[ns, tz=-4:00]
datetime: [[2020-01-01 04:00:00.000000000,2020-01-01
05:00:00.000000000,2020-01-01 06:00:00.000000000]]
```

Since pandas is used so extensively in the Python ecosystem and already provides utilities for reading and writing CSV, Parquet, and other file types, it may not necessarily be clear what advantages Arrow provides here other than interoperability. That's not to say that providing interoperability for pandas with any utility built for Arrow isn't a huge benefit – it is! But this integration shines when you're considering memory usage and the performance of reading, writing, and transferring the data.

Making pandas run fast

With all the optimizations and low-level tweaks that Arrow has to ensure performant memory usage and data transfer, it makes sense for us to compare reading in data files between the Arrow libraries and the pandas library. Using the IPython utility, it's really easy to do timing tests for comparison. We're going to use the same sample data files we did for the examples of reading data files to do the tests:

```
In [1]: import pyarrow as pa
In [2]: import pyarrow.csv
In [3]: %timeit table = pa.csv.read_csv('train.csv')
177 ms ± 3.03 ms per loop (mean ± std. dev. Of 7 runs, 1 loop
each)
```

The preceding output shows the results of using the timeit utility to read the CSV file in using pyarrow seven times and getting the average and standard deviation of the time each took. On my laptop, it took only 177 milliseconds on average to create an Arrow table from the CSV file, which is around 192 megabytes in size. To keep a fair comparison, we also need to time how long it takes to create the pandas DataFrame from the Arrow table so that we're comparing apples to apples:

```
In [4]: table = pa.csv.read_csv('train.csv')
In [5]: import pandas as pd
In [6]: %timeit df = table.to_pandas()
509 ms ± 10.7 ms per loop (mean ± std. dev. Of 7 runs, 1 loop
each)
```

At around 509 milliseconds, we see it took much longer to convert the table into a DataFrame than it took to even read the file into the Arrow table. Now, let's see how long it takes to read it in using the pandas read_csv function:

```
In [7]: %timeit df = pd.read_csv('train.csv')
3.49 s ± 193 ms per loop (mean ± std. dev. Of 7 runs, 1 loop
each)
```

Wow! Look at that! On my laptop, it took an average of 3 and a half seconds to read the file using pandas directly. Even combining the cost of reading the file in and converting it from Arrow into a DataFrame, that's just over an 80% difference in performance with this fairly small (by data analysis standards) file containing 1,458,644 rows and 11 columns. I'll give pandas a fighting chance, though. We can try reading from a compressed version of the CSV file, causing there to be added processing that must be performed to decompress the data before it can be parsed to create the final objects. The following chart contains the final times from using the `timeit` utility, not just for reading the file and its compressed form, but also for writing the CSV file from the data:

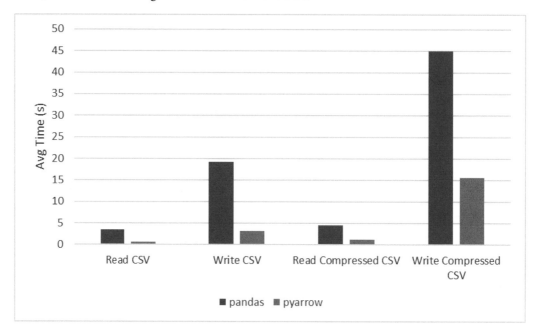

Figure 2.7 – Runtime comparison for reading and writing a CSV file

You might be wondering about the other file formats besides CSV and how the performance compares between pandas and `pyarrow`. If you look at the documentation for the functions in pandas that deal with Parquet and ORC file formats, you'll find that in both cases, it just delegates calls out to the `pyarrow` library and uses it to read the data in. For the JSON use case, the structure and format of the data expected by pandas is different than what is expected by `pyarrow`, so it's not an equivalent use case. Instead, you should choose based on which conforms to what you need. This usually depends on the source of the data you'll be using.

Occasionally, when you're performing the conversions between Arrow arrays or tables and pandas DataFrames, memory usage and performance issues can rear their ugly heads. Because the internal representation of the raw data is different between the two libraries, there are only a limited number of situations where the conversion can occur without you having to copy data or perform computations. At worst, the conversion can result in having two versions of your data in memory, which is potentially problematic, depending on what you're doing. But don't fret! We're going to cover a few strategies to mitigate this problem next.

Keeping pandas from running wild

In the previous section, we saw it took a little more than 500 ms to create a pandas DataFrame from the Arrow table of our CSV data. If that seemed to be a little slow to you, it's because it had to copy all those strings we have in the data. The functions for converting Arrow tables and arrays into DataFrames have an argument named `zero_copy_only` that, if set to `true`, will throw an `ArrowException` if the conversion requires the data to be copied. It's kind of an *all-or-nothing* situation that should be reserved for only if you need to micromanage your memory usage. The requirements that need to be met for a zero-copy conversion are as follows:

- Integral (signed or unsigned) data types, regardless of the bit width, or a floating-point data type (`float16`, `float32`, or `float64`). This also covers the various numeric types that are represented using this data, such as timestamps, dates, and so on.

- The Arrow array contains no null values. Arrow data uses bitmaps to represent null values, which pandas doesn't support.

- If it is a chunked array of data, then it needs to be only a single chunk because pandas requires the data to be entirely contiguous.

Two options are provided by the pyarrow library to limit the potential copies of data during conversion – split_blocks and self_destruct. Because pandas uses NumPy under the hood for its computations, it likes to collect columns of the same data type in two-dimensional NumPy arrays because it speeds up the – already very speedy – operations on many columns at once, such as gathering the sum of multiple columns. The following diagram shows a very simplified visual as to how the memory of a DataFrame is managed in pandas. There's an object called a **Block Manager** that handles memory allocations and keeps track of where the underlying arrays of data are. Unfortunately, if you are gradually building up a DataFrame column by column every so often, the Block Manager is going to consolidate those individual columns into groups called **blocks**, and that consolidation will require copying the data internally to put the block together:

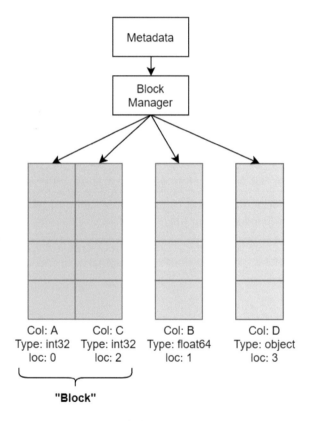

Figure 2.8 – Simplified DataFrame memory layout

The `pyarrow` library tries very hard to construct the exact *consolidated* blocks that would be expected so that pandas won't perform extra allocations or copies after converting them into a DataFrame. The downside to doing this is that it requires copying the data from Arrow, which means your *peak* memory usage would be double the full size of your data. The previously mentioned `split_blocks` option for conversion produces a single *block* for each column instead of performing the consolidation beforehand if set to `True`. Keep in mind that plenty of pandas operations are going to trigger it to start consolidating internally anyway, but this is going to both speed up the conversion process and potentially avoid the worst-case scenario of completely doubling the memory usage for your data. With this option set, if your data meets the criteria for a zero-copy conversion, you will get a true zero-copy operation.

Let's see this in action:

1. First, we must import the libraries we need – that is, `pandas`, `pyarrow`, and `numpy`:

    ```
    import pandas as pd
    import pyarrow as pa
    import numpy as np
    ```

2. Then, we must create a whole bunch of random floating-point data to test with as NumPy arrays:

    ```
    nrows = 1_000_000
    ncols = 100
    arr = np.random.randn(nrows)
    data = {'f{}'.format(i): arr for i in range(ncols) }
    ```

3. Now, we must time our conversions – let's see how it goes:

    ```
    In [8]: %timeit df = pd.DataFrame(data)
    157 ms ± 13.6 ms per loop (mean ± std. dev. of 7 runs, 1
    loop each)
    In [9]: %timeit df = pa.table(data).to_pandas()
    115 ms ± 4.91 ms per loop (mean ± std. dev. of 7 runs, 10
    loops each)
    In [10]: %timeit df = pa.table(data).to_pandas(split_
    blocks=True)
    3.18 ms ± 37.3 µs per loop (mean ± std. dev. of 7 runs,
    100 loops each)
    ```

Sorcery! Of course, if you followed these conversions up with a bunch of pandas operations, the 100 milliseconds that you saved on the conversion may instead show up when the next consolidation happens, but the numbers are pretty impressive! Even in the case where Arrow does the consolidation, the conversion was faster than just creating the DataFrame from the NumPy arrays in the first place by around 26%. One of the reasons that Arrow does all this work when constructing DataFrames, and doing it as fast and efficiently as possible, is to prevent everyone from having to come up with converters for DataFrames. Components, utilities, and systems can just produce Arrow formatted data in whatever language they want (even if they don't depend on the Arrow libraries directly!) and then use `pyarrow` to convert it into a pandas DataFrame. Don't go writing a converter – the Arrow library is likely going to be much faster than any custom conversion code and you will end up with less code to maintain. It's a win-win!

But what about the ominous-sounding `self_destruct` option? Normally, when you copy the data, you end up with two copies in memory until the variable goes out of scope and the Python garbage collector cleans it up. Using the `self_destruct` option will blow up the internal Arrow buffers one by one as each column is converted for pandas. This has the potential of releasing the memory back to your operating system as soon as an individual column is converted. The key thing to remember about this is that your `Table` object will no longer be safe to use after the conversion and trying to call a method on it will crash your Python process. You can also use both options together which will, in some situations, result in significantly lower memory usage:

```
>>> df = table.to_pandas(split_blocks=True, self_destruct=True)
>>> del table # not necessary but good practice
```

> **Note**
>
> Using `self_destruct` is not necessarily guaranteed to save memory! Because the conversion is happening with each column as it is converted, freeing the memory is also happening column by column. In the Arrow libraries, it is possible, and frequently likely, that multiple columns could share the same underlying memory buffer. In this situation, no memory will be freed until all of the columns that reference the same buffer are converted.

We've talked a lot about *zero-copy* up to this point with it coming up here and there as I've introduced various ways Arrow enables transferring data around. The nature of Arrow's columnar format makes it very easy to stream and shift raw buffers of memory around or repurpose them to increase performance. Usually, when data is being passed around, there is a need to serialize and deserialize information, but you'll remember that previously, I said that Arrow allows you to skip the serialization and deserialization costs.

To ensure efficient memory usage when you're dealing with all these streams and files, the Arrow libraries all provide various utilities for memory management that are also utilized internally by them. These helper classes and utilities are what we're going to cover next so that you know how to take advantage of them to make your scripts and programs as lean as possible. We're also going to cover how you can share your buffers across programming language boundaries for improved performance, and why you'd want to do so.

Sharing is caring... especially when it's your memory

Earlier, we touched on the concept of slicing Arrow arrays and how they allow you to grab views of tables or record batches or arrays without having to copy the data itself. This is true down to the underlying buffer objects that are used by the Arrow libraries, which can then be used by consumers, even when they aren't working with Arrow data directly to manage their memory efficiently. The various Arrow libraries generally provide memory pool objects to control how memory is allocated and track how much has been allocated by the Arrow library. These memory pools are then utilized by data buffers and everything else within the Arrow libraries.

Diving into memory management

Continuing with our examination of the Go, Python, and C++ implementations of Arrow, they all have similar approaches to providing memory pools for managing and tracking your memory usage. The following is a simplified diagram of a memory pool:

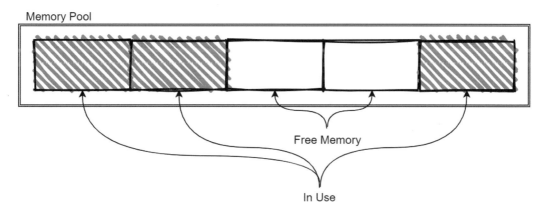

Figure 2.9 – Memory pool tracking memory

As more memory is needed, the pool is expanded as it allocates more memory. When memory is freed, it is released back to the pool so that it can be reused by future allocations. The exact management strategy will vary from implementation to implementation, but the basic idea is still like what's shown in the preceding diagram. The memory pools are typically used for the longer-lived and larger-sized data, such as the data buffers for arrays and tables, whereas the small, temporary objects and workspaces will use the regular allocators for whatever programming language you're working in.

In most cases, a default memory pool or allocator will be used (which you can see in several of the previous code examples), but many of the APIs allow you to pass in a specific memory pool instance to perform allocations with, as follows:

C++

The `arrow::MemoryPool` class is provided by the library for manipulating or checking the allocation of memory. A process-wide default memory pool will be initialized when the library is first initialized. This can be accessed in code via the `arrow::default_memory_pool` function. Depending on how the library was compiled and the `ARROW_DEFAULT_MEMORY_POOL` environment variable, the default pool will either be implemented using the `jemalloc` library, the `mimalloc` library, or the standard C `malloc` functions. The memory pool itself has functions to manually release unused data back to the operating system (best effort and only if the underlying allocator holds onto unused memory), to report the peak amount of memory allocation for the pool, and to return the current number of bytes allocated but haven't been freed through the pool.

> **Memory Allocators**
>
> The benefit of using custom allocators such as `jemalloc` or `mimalloc` is the potential for significant performance improvements. Depending on the benchmark, both have shown lower system memory usage and faster allocations than the old standby of `malloc`. It's worth testing your workloads with different allocators to see if you may benefit from them!

For manipulating buffers of data, there is the `arrow::Buffer` class. Buffers can be pre-allocated, similar to using STL containers such as `std::vector` via the `Resize` and `Reserve` methods by using a `BufferBuilder` object. These buffers will either be marked as `mutable` or not based on how they were constructed, indicating whether or not they can be resized and/or reallocated. If you're using I/O functionality such as an `InputStream` object, it's recommended to use the provided `Read` functions to read into a `Buffer` instance because in many cases, it will be able to slice the internal buffer and avoid copying additional data. The following diagram shows an allocated buffer with a length and capacity, along with a sliced *view* of the buffer. The slice knows that it does not own the memory it points to, so when it is cleaned up, it won't attempt to free the memory:

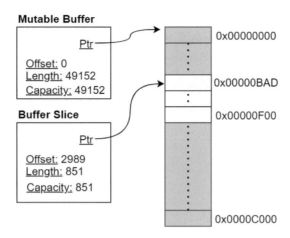

Figure 2.10 – Mutable buffer and slice

Python

Because the Python library is built on top of the C++ library, all of the functionality mentioned previously regarding memory pools and buffers is also available in the Python library. The pyarrow.Buffer object wraps the C++ buffer type to allow the other, higher-level classes to interact with memory that they may or may not own. Buffers can create parent-child relationships with other buffers by referencing each other via slices and memory views, so that memory can be easily shared across different arrays, tables, and record batches instead of copied. Anywhere that a Python buffer or memory view is required, a buffer can be used without you having to copy the data:

```
>>> import pyarrow as pa
>>> data = b'helloworld'
>>> buf = pa.py_buffer(data)
>>> buf
<pyarrow.lib.Buffer object at 0x000001CB922CA1B0>
```

No memory is allocated when calling the py_buffer function. It's just a zero-copy view of the memory that Python already allocated for the data bytes object. If a Python buffer or memory view is required, then a zero-copy conversion can be done with the buffer:

```
>>> memoryview(buf)
<memory at 0x000001CBA8FECE88>
```

Lastly, there's a to_pybytes method on buffers that will create a new Python bytestring object. This will make a copy of the data that is referenced by the buffer, ensuring a clean break between the new Python object and the buffer.

Once again, since everything is backed by the C++ library, the Python library has its own default memory pool that can tell you how much data has been allocated so far. We can allocate our own buffer and see this happen:

```
>>> pa.total_allocated_bytes()
0
>>> buf = pa.allocate_buffer(1024, resizable=True)
>>> pa.total_allocated_bytes()
1024
>>> buf.resize(2048)
>>> pa.total_allocated_bytes()
2048
>>> buf = None
>>> pa.total_allocated_bytes()
0
```

You can also see that once the memory has been garbage collected, it is freed and the memory pool reflects that it's no longer allocated.

Golang

As with the Python and C++ libraries, the Go library also provides buffers and memory allocation management with the `memory` package. There is a default allocator that exists that can be referenced by `memory.DefaultAllocator`, which is an instance of `memory.GoAllocator`. Because the allocator definition is an interface, custom allocators would be easy to build if desired for given projects. If the C++ library is available, the `"ccalloc"` build tag can be provided when you're building a project using the Go Arrow library. Here, you can use CGO to provide a function, `NewCgoArrowAllocator`, which creates an allocator that allocates memory using the C++ memory pool objects rather than the default Go allocators. This is important to utilize if you need to pass memory back and forth between Go and other languages to ensure that the Go garbage collector doesn't interfere.

Finally, there is the `memory.Buffer` type, which is the primary unit of memory management in the Go library. It works similarly to the buffers in the C++ and Python libraries, providing access to the underlying bytes, being potentially resizable, and checking their length and capacity when wrapping slices of bytes.

Managing buffers for performance

With this memory and buffer management, we can imagine a couple of scenarios where this can all come together to ensure superior performance, as follows:

- Suppose you want to perform some analysis on a very large set of data with billions of rows. A common way to improve this performance would be to parallelize the operations on subsets of rows. By being able to slice the arrays and data buffers without having to copy the underlying data, this parallelization becomes faster and has lower memory requirements. Each batch you operate on isn't a copy – it's just a view of the data, as shown in the following diagram. The dotted lines on the sliced columns indicate that they are just views over a subset of the data in their respective column, in the same way that the preceding diagram demonstrates a sliced buffer. Each slice can be safely operated on in parallel:

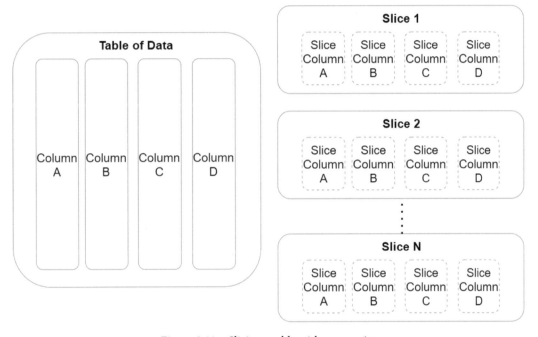

Figure 2.11 – Slicing a table without copying

- Maybe you have a series of columns of data and you want to incrementally filter out rows where every column is null. The naive approach would be to simply iterate the rows and copy the data to a new version of each column if at least one of them is not null at that index. This could become even more complex if you're dealing with nested columns. Instead, when using Arrow arrays, you could use the validity bitmap buffers to speed this up! Just perform a bit-wise `or` operation with all the bitmaps to get a single bitmap that represents the final filtered indexes. Then, rather than having to progressively build up a filtered copy of every single column, you could do it column by column to achieve better CPU cache hits and memory locality. The following diagram shows this process visually. Depending on the total size of the data and the number of rows in the result, it may make more sense to just take slices of each group of rows instead of copying them to new columns. Either way, you are in control of how and when the memory is used and freed:

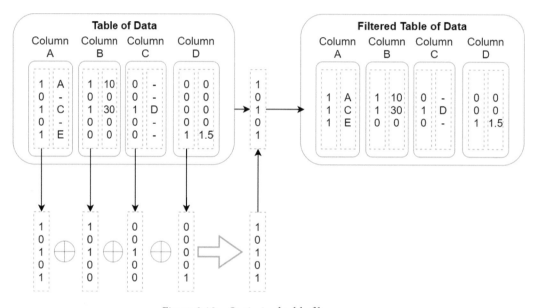

Figure 2.12 – Optimized table filter process

If you're able to pass the address of some buffer of data around, and you know that Arrow's memory format is language agnostic, that means that with just a bit of metadata, you can even share tables of data between different runtimes and languages. *Why would you want to do that?* I hear you ask. Well, let's see how that could be useful…

Crossing the boundaries

One of the more common workflows when it comes to data science can be seen in the following diagram:

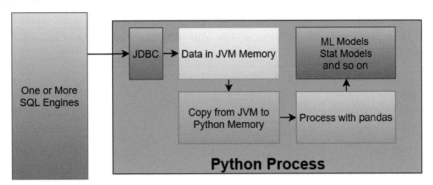

Figure 2.13 – Example data science workflow

The steps of this workflow are as follows:

1. Data is queried from one or more SQL engines from a Python process using a JDBC driver via some library.

2. The rows of data, now residing in JVM memory, are *copied* into Python memory.

3. The data, now in Python memory, is then processed in some way with pandas.

4. The results of the analysis with pandas are fed into the various models being utilized, such as a machine learning model or some other statistical model.

For large datasets, the most expensive part of this workflow is copying the data from the JVM to Python memory and converting the orientation in pandas from rows into columns. To improve workflows like this, the Arrow libraries provide a stable C data interface that allows you to share data across these boundaries without copying it by directly sharing pointers to the memory. Here, the data is located rather than you creating a huge number of intermediate Python objects. The interface is defined by a couple of header files that are simple enough that they can be copied into any project that is capable of communicating with C APIs, such as by using **foreign function interfaces**, or **FFIs**.

In this particular workflow, there is also a JDBC adapter for Arrow in the Java library that retrieves the results, converts the rows into columns in the JVM, and stores data as Arrow record batches in *off-heap* memory, which is not managed by the JVM itself. This native memory layout can then use the C data interface to inform the `pyarrow` library of pointers to the raw data buffers and logical structure so that the library can interpret the memory in place properly and use it. The following diagram shows the new workflow using these interfaces:

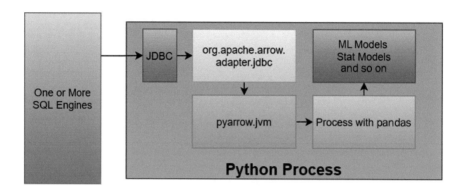

Figure 2.14 – Example data science workflow with memory sharing

This time, the workflow is like this:

1. Data is queried from one or more SQL engines from a Python process using a JDBC driver via some library.

2. As the rows of data come in, they are converted into columnar formatted Arrow record batches with the raw data stored "off-heap" and not managed by the JVM.

3. Instead of copying the data, the Arrow data is accessed directly in Python via the pointers to the data that have already been allocated by the JVM. No intermediate Python objects are created and no copies are made of the raw data.

4. We can now perform the conversion into pandas DataFrames, as we've seen previously, on the Arrow record batches.

5. Finally, those DataFrames are passed to the desired libraries to populate models with the analyzed data.

This may not seem like a lot, but in practice, it can result in humongous performance speedups. Utilizing Dremio as the SQL engine and the sample NYC Taxi dataset, I compared the performance of the two approaches:

- With the former approach, a fairly simple query on the dataset that pulls ~623k rows and 6 columns from Dremio and creates a DataFrame from it took, on average, 1 minute and 5 seconds.

- With the latter approach, while sharing the memory to avoid the copies, the same query took around 573 milliseconds. That's about 113 times faster or an 11,243.8% improvement.

If your result set is small enough, then the benefit of the shared memory approach won't be as large and may not be worth the extra complexity and dependency. The following table shows the performance of the two approaches with different numbers of rows, all at 6 columns each. We can see that if you've got around less than 10,000 rows, even if the relative numbers show significant speedups, the absolute amount of time isn't that much, depending on your workflow:

# Rows	Traditional (Copy)	Shared Memory (No Copy)	Speedup	% Improvement
950	274 ms	144 ms	1.90x	90.27%
10,000	1.29 s	175 ms	7.37x	637.14%
198,143	26.8 s	403 ms	66.50x	6550.12%
623,418	1 min 5 s	573 ms	113.44x	11243.80%

Figure 2.15 – Performance comparison of traditional versus shared memory

Just out of pure curiosity, I tested both workflows with the full dataset in the Parquet file I was using, which comes out to a bit more than 62 million rows of data. The workflow that performs the copying wound up taking a little over 3 hours; utilizing the shared memory utilities across the C data interface only took around 58.7 seconds. This is an astounding ~184 times speedup or ~18,520% improvement!

If you haven't guessed yet, the primary target audience for the C data interface is those developers building libraries, tools, and utilities that use Arrow. Several packages exist already that take advantage of these interfaces, such as the `reticulate` methods of the `arrow` R package (`https://rstudio.github.io/reticulate/articles/python_packages.html`) for passing data between R and Python in the same process and the `pyarrow.jvm` module I used previously. As more developers and library builders take advantage of the C data interface for passing data around via sharing memory, we'll see the overall performance of common data tasks rocket into the stratosphere, leaving more CPU cycles and memory to be used for performing the necessary analytics computations, rather than on copying data over and over just to make it accessible in the tools you want to use.

If you are one of those library and utility developers or are an engineer working on passing data for other purposes, take advantage and play around with the interface. In addition to the raw data, there is also support for streaming data via the C interface so that you can stream record batches directly into shared memory instead of copying them. At the time of writing, facilities for using the C data interface exist in the C++, Python, R, Rust, Go, Java, C/GLib, and Ruby implementations of the Arrow library. Go take advantage of this awesome way to share data between tools! Go!

Summary

At this point, not only should you be fairly well acquainted with a variety of topics and concepts regarding the usage of the Apache Arrow libraries, but you should also know how to start integrating them into your daily workflows. Whether you're taking advantage of the filesystem abstractions, data format conversions, or zero-copy communication benefits, Arrow can slot into a huge number of parts of any data workflow. Make sure you understand the concepts that have been touched on so far involving the formats, communication methods, and utilities provided by the Arrow libraries before moving on. Play around with them and try out different strategies for managing your data and passing it around between tools and utilities. If you're an engineer building out distributed systems, try using the Arrow IPC format (which we will learn about in detail in *Chapter 4, Format and Memory Handling*) and compare that with whatever previous way you passed data around. Which is easier to use? Which is more performant?

The next chapter, *Data Science with Arrow*, kind of wraps up the first big part of this book by diving more into specific examples of where and how Arrow can enable and enhance data science workflows, as we saw with the memory sharing through the C data interface, which provides huge performance improvements to a fairly standard workflow. We're going to address using **ODBC/JDBC** more directly, using **Apache Spark** and **Jupyter**, and even strategies and utilities for using **Elasticsearch** and providing interactive charts and tables powered by Arrow.

Ready? Let's do this!

3
Data Science with Apache Arrow

So far, we've covered the **Apache Arrow** format and how to read various types of data from local disks or cloud storage into Arrow-formatted memory, but if you aren't the one actually building tools and utilities for others to use, then what does this mean for you? You'll be able to benefit from things that people will build using Arrow, such as new fancy libraries, performance enhancements, and utilities. But, how can you materially change your workflow to get some of these improvements right now? That's what we're going to be covering in this chapter, specific examples of Arrow enhancing existing data science workflows and enabling new ones.

In this chapter, we'll look at the following topics:

- How **Open Database Connectivity** (**ODBC**) is being improved upon and will eventually, hopefully, be rendered obsolete by Arrow communication protocols

- Leveraging the topics we covered in the previous chapters with Apache Spark and Jupyter notebooks

- Usage of **Perspective**, an interactive analytics and data visualization component for web and Python/JupyterLab

- An example of a full stack application using Arrow as its internal data format

Technical requirements

With the exception of the last section of the chapter, this chapter is more focused on specific examples rather than code snippets, but if you want to try performing the same tests as the examples, you'll need the following:

- An internet-connected computer.

- A single- or multiple-node Apache Spark cluster also running Jupyter. Docker is the easiest way to set this up, which is what we'll use in this chapter.

Let's begin!

ODBC takes an Arrow to the knee

Open Database Connectivity (**ODBC**) is a standardized **Application Programming Interface** (**API**) for accessing databases originally designed and built in the early 1990s. The development of ODBC intended to enable applications to be independent of their underlying database by having a standardized API to use that would be implemented by database-specific drivers. This allowed a developer to write their application and potentially easily migrate to a different database by simply specifying a different driver. In 1997, the **Java Database Connectivity** (**JDBC**) API was developed to provide a common API for Java programs to manage multiple drivers and connect either by bridging to an ODBC connection or by other types of connections, which all have different pros and cons. Almost 30 years later, these technologies are still the de facto standard way to communicate with **Structured Query Language** (**SQL**) databases.

That all being said, computing, and data in particular, have changed significantly in that time frame. Back then, computers didn't have the dozens of cores that they have today, and systems were much more monolithic. Big data's rise, alongside the increase in distributed systems and the emergence of data science as a full profession, has shown the cracks in the promises of performance and scalability from ODBC and JDBC. Unfortunately, it's going to take a while for everything to follow suit to new technologies, so there needs to be a stepping-stone, an intermediate step, to help push things towards leveraging new technologies such as Arrow.

In the context of data science, most will interact with ODBC or JDBC when working with loading data for analysis into scripts or tools. **Business intelligence** (**BI**) utilities nearly universally accept ODBC and JDBC interfaces as their primary way to interact with data sources. It makes sense, as they only have to implement their code once in terms of the ODBC standard and that gives them access to any data source that publishes an ODBC driver. Some of the big names in this space would be tools such as Tableau and Power BI, both of which support ODBC data source access. Supporting native Arrow data, Parquet files, and other communications would mean faster data access, quicker computations, and snappier interactive dashboards for users. How does it do that? Well, by reducing and eliminating the translations and copies of data being made at every level through direct support of Arrow in all stages. We've already mentioned in *Chapter 2, Working with Key Arrow Specifications*, one such example: the **Arrow-JDBC adapter**.

Lost in translation

Even when systems speak the same standard protocol, there might be a whole bunch of translations and copies happening under the hood. ODBC, for all its benefits, was still designed during a time when it was much more common to be requesting wide tables with large numbers of columns and fewer rows as compared to modern data analysis. While it enabled connectivity between different disparate systems, there's still a lot of translating and copying that has to happen in the ODBC drivers for everything to work correctly. *Figure 3.1* shows a comparison between a standard data science workflow using typical ODBC or JDBC and using the Arrow-JDBC adapter.

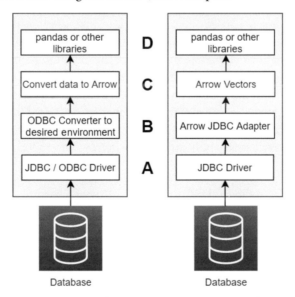

Figure 3.1 – Typical ODBC versus Arrow JDBC adapter

Look first at the left side of *Figure 3.1*, the typical case when using JDBC. There are three points where data has to be translated between formats, as follows:

1. First, data is translated inside the JDBC/ODBC driver from whatever format the database speaks natively into the JDBC/ODBC standards.

2. Next, data has to be translated into the necessary objects/memory for your choice of programming language/environment. For example, if you're using Python and pandas, you have to either use ODBC or Python-native drivers (lower performance) or a JDBC driver, which then has to convert the JDBC objects to Python objects, and this has a high cost.

3. Finally, however you got your data into your environment, if the interface didn't spit out Arrow data objects, then once again there's a translation to Arrow before you can finally interact with the data in pandas. (Sure, you can go straight to pandas, but we've already shown that the creation of pandas from Arrow has a negligible cost, so it doesn't save you anything.)

Compare this with the workflow on the right side of *Figure 3.1*:

1. If the underlying database doesn't speak Arrow natively, there's a translation from the database data into JDBC objects.

2. The Arrow-JDBC adapter will then convert the JDBC objects directly into Arrow vectors in memory that is not managed by the **Java Virtual Machine** (**JVM**).

3. The addresses of the vectors can be passed directly into Python, which can then reference the memory exactly where it is (as shown in *Chapter 2, Working with Key Arrow Specifications*) rather than having to translate or copy the data.

By reducing the translations and copies, we reduce the CPU usage, memory usage, and run time. In short, it goes much faster and requires fewer resources! This could apply directly to tools such as Tableau and Power BI if they supported Arrow natively. We're starting to see this happen as more and more companies start enabling Arrow data as the memory format for ODBC and JDBC drivers. Here's a short list of a couple of tools and companies that have already built support for Arrow into their clients, drivers, and connectors:

*   **Snowflake** updated their ODBC drivers and Python client to convert their internal memory format to Arrow for data transfer and saw between 5x and 10x performance improvements depending on the use case (https://www.snowflake.com/blog/fetching-query-results-from-snowflake-just-got-a-lot-faster-with-apache-arrow/).

- Google's **BigQuery** added support for pulling data using Arrow record batches and users saw from 15x to 31x performance improvements for retrieving data into `pandas` DataFrames from the BigQuery Storage API (`https://medium.com/ google-cloud/announcing-google-cloud-bigquery-version-1- 17-0-1fc428512171`).

- **Dremio Sonar's** JDBC and ODBC drivers have always utilized Arrow to transfer data to users and since Arrow is Dremio Sonar's internal memory format (unlike BigQuery and Snowflake). There is zero data conversion from when the data is read to when the result set is returned to the client.

This is, of course, not a full list, just what I was able to find easily or am already using myself. I'm sure that by the time this book is in your hands, there will likely be even wider support. But, eventually, we may see ODBC and JDBC as a protocol replaced by something better. (Yes, I'm alluding to something but you'll have to keep reading to find out what!)

With ODBC/JDBC as the primary connector used to retrieve data, the other big heavyweight in the data science space is Apache Spark, combined with the Jupyter Notebook, which is one of the most common distributed computing platforms used by data scientists. Even if they aren't using it directly, Spark also is the underlying technology of (or used by) a large number of commercial products such as AWS Glue, Cloudera, and Databricks. Adding Arrow support to Spark at a low level, in conjunction with Parquet files, has resulted in enormous performance gains that are easy to replicate and show off. Follow along!

SPARKing new ideas on Jupyter

Apache Spark is an open source analytics engine for distributed processing across large clusters to take advantage of parallelism and fault tolerance that can come from such designs. It is also very likely, in my opinion, the most loved and simultaneously hated piece of software since the invention of JavaScript! The love comes from the workflows it enables, but it is notoriously fragile and difficult to use properly. If you aren't familiar with Spark, it is commonly used in conjunction with Scala, Java, Python, and/or R in addition to being able to run distributed SQL queries. Because Python is easy to pick up and very quick to write, data scientists will often utilize Jupyter notebooks and Python to quickly create and test models for analysis.

This workflow is excellent for quickly iterating on various ideas and proving their correctness. However, engineers and data scientists often find themselves beholden by the fact that, frankly, Python is pretty slow. In addition, unless you have access to a large cluster with a huge number of cores, Spark can also be fairly slow depending on the calculations and use case. That brings us to the question of how we can simultaneously make it easier to write code for the calculations we want, and improve the performance of those calculations. The answer is integration with Arrow and Parquet and taking advantage of columnar formats.

Understanding the integration

First thing's first, I should point out that this isn't a case of Spark versus Arrow, but rather where Arrow can be used to enhance existing Spark pipelines. Many Apache Spark pipelines would never need to use Arrow, and Spark has its own in-memory DataFrame format that is distinct from Arrow's. Converting between the two would introduce a performance drop, so any benefits need to be considered and weighed against this. With all of that said, where this marriage works beautifully is when it comes to switching your pipelines and data to different languages and libraries, such as when you use a `pandas` user-defined function as part of your Spark pipeline. In this situation, Spark can utilize Arrow for performing the conversion and communication for the benefits we saw in the last chapter when converting. *Figure 3.2* can help explain this a bit more by showing a simplified representation of how PySpark works.

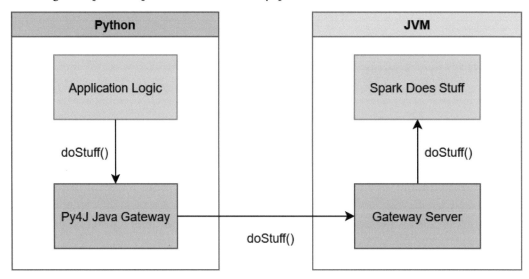

Figure 3.2 – PySpark Using Py4J to communicate

When you run PySpark, two processes are started up for you, the Python interpreter itself and a JVM process. This is because Spark is written using Scala/Java, not Python. All the heavy lifting that Spark does is actually done outside of the Python process, with Python providing an interface to send commands to Spark via the Py4J bridge. The problem is that when you want to interact with the data in Python, then send it to Spark, and then get the results back, you need to send the data across this bridge somehow. Imagine loading a 4 GB `pandas` DataFrame in Python, manipulating it a bit, and then sending it to Spark for computations and further analysis. *Figure 3.3* shows what happens under the hood:

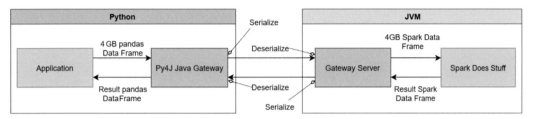

Figure 3.3 – Sending data back and forth to Spark from PySpark

In *Figure 3.3*, you can see that the 4 GB of data will need to get serialized somehow into a stream of bytes, passed to the JVM process to get deserialized so Spark can operate on it, only for the results from Spark to go through the same process in reverse. When you're dealing with large datasets, optimizing this passing of the data can save you a ton of time and computing resources! Also, keep in mind that since `pandas` DataFrames and Spark DataFrames are different formats, there's still a conversion to be done there as well. This is where Arrow can come in and speed things up.

Essentially, any time you want to use a library that isn't using Spark's native in-memory format, you are going to have to do a translation between those formats. This includes some Java libraries and any non-Java library (such as running Python user-defined functions). There are some operations that are faster with Arrow's format than with Spark's, and vice versa, but in most cases, it's only worth it if you are doing a lot of work in a non-Spark format such as `pandas`, which happens frequently concerning data scientists since pandas is a lot more friendly and easy to use than Spark itself.

In this example, we're going to use a slice of one of the files from the free and open *NYC Taxi* dataset, which is included in the `sample_data` folder of the GitHub repository that accompanies this book, which we've used before (such as with the exercises at the end of *Chapter 1, Getting Started with Apache Arrow*). I've intentionally only grabbed a slice of the file instead of the entire thing since this is to showcase examples that will be easy to run and replicate using Docker rather than needing your own Spark cluster. There are two main use cases we're going to look at:

- Getting the data into and out of Spark from the raw CSV file
- Performing a normalization calculation on one or more numeric fields in the dataset

Before we dive into the code first, let's spin up our development environment with Docker.

Everyone gets a containerized development environment!

Instead of fiddling with installing Apache Spark and Jupyter ourselves, we can launch a consistent and useful development environment using Docker. No manually dealing with dependencies, just an easy-to-share image name and you can replicate the examples. Oh, Docker. How much do we love you? Let us count the ways!

1. The Docker Hub community provides pre-packaged development environment containers that are easy to test and use.

2. We don't have to fight and figure out the proper way to install Spark and all of its dependencies; just use a ready-made image.

3. We can ensure that the environment I'm showing these examples with is easily set up by any reader that wants to follow along and see for themselves by referring to the specific Docker image.

4. You can put Docker inside of Docker, so you can docker while you docker... *never mind.*

If you haven't done so yet, make sure to install Docker on your development machine. For Windows, I find Docker Desktop is the easiest way to set it up and is also free (with restrictions). Most Linux package managers will have Docker available for installation also. Once it's installed, you can launch the development container we're going to use with the following command:

```
$ docker run -d -it -v ${PATH_TO_SAMPLE_DATA}/chapter3:/home/
jovyan/work -e JUPYTER_ENABLE_LAB=yes -p 8888:8888 -p 4040:4040
jupyter/pyspark-notebook
```

`PATH_TO_SAMPLE_DATA` should be an environment variable containing the path to a local clone of the GitHub repository for this book, which will contain a Jupyter notebook that can be opened in the directory named `chapter3`. This will start the Docker image in a detached state, so it doesn't start dumping its logs right into your terminal, and bind the local ports `8888` and `4040` for use. Feel free to pick different local ports for binding if you prefer.

After it starts up, make sure to look at the logs though, as you'll need to get the URL to start your Jupyter session from those logs. *Figure 3.4* shows you what to look for in the logs. The highlighted line in the screenshot is the URL you will need to copy and paste into your browser in order to access Jupyter and open the notebook in the repository:

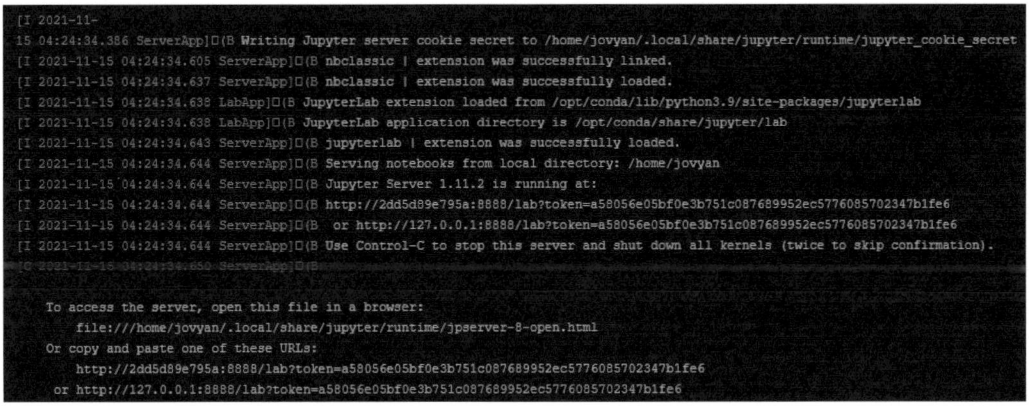

Figure 3.4 – Jupyter Docker logs

After opening up the notebook named `chapter3.ipynb`, you'll be greeted by the first cell of the notebook, which sets up the PySpark environment for you. The Docker image being used already includes the `pyarrow` module in the image, so it's already accessible for us to use. By clicking on the first cell and pressing the *Shift + Enter* keys, you'll start up the Spark master and executor, which will also download the necessary package for accessing AWS S3 from Spark. It should look similar to *Figure 3.5*:

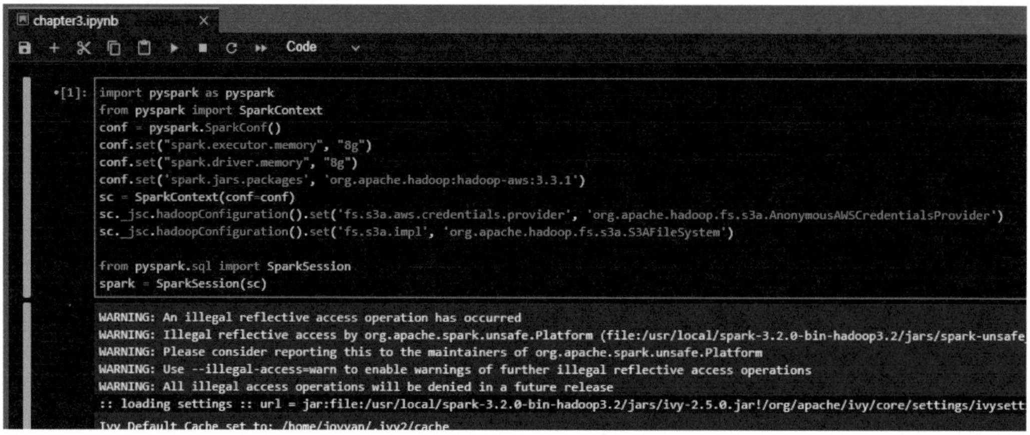

Figure 3.5 – Screenshot of provided Jupyter notebook

Now, you're all set to try running the examples I'm going to walk you through. You can see exactly how you'd be able to benefit from the Arrow integration in Spark. Let's begin!

SPARKing joy with Arrow and PySpark

So, looking at the files that are included, there are two of interest: `sliced.csv` and `sliced.parquet`. These are the aforementioned slices of the *NYC Taxi* dataset that we're going to use for these examples.

Setting Up the Data

The `sliced.parquet` file is included in the GitHub repository `sample_data` directory. The first cell of the Jupyter notebook for `Chapter3` contains some quick code to write out the CSV file from the Parquet file. This way you don't have a large file to download.

The CSV file is around 511 MB, while the Parquet file is only 78 MB. Important to note is that they both contain the exact same data! That difference in file size is all down to the benefits of a binary, columnar storage format such as Parquet and the compression it uses. In addition to showing how to get our data into Spark from the CSV file, we're also going to see how much faster it is to get the same data usable from a Parquet file instead.

Step 1 – Making the data usable

The first thing I want you to do is to think back to the previous chapter and try to read that `sliced.csv` file into a `pandas` DataFrame Remember that *Shift + Enter* will run the code in the cell, or you can switch to just using a direct interactive console if you prefer it over the notebook. One cool thing you can use here is by prefacing a single line with `%time` before executing it, you'll get timing information printed out after execution. For multi-line cells, you just use an extra percentage sign, `%%time`. So, let's read that file into a DataFrame:

```
%%time
import pyarrow as pa
import pyarrow.csv

pdf = pa.csv.read_csv('../sample_data/sliced.csv').to_pandas()
```

This is the output I get on my laptop. Your exact time might vary based on the specs of the machine you run the examples on:

```
CPU times: user 5.76 s, sys: 1.86, total: 7.63
Wall time: 1.86 s
```

> **Note**
>
> In case you are unfamiliar with the terms, **wall time** is the amount of time that elapsed if you used a stopwatch and timed the whole command. **User** time is the amount of CPU time utilized; on a machine with multiple cores, this can be much larger than the wall time. In this case, we know that by default, `pyarrow` is going to use multiple threads to read the CSV file, leading to a larger *user* time than *wall* time. **Sys** time is the time taken by the kernel to execute system-level operations such as context switching and resource allocation.

You may notice this as different from the output I used for timing in previous examples; the difference there is the usage of %timeit versus %time. Using %timeit will run the command several times in a loop and then give the average and standard deviation of the runtimes and tell you how many times it ran. Using %%timeit on the same code, I get the following output:

```
1.85 s ± 31.2 ms per loop (mean ± std. dev. of 7 runs, 1 loop
each)
```

Either way, we see that it takes nearly 2 seconds on average (on my laptop) to read this CSV file into a pandas DataFrame using pyarrow. But remember, we need a *Spark DataFrame* for Spark to use it! The way to do that is with a very helpful method on the spark session object called createDataFrame. Unfortunately, on a 3.5 million row by 21 column pandas DataFrame this is actually a potentially very expensive operation. On my machine, it ends up taking over an hour! Wow! What about if we just read it directly using Spark's own functions? Run this in a cell of the Jupyter notebook:

```
%time df = spark.read.format('csv').load('../sample_data/
sliced.csv',

                                    inferSchema='true',
                                    header='true')
```

This is the output I get on my machine:

```
CPU times: user 9.98 ms, sys: 637 µs, total: 10.6 ms
Wall time: 4.26 s
```

Well, that's quite the difference there. That's the cost of translation that I mentioned earlier regarding the different DataFrame formats. However, recent releases of Spark have added support to utilize pyarrow support to supercharge these operations and reduce copies. You can enable this behavior by running the following:

```
spark.conf.set("spark.sql.execution.arrow.pyspark.enabled", "true")
```

That's all. With this configuration set, we see a huge difference in how long it takes:

```
%time df = spark.createDataFrame(pa.csv.read_csv('../sample_
data/sliced.csv').to_pandas())
```

The output is as follows:

```
CPU times: user 6.2 s sys: 2.64 s, total 8.84 s
Wall time: 3.35 s
```

By enabling the usage of Arrow optimizations with Spark, we can benefit from Arrow's extremely fast reading of the CSV file and we are faster than natively reading it in Spark (at least with a single executor) but are still able to get a Spark DataFrame at the end. There's also one additional benefit of using the `pyarrow` library to perform our CSV reading, the default type inference.

There are two columns in our CSV file that consist of timestamps: `tpep_pickup_datetime` and `tpep_dropoff_datetime`. The fastest way to read in the file with Spark is to treat all the columns as strings or if you know the schema of the file beforehand. That way Spark will lazily load your file and only read it when you run a function that expects results. If you want to let the schema get figured out by reading the file, you can set the `inferSchema` option to `true`, as we did in the previous example. While Spark does provide mechanisms to specify custom parsing of the CSV, the default behavior doesn't recognize the timestamp columns as such, inferring them to just be a `string` typed column when using the native spark parsing:

```
df.printSchema()
```

The output is as follows:

```
root
 |-- VendorID: integer (nullable = true)
 |-- tpep_pickup_datetime: string (nullable = true)
 |-- tpep_dropoff_datetime: string (nullable = true)
 ...
```

But, the `pyarrow` module has better default parsing and automatically recognizes those columns as timestamps, keeping them typed when converting to a `pandas` DataFrame. This means that the resulting Spark DataFrame maintains treating them as timestamps off the bat instead of having to separately cast them after reading the data in. This also applies to other types of parsing and type handling where the Arrow library is different, such as identifying certain columns as `long` whereas Spark reads them in as `integer`:

```
root
 |-- VendorID: long
 |-- tpep_pickup_datetime: timestamp (nullable = true)
 |-- tpep_dropoff_datetime: timestamp (nullable = true)
```

Make sure to keep these differences in mind when using this, but don't forget about the customization options that exist for controlling what types get used, as seen in the previous chapter and the documentation.

While this is a fairly trivial example of converting a pandas DataFrame into a Spark DataFrame with the advent of so many libraries and modules that work directly with the `pandas` library, there are many cases where your pre-analysis operations for cleaning or manipulating the data will leave you with a `pandas` DataFrame at the end. This integration with Spark ensures superior performance for those cases where it isn't feasible to simply read the data directly into Spark natively due to your data pipeline's configuration.

Keep in Mind!

This is still an example of only using a single executor with my local machine. The benefit of Spark in general is the parallelization across multiple machines and cores, which I'm not using in the example here. You can still benefit from it using the Arrow library, but it's not as straightforward. The same is true for the Parquet version. If your dataset is large enough, you should use separate Spark tasks to create multiple smaller DataFrames and utilize the `block_size` and `skip_rows_after_names` read options for the CSV reader or read smaller row groups from the Parquet files.

Because of the optimizations and lazy loading, the speedup isn't as obvious with the Parquet file version just from reading it in. Regardless of whether you're using `pyarrow` directly or using Spark, it's going to read the Parquet file into your DataFrame in less than a second. But, if we use `describe().show()` to force Spark to read the entire file and perform some operations on it, we can see the benefits by using `pyarrow` to read the Parquet file over Spark's native parquet reader:

```
%%time
df = spark.read.format('parquet').load('../sample_data/sliced.parquet') # using pyspark native reader
df.describe().show()
```

We get the following output, though I've omitted the data itself to just show the resulting CPU and wall time that is reported:

```
...
CPU times: user 12.7 ms, sys: 247 µs, total: 12.9 ms
Wall time: 32.7 s
```

Looking at the timing information from using the Spark native reader, we can see how the work is done by the Spark driver and executors rather than the Python process. Despite the 32-second wall time, the CPU time reported is only a few milliseconds because all the work is done by the JVM process and Spark processes, and then just the results are sent back over from the JVM to the Python process. If we use `pyarrow` to read the file instead, we see the difference:

```
%%time
df = spark.createDataFrame(pq.read_table('../sample_data/sliced.parquet').to_pandas()) # using pyarrow
df.describe().show()
```

Once again, omitting the raw data, we get the following times as output:

```
...
CPU times: user 2.54 s, sys: 1.38 s, total: 3.92 s
Wall time: 12.3 s
```

Our timing shows a total of 3.92 seconds spent by the Python process as opposed to the 12.9 milliseconds from before. This is because the work to read the Parquet file is being done in Python by the pyarrow module, but the zero-copy benefits of the conversion and enabling Arrow in Spark make the data translation very fast. If we look at the Spark visualization of the execution plan for each side by side in *Figure 3.6*, it helps us understand what's going on:

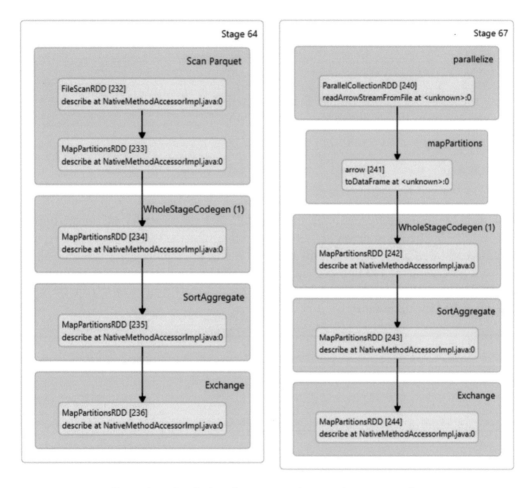

Figure 3.6 – Spark plans for native read versus Arrow -> pandas

Comparing the execution plans, the differences that we can see are the `ParallelCollectionRDD` and Arrow `toDataFrame` steps instead of `FileScanRDD`. It looks like Spark does a better job parallelizing the tasks when streaming arrow record batches than if Spark is doing the read directly. The `pyarrow` module reads the entire Parquet file into memory and then uses the Arrow **inter-process communication** (**IPC**) format to pass it to Spark in an easy to parallelize way. This becomes even more apparent if we look at the execution timelines for the two cases, as in *Figure 3.7*:

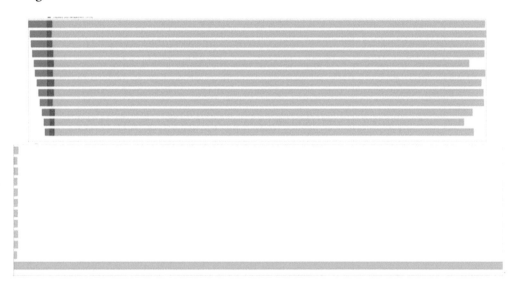

Figure 3.7 – Spark execution timelines for native and DataFrame Parquet

Can you guess which screenshot is from the run that used Arrow to read the file and pass the DataFrames? I'll give you a second... Yes, the top one. What you're looking at is how Spark chose to split the tasks up across different worker processes the driver used. The colors in the images represent how the time was spent by the executors. The blue sections are the scheduler delay and the red sections are the time deserializing the task. The green section is what we're most interested in, the time spent actually executing the task.

In both cases, Spark split up the work into 12 tasks, but in the case where it was streaming the Arrow record batches that were already read, instead of reading the file itself, the work got distributed much more evenly across all the workers, which each took a chunk of work. When Spark read the file itself, it only parallelized the read of the Parquet file to gather all the data into one executor that did all the computations resulting in the extra computation time it took.

For the purposes of the next steps, we only need a subset of the columns, which further improves our read performance:

1. First we have the Spark native version:

    ```
    %%timeit
    df = spark.read.format('csv').load('../sample_data/
    sliced.csv',
                                    inferSchema='true',
                    header='true').select('VendorID',
    'tpep_pickup_datetime', 'passenger_count',
    'tip_amount', 'fare_amount', 'total_amount')
    5.28 s ± 216 ms per loop (mean ± std. dev. of 7 runs, 1
    loop each)
    ```

2. Then, using pyarrow and converting to a pandas DataFrame first:

    ```
    % % timeit
    df = spark.createDataFrame(pa.csv.read_csv('../sample_
    data/sliced.csv',
        convert_options = pa.csv.ConvertOptions(
            include_columns =
                ['VendorID', 'tpep_pickup_datetime',
                'passenger_count', 'tip_amount',
                'fare_amount', 'total_amount'
                ])
    ).to_pandas())
    1.98 s± 104 ms per loop(mean± std.dev.of 7 runs, 1 loop
    each)
    ```

By taking advantage of the Arrow library's better read performance and the zero-copy conversion, we can demonstrate a significant performance improvement over using the native Spark loading functions.

Step 2 – Adding a new column

We're going to normalize our total_amount column by grouping rows based on the vendor ID and the month in which the trip occurred. Since we only have a full timestamp, we first need to add a column to our DataFrame that extracts the month from the timestamp.

For our DataFrame created by the Spark native reader that didn't automatically figure out the column as a timestamp type, we first need to cast that column to the right type before we can extract the month:

```
from pyspark.sql.functions import *
# import the functions we want to use like 'month',
# 'to_timestamp' and 'col'. Very useful.

df = df.withColumn('tpep_pickup_datetime',
                   to_timestamp(col('tpep_pickup_datetime'),
                   'yyyy-MM-dd HH:mm:ss')) # the datetime format
```

With our properly typed datetime column in hand, we can add our new column, which extracts the month as a number so we can group by it easily:

```
df = df.withColumn('pickup_month',
                   month(col('tpep_pickup_datetime')))
```

Now, we can finally perform our normalization. Hold on to your hats, this is a doozy! We're going to use a **user-defined function** (**UDF**). You could do this with the native Spark intrinsic functions, but doing the normalization as a UDF is a stand-in for whatever complex logic you might have that is written in Python already. This allows you to avoid re-writing it or to benefit from the ease of writing Python without sacrificing performance. The reason why they exist is simply that there are a lot of computations and logic that are much more easily expressed using Python than with Spark's built-in functions, such as the following:

- Weighted mean
- Weighted correlation
- Exponential moving average

Now, let's move on to *Step 3*.

Step 3 – Creating our UDF to normalize a column

For this example, we're going to do a simple normalization of the `total_amount` column. The standard formula for normalization is as follows:

$$\frac{(values - values.mean)}{values.std}$$

> **Note**
>
> Before I continue, I want to first acknowledge that I adapted this example from a fantastic webinar presentation given by Julien Le Dem and Li Jin that introduced this functionality. They go into significantly more detail, making the webinar a very worthwhile watch, so please give it a look when you have a chance. You can find it here: `https://www.dremio.com/webinars/improving-python-spark-performance-interoperability-apache-arrow/`.

The interesting thing to remember is that when you create a UDF in PySpark, it will execute your function in Python, not in the native Java/Scala that Spark runs in. As a result, UDFs are much slower to run than their built-in equivalents but are easier and quicker to write.

There are two types of UDFs:

- **Row-oriented functions** – Operate on a single row at a time:

    - `lambda x: x + 1`

    - `lambda date1, date2: (date1 - date2).years`

- **Grouped functions** – Need more than one row to compute:

    - Compute a weighted mean grouped by month

For the purposes of our example, and to show off the benefits of Apache Arrow, we're going to focus on the grouped UDF.

When building our user-defined monthly data normalization function, it's going to require a bunch of boilerplate code to pack and unpack multiple rows into a nested row that we can compute across. Because of this, performance is affected, as Spark first has to materialize the groups and then convert them to Python data structures so it can run the UDF, which is expensive. Let's take a crack at this; try working through the example here before looking at the notebook that has the solutions:

1. First, to save ourselves some typing, let's import the PySpark SQL type functions:

    ```
    from pyspark.sql.types import *
    ```

2. Next, we need to create a `struct` column to represent our nested rows:

    ```
    group_cols = ['VendorID', 'pickup_month']
    non_group_cols = [col for col in df.columns if col not in
                    group_cols]
    s = StructType([f for f in df.schema.fields if f.name in
                    non_group_cols])
    cols = list([col(name) for name in non_group_cols])
    df_norm = df.withColumn('values', struct(*cols))
    ```

3. Now, we need to use our grouping definition to aggregate the values in the DataFrame:

    ```
    df_norm = (df_norm
                    .groupBy(*group_cols)
                    .agg(collect_list(df_norm.values)
                    .alias('values')))
    ```

4. See what I mean with all the boilerplate? Okay, next, we need to actually define our UDF to perform the normalization:

    ```
    s2 = StructType(s.fields + [StructField('v', DoubleType())])

    @udf(ArrayType(s2))
    def normalize(values):
        v1 = pd.Series([r.total_amount for r in values])
        v1_norm = (v1 - v1.mean())/v1.std()
        return [values[i] + (float(v1_norm[i]),)
                        for i in range(0, len(values))]
    ```

5. We're almost there. We've got our normalization function, so we just have to apply it, explode the columns, and drop the extra columns we only needed for the calculation:

```
df_norm = (df_norm.withColumn('new_values',
                normalize(df_norm.values))
              .drop('values')
              .withColumn('new_values',
                    explode(col('new_values')))))

for c in [f.name for f in s2.fields]:
    df_norm = df_norm.withColumn(c,
                    col('new_values.{0}'.format(c)))

df_norm = df_norm.drop('new_values')
df_norm.show()
```

The highlighted line is what kicks off Spark to perform the work and start calculating everything. Before that point, it's just creating the plan until we want it to show us the results.

With everything in place, we can toss the `%%time` magic as the first line, and then run it so we can see how long it takes:

```
CPU times: user 74ms, sys: 53.5 ms, total: 127 ms
Wall time: 3min 9s
```

Okay. So that took a bit to run. Notice that the CPU timing shows that the Python process only spent about `127` milliseconds to construct the plan and send it to the JVM. The 3 minutes of runtime all took place within the JVM process and the Python processes Spark kicked off to run the UDF we created. For such a simple calculation, 3 minutes seems like a long time, even if it is for 3.5 million rows. Why did it take so long? Let's see the reasons in the following points:

- We had to pack and unpack the nested rows to get the data where we needed it.

- There was lots of serialization/deserialization to pass the data around. Spark, by default, is going to use the Python `pickle` protocol.

- The computation is still technically a *scalar* computation, so we're paying the costs of overhead for the Python interpreter and working with the row-by-row model instead of a column-oriented model.

Can we do better than this and also clean it up to remove a lot of the boilerplate? Of course we can, otherwise, I wouldn't have used this as an example!

Step 4 – Throwing out step 3 and using a vectorized UDF instead

First, I'm going to show the vectorized computation example, then I'll explain the differences in depth. So, let's take a look.

Are you ready? Here's the vectorized UDF and how to use it:

```
schema = StructType(df.schema.fields +
                    [StructField('v', DoubleType())])


def vector_normalize(values):
    v1 = values.total_amount
    values['v'] = (v1 - v1.mean())/v1.std()
    return values


group_columns = ['VendorID', 'pickup_month']
df_pandas_norm = df.groupby(*group_columns)
                   .applyInPandas(vector_normalize,
                                  schema=schema)
df_pandas_norm.show()
```

That's it. That's everything. You should see the same output that you saw for *Step 3*, only much faster. How much faster? Well, shove the magic `%%time` keyword on that UDF, and let's find out together:

```
CPU times: user 22.1 ms, sys: 16.9 ms, total: 39 ms
Wall time: 3.57 s
```

That's 3.57 seconds instead of 3 minutes and 9 seconds. That's a huge 98.11% reduction in the time to calculate! So, how do we do it? Why does this run so much faster? The devil is in the details.

Step 5 – Understanding what's going on

To understand why vectorization of the calculation provides such a huge benefit, first, you have to understand how PySpark UDFs get calculated in the first place. *Figure 3.8* is a simplified diagram of this execution:

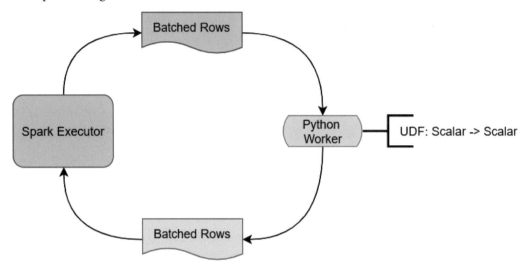

Figure 3.8 – PySpark UDF execution

During the execution of a UDF, the Spark executor running on Java/Scala is going to stream batches of rows to a Python worker. That worker is simply going to use a `for` loop to invoke the UDF on each row it gets and send back the results as another batch of rows. Given that the Spark executor is running in an entirely different programming language and runtime environment from the Python worker, you can guess that one of the big pieces of overhead is the serialization and deserialization of the data to send it back and forth between the environments. On top of that, since this is still a scalar computation, looping on a row-by-row basis isn't the most efficient way to perform the calculation. But, if we can take advantage of the vectorized, columnar computations that are implemented in pandas and eliminate the serialization/deserialization as seen in *Figure 3.9*, we end up with superior performance:

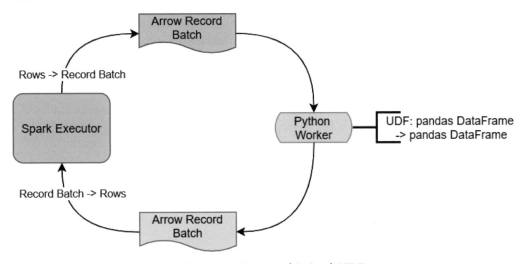

Figure 3.9 – Vectorized PySpark UDF

There are also other ways to leverage the vectorized computing for pandas within Spark:

- mapInPandas can be used instead of applyInPandas for applying a function through an iterator instead of a group-based operation, such as filtering rows by some criteria.

- When not grouping the data by some value, a simple pandas UDF can be used for performing vectorized *element-wise* operations, such as multiplying one column by another as a faster alternative to traditional Spark UDFs.

- Performing grouped aggregations, such as just calculating the mean/standard deviation of a given column, can be sped up using pandas_udf in conjunction with Windows functions and otherwise, instead of the traditional udf decorator.

Deeper information can be found in the Spark Python documentation for working with pandas and Arrow, but hopefully, the previous examples can get you started showing the power of utilizing the vectorized columnar calculations for your UDFs.

Step 6 – Profiting from our hard work

At the end of the day, the common development environment for data scientists of Jupyter and Apache Spark is yet another tool that is able to leverage Arrow for performance. As we can see, every step of the process, from loading the data files to performing computations on them, has the potential to benefit from the common memory format Arrow provides. After you've done your data normalization, cleanup, and any other modifications to the dataset that you want to do, what do we do next?

Raw data and numbers are all well and good, but to really get your point across, you want to provide charts and visual aids with your data. Well, there's a handy library called **Perspective** that utilizes Arrow built for visualizing data with charts and graphs and interactively manipulating those visuals. It's an open source interactive analytics and data visualization component that also includes a plugin for Jupyter allowing us to embed a widget to play with. The next section will show you how to take the data you've just prepared and feed it directly into Perspective to create useful charts and visuals directly from the Arrow formatted data.

Interactive charting powered by Arrow

Perspective was originally developed at J.P. Morgan and was open sourced through the **Fintech Open Source Foundation** (**FINOS**). The goal of this project was to make it easy to build analytics entirely in the browser that were user-configurable, or by using Python and/ or Jupyter to create reports, dashboards, or any other application both with static data and streaming updates. It uses Apache Arrow as its underlying memory handler with a query engine built in C++ that is then compiled both for WebAssembly (for the browser/Node.js) or as a Python extension. While I highly encourage looking into it further, we're just going to cover using the `PerspectiveWidget` component for a Jupyter notebook to further analyze and play with the data we were using for the Spark examples, the NYC Taxi dataset.

Before we dive in, make sure that your Jupyter notebook is either still running, or you've spun it back up, as we're going to utilize it for this exercise. One of the cool, magic things Jupyter exposes is the ability to run commands as part of your notebook. In a cell of your notebook, you can place the following command to install the Python Perspective library:

```
!pip install perspective-python
```

Then, press the *Shift + Enter* keys to execute that and install it. Now, we can install the extension for the widget:

```
!jupyter labextension install @finos/perspective-jupyterlab
```

You're going to need to refresh your browser view of the Jupyter notebook after it finishes installing and rebuilding; you could also install this via the Jupyter UI. Also, make sure that you have the `ipywidgets` extension installed, which you can install with this command if you don't:

```
!jupyter labextension install @jupyter-widgets/jupyterlab-
manager
```

Just like the Perspective widget extension, you can install this from the Jupyter UI if you prefer.

With our freshly refreshed instance of Jupyter running with the extensions, we're now ready to get a widget up to play with. Just follow along with these steps:

1. First, we're going to import our data into an Arrow table in memory just like before. Try doing it yourself before reading further:

    ```
    import pyarrow as pa
    import pyarrow.csv


    arrow_table = pa.csv.read_csv('../sample_data/sliced.csv')
    ```

2. Next, we import the dependencies we're going to need for Perspective:

    ```
    from perspective import Table, PerspectiveWidget
    from datetime import date, datetime
    import pandas as pd
    ```

3. There are a few ways we could go from here. Perspective tables can be created from a pandas DataFrame or a dict object, but the most efficient by far is to just use Arrow directly. Perspective isn't able to take an Arrow table object directly, but it can read the Arrow IPC format if we just give the constructor the raw bytes:

    ```
    sink = pa.BufferOutputStream() # create our buffer stream
    with pa.ipc.new_stream(sink, arrow_table.schema) as
    writer:
        writer.write_table(arrow_table) # write the table as
    IPC


    buf = sink.getvalue() # get a buffer of the resulting bytes
    ```

    Another alternative might be to have our dataset as a .arrow file written somewhere, which is just the Arrow IPC file format, as we've already covered.

4. Finally, we can create our Perspective table, and to cut down on the render time, let's filter out some rows to bring it down to just under a million rows for us to play with:

    ```
    table = Table(buf.to_pybytes())
    view = table.view(filter=[
                        ['tpep_pickup_datetime', '<', '2015-01-
    10']])
    display(view.num_rows())
    ```

    Running this gives us the output of the number of rows:

    ```
    977730
    ```

5. To create our widget from this view, we just call the `to_arrow` function on it to flatten it out to a new table for the widget to run over. In an actual production scenario, you might use a Python Tornado server to host the data remotely or to perform real-time updates of the data, but for now, a static dataset is fine:

```
widget = PerspectiveWidget(view.to_arrow())
widget
```

That's all that's necessary to get our initial widget drawn. Various arguments exist for the constructor so that you can control the initial state of the widget, such as the following:

-   The initial view (**Datagrid**, **Bar chart**, **Scatterplot**, **Heatmap**, **Treemap**, **Sunburst**, and so on)

-   The initial pivots of the rows and columns for grouping and splitting the dataset

-   The initial sort order

-   An initial subset of columns to display instead of showing all of them

-   Further filters and custom columns derived from the existing columns

Figure 3.10 is a screenshot of this widget in action, where I've added some custom columns to split the pickup timestamp into the hour of the day and the day of the week:

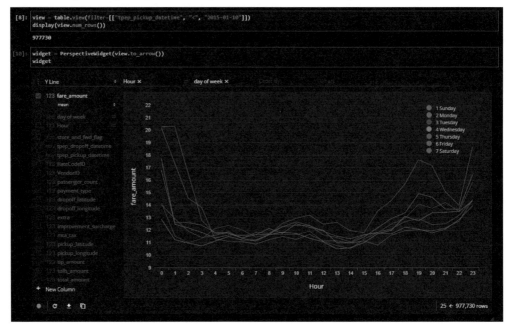

Figure 3.10 – Perspective widget inside of JupyterLab

Looking at *Figure 3.10*, you can see that I've grouped the input data by the fare amount field to create a chart showing the mean fare amount per hour for each day of the week. There are a lot of different options for how you want to display the data visually, enabling users to interactively manipulate what you're grouping by, splitting by, and so on. Another quick example is shown in *Figure 3.11*, which contains a heatmap for the average number of passengers per hour based on the days of the week. All I did was change the settings and wait a couple of seconds for the widget to update:

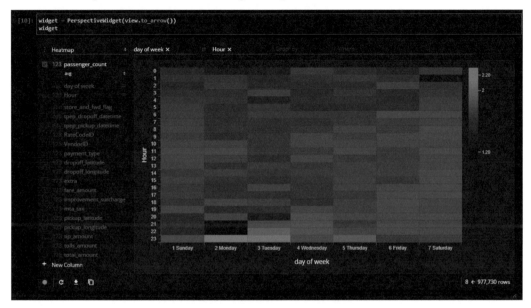

Figure 3.11 – Perspective widget heatmap

In this situation, the performance of this interactive charting widget is going to be directly connected to the power of your machine/given to your Docker machine running Jupyter. If you desire a bit more horsepower, you could use the Perspective documentation to create a server and build your own UI using the building blocks it provides. But this isn't a book about Perspective; I'm just using it as an example of what people have done and can do using Arrow.

While Perspective is an excellent example of adopting Arrow for an interactive data visualization solution, it's not the only attempt at this. A couple of other visualization solutions for Arrow formatted data that I've come across are as follows:

- **Falcon**: A visualization tool for linked interactions across multiple aggregate visualizations (`github.com/vega/falcon`)

- **Vega**: An ecosystem of tools for interactive web-based visualizations (`github.com/vega`)

- **Graphistry**: A company providing utilities and specialized hardware to use GPUs to accelerate visualization of large datasets using Arrow and remote rendering (`graphistry.com/data-science`)

After covering all these analytics use cases, there's one use case that we're leaving out a bit: **searching**. While Arrow can supercharge your analytics engines, improve your data transfer, and make it seamless to share data between programming languages, very few tools are able to beat the power of **Elasticsearch** when it comes to just performing searches and simple aggregations. Recently, I worked on an application whose analytics were powered on analytics engines using Apache Arrow, but we found that after pre-calculating all the data, Elasticsearch was the best method to return pages of data to the UI.

Stretching workflows onto Elasticsearch

If what you need is primarily searching and filtering large amounts of data rather than heavy analytical computations, chances are you've probably looked into Elasticsearch. Even if you do need heavy computations, you might be able to pre-calculate large amounts of data and store it in Elasticsearch to fetch later to speed up your queries. However, there's a slight issue: Elasticsearch's API is entirely built in JSON, and Arrow is a binary format. We also don't want to sacrifice our fast data transportation using Arrow's IPC format if we can avoid it!

I recently worked on a project where the solution we came up with was to have a unified service interface that used Arrow, but heuristically determine when a request would be better serviced by an Elasticsearch query and simply convert the data from the JSON returned by Elasticsearch to Arrow. If this seems overly complicated, here's what this solution achieved for us:

- A unified interface for consumers:

  - Regardless of the underlying data source, our consumers got data using the Arrow IPC format with a proper schema.

- Separation of concerns:

  - If something better comes along for this particular use case, we can easily replace Elasticsearch with it and consumers won't have to care or be affected.

- An optimized interface for bulk fetches that use Arrow the whole way through:

  ▪ Elasticsearch works best if the result data from a given fetch is relatively small rather than trying to fetch your entire dataset at once. That small result set is quick to convert to Arrow from JSON. Big bulk fetches that would be very expensive to convert instead come from a bulk interface that just returns Arrow natively.

Since the data is stored using Parquet files or accessed by a native Arrow format interface, the first thing we had to do was work out how to get the data indexed by Elasticsearch in the first place. Thankfully, this turned out to not be difficult, as several Arrow libraries have easy conversions to JSON that work very well for mapping to Elasticsearch documents. Once all of the data was indexed, the service we built would determine whether to query Elasticsearch or a different source based on the request, and if Elasticsearch was queried, the JSON response would get converted back to Arrow before it was returned. Visually, the architecture looked like *Figure 3.12*:

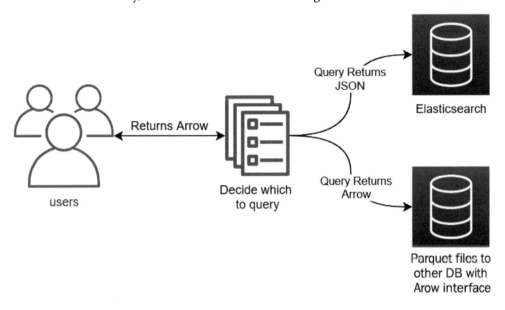

Figure 3.12 – Service architecture including Elasticsearch

Let's take a look at the interaction with Elasticsearch and how the conversion to and from JSON works in this case. We'll launch an instance of Elasticsearch locally using Docker with the following command:

```
$ docker run --rm -it -p 9200:9200 -p 9300:9300 -e "discovery.
type=single-node" docker.elastic.co/elasticsearch/
elasticsearch:7.15.2
```

After it starts up and is running, you can visit http://localhost:9200 in your browser to confirm it is up and running. You should see something similar to this in your browser:

```
{
    "name": "21c57c172ae9",
    "cluster_name": "docker-cluster",
    "cluster_uuid": "ZAm29KdFS6e2osGXY44vvQ",
    "version": {
        "number": "7.15.2",
        "build_flavor": "default",
        "build_type": "docker",
        "build_hash": "93d5a7f6192e8a1a12e154a2b81bf6fa7309da0c",
        "build_date": "2021-11-04T14:04:42.515624022Z",
        "build_snapshot": false,
        "lucene_version": "8.9.0",
        "minimum_wire_compatibility_version": "6.8.0",
        "minimum_index_compatibility_version": "6.0.0-beta1"
    },
    "tagline": "You Know, for Search"
}
```

With an Elasticsearch instance now running locally on your laptop, we can start filling it with data for us to query. Keep in mind that Elasticsearch is not intended to be the source of truth for your data; it's an optimization for querying with particular workflows. Referencing the architecture diagram from *Figure 3.12*, we created automated jobs that performed updates of the data in Elasticsearch when the underlying data in Parquet files changed or updated.

Indexing the data

Using the Parquet files or database that returns native Arrow as the source of truth, Elasticsearch can be easily populated after converting the Arrow data to JSON, as long as you take care when handling the data types. When creating an index in Elasticsearch, you have two choices for handling the data types: dynamic mapping and explicit mapping. Because of the flexible nature of JSON, when converting from Arrow, it makes more sense to use an explicit mapping since you already know the data types via the Arrow schema. You can see the data types that Elasticsearch supports in the documentation available online (`https://www.elastic.co/guide/en/elasticsearch/reference/current/mapping-types.html`). Most of the type mapping can be handled with some simple mappings, but for other types such as dates, times, and strings, you'll want to include extra information to handle the mapping. I'm going to use **Go** for these examples, but conceptually, this would work with the Arrow library in any language:

1. First, let's create a struct to make it easy to marshal the mapping to JSON:

    ```go
    type property struct {
        Type   string     `json:"type"`
        Format string     `json:"format,omitempty"`
        Fields interface{} `json:"fields,omitempty"`
    }
    ```

    If you're unfamiliar with Go, the `` `json:"format,omitempty"` `` tags in the `struct` definition define how an instance of this struct would get marshaled to JSON. The `omitempty` tag tells the marshaller to leave out this field if it is *empty*, which is defined differently based on the type. For a string, *empty* is just when the length is `0`. For `interface{}`, *empty* is when the value is `nil`.

2. For this example, we're going to create a static keyword field definition with defaults to use for string values, but this could be replaced by more specific options if desired:

    ```go
    var keywordField = &struct{
        Keyword interface{} `json:"keyword"`
    }{struct {
        Type       string `json:"type"`
        IgnoreAbove int   `json:"ignore_above"`
    }{"keyword", 256}}
    ```

3. Now, let's create our simple mapping for the primitive values:

```go
import (
    ...
    "github.com/apache/arrow/go/v7/arrow"
    ...
)


var primitiveMapping = map[arrow.Type]string{
    arrow.BOOL:      "boolean",
    arrow.INT8:      "byte",
    arrow.UINT8:     "short", // no unsigned byte type
    arrow.INT16:     "short",
    arrow.UINT16:    "integer", // no unsigned short
    arrow.INT32:     "integer",
    /* the rest of the arrow types */
}
```

4. Finally, let's construct a function that converts an Arrow schema to mapping for JSON conversion. For this example, I'm not going to handle nested types such as Union, List, Struct, or Map columns, but they could be easily handled with Elasticsearch's type system, which allows array and object types:

```go
func createMapping(sc *arrow.Schema) map[string]property {
    mappings := make(map[string]property)
    for _, f := range sc.Fields() {
        var (
            p property
            ok bool
        )
        if p.Type, ok = primitiveMapping[f.Type.ID()]; !ok {
            switch f.Type.ID() {
            case arrow.DATE32, arrow.DATE64:
                p.Type = "date"
                p.Format = "yyyy-MM-dd"
            case arrow.TIME32, arrow.TIME64:
                p.Type = "date"
                p.Format = "time||time_no_millis"
```

```
              case arrow.TIMESTAMP:
                  p.Type = "date"
                  p.Format = "yyyy-MM-dd HH:mm:ss||yyyy-
MM-dd HH:mm:ss.SSSSSSSSS"
              case arrow.STRING:
                  p.Type = "text" // or keyword
                  p.Fields = keywordField
              }
          }
          mappings[f.Name] = p
      }
      return mappings
  }
```

Walking through the code snippet, the first highlighted section checks whether the type of the field is in our primitive mapping. If it isn't, then we have to handle the type separately. The next several highlighted lines specify the expected string format that the JSON conversion will output the date, time, or timestamp to so that Elasticsearch knows what to expect for ingesting documents. In the case of a string, we can use either the `text` or `keyword` type and use the keyword field definition we made to tell Elasticsearch to index the value accordingly.

5. We've got our helper functions, so now we need some data. Let's read from the Parquet file in the sample data named `sliced.parquet`. Many of the official Parquet libraries provide an easy reader that reads data directly into Arrow record batches; the Go library does this through a module named `pqarrow`:

```
import (
    ...
    "github.com/apache/arrow/go/v7/arrow/memory"
    "github.com/apache/arrow/go/v7/parquet/file"
    "github.com/apache/arrow/go/v7/parquet/pqarrow"
    ...
)


func main() {
    // the second argument is a bool value for memory
mapping
    // the file if desired.
```

```
        parq, err := file.OpenParquetFile("../../sample_data/
sliced.parquet", false)
        if err != nil {
            // handle the error
        }
        defer parq.Close()

        props := pqarrow.ArrowReadProperties{BatchSize: 50000}
        rdr, err := pqarrow.NewFileReader(parq, props,
                                            memory.
DefaultAllocator)
        if err != nil {
            // handle error
        }
        ...
}
```

The pqarrow module provides helper functions that can read an entire file into memory as an Arrow table, but we want to limit the amount of memory we're using. So, rather than pulling the entire file into memory at one time, we create a Parquet file reader and wrap that with a pqarrow reader. We create a properties object and define the batch size to use, which is the number of rows that will be read from a column per read. Higher batch sizes can speed up the indexing but will require more memory.

6. We're going to stream our records out of the file and to Elasticsearch, which means we're going to utilize a goroutine to concurrently read record batches and use the bulk index API of Elasticsearch. In order to ensure graceful failures, we're going to need a context and a cancel function. We can then use that context to create a record reader as per the highlighted lines as follows:

```
import (
    "context"

    ...
)

func main() {
    ...
    ctx, cancel := context.WithCancel(
        context.Background())
```

```go
    defer cancel()
    // leave these empty since we're not filtering out any
    // columns or row groups. But if you wanted to do so,
    // this is how you'd optimize the read
    var cols, rowgroups []int
    rr, err := rdr.GetRecordReader(ctx, cols, rowgroups)
    if err != nil {
        // handle the error
    }
    ...
}
```

7. Huzzah! We can create our index in Elasticsearch now. For ease of use, the default client expects an environment variable to be set named ELASTICSEARCH_URL, which is the address of the Elasticsearch instance. If you're following along and used Docker to launch your instance, you can set the environment variable to the http://localhost:9200 value. First, let's add the necessary imports; your editor might be smart enough to do this automatically:

```go
import (
    "net/http"

    ...

    "github.com/elastic/go-elasticsearch/v7"
    "github.com/elastic/go-elasticsearch/v7/esutil"

    ...
)
```

Now, we add the creation of an Elasticsearch client to the main function:

```go
    ...
    es, err := elasticsearch.NewDefaultClient()
    if err != nil {
        // handle the error
    }
    ...
```

Finally, we create our Elasticsearch index mappings from the schema of our RecordReader and create the index itself:

```go
    ...
    var mapping struct {
```

```
        Mappings struct {
                Properties map[string]property
`json:"properties"`
        } `json:"mappings"`
    }
    mapping.Mappings.Properties = createMapping(rr.Schema())
    response, err := es.Indices.Create("indexname",
                        es.Indices.Create.WithBody(
                            esutil.NewJSONReader(mapping)))
    if err != nil {
        // handle error
    }
    if response.StatusCode != http.StatusOK {
        // handle failure response and return/exit
    }
    // Index created!
    ...
```

Creating the index is straightforward as per the highlighted lines. We get the Arrow schema from the record reader and create an Elasticsearch client, then use our function to construct the mappings. The official Elasticsearch library provides a very useful utility package called esutil, which contains helpers such as the NewJSONReader function we call to convert the mapping struct to a JSON object and create io.Reader to send the request. If all goes well, the response should have the HTTP response code of 200, represented by the http.StatusOK constant.

8. We're almost done! We've got our index created and we've got our record reader to pull batches of rows from the file. We just need to use the bulk indexer API to stream all of this into our instance. I know this is my longest code step list so far but stay with me now! This is the cool part. First, the extra imports we're going to need to finish this up are as follows:

```
import (
    ...
    "bufio"
    "io"
    "strings"
    "fmt"
```

```
    ...
        "github.com/apache/arrow/go/v7/arrow/array"
)
```

9. Then, we create our bulk indexer. There are a lot of options that exist on the indexer object to control the amount of parallelism it can use, how often to flush the data, and so on. We're just going to use the defaults for those options for now, but feel free to play with them:

```
    ...
    indexer, err := esutil.NewBulkIndexer(esutil.
    BulkIndexerConfig{
                        Client: es, Index: "indexname",
                        OnError: func(_ context.Context, err
    error) {
                            fmt.Println(err)
                        },
                    })
    if err != nil {
        // handle error
    }
```

10. Let's start actually reading from the file into a pipe that we'll read lines from. Using array.RecordToJSON will convert the records to JSON with each row as a single-line JSON object, just as we saw in the previous chapter. We use the go func syntax to start a goroutine running concurrently with our indexer:

```
    pr, pw := io.Pipe() // to pass the data
    go func() {
      for rr.Next() {
        if err := array.RecordToJSON(rr.Record(), pw); err !=
    nil {
            cancel()
            pw.CloseWithError(err)
            return
        }
      }
      pw.Close()
    }()
```

11. We can use `bufio.Scanner` to grab the JSON data line by line to send to Elasticsearch's bulk index API. Just initialize it to read from the read side of the pipe we created and we're off to the races! The highlighted lines are how we add the items to the bulk indexer, and the `Scan` method will return `false` when we hit the end of the data:

```go
scanner := bufio.NewScanner(pr)
for scanner.Scan() {
    err = indexer.Add(ctx, esutil.BulkIndexerItem{
        Action: "index",
        Body: strings.NewReader(scanner.Text()),
        OnFailure: func(_ context.Context,
                        item esutil.BulkIndexerItem,
                        resp esutil.
BulkIndexerResponseItem,
                        err error) {
            fmt.Printf("Failure! %s, %+v\n%+v\n", err, item,
resp)
        },
    })
    if err != nil {
        // handle the error
    }
}

if err = indexer.Close(ctx); err != nil {
    // handle error
}
...
```

Okay, so that was a bit more complicated than I may have made it seem. The full code can be found in the GitHub repository for the book and I encourage you to try it out and play with the different settings and tweaks to control the performance, memory usage, and so on. Since you've seen the code to convert Arrow record batches to JSON for indexing into Elasticsearch, you should be able to build the reverse yourself! Write something that can take the response from an Elasticsearch query, which would be JSON objects, and reconstruct the Arrow record batches from it. Because of the format of Elasticsearch responses, it's not quite as simple as just directly using the JSON reader in the Arrow library. After you attempt this, you can take a look at the GitHub repository's `Chapter3` directory for the solution.

Building the full service end to end is a bit outside the scope of this chapter, but I highly recommend taking a stab at it, as it makes a great exercise in most of the things we've covered so far. It's also pretty fun and a cool thing to see when it works, as it's extremely performant, if you like that sort of thing.

Summary

With Jupyter, Spark, and ODBC as some of the most ubiquitous utilities in data science, it only makes sense to cover Arrow from the perspective of its integration with these tools. Many of you will likely not use Arrow directly in these cases, but rather benefit from the work being done by others utilizing Arrow. But, if you're a library or utility builder, or just want to tinker a bit to see whether you can improve the performance of some different tasks, this chapter should have given you a lot of information to chew on and hopefully a bunch of ideas to try out, such as converting Arrow on the fly to populate an Elasticsearch index but maintain a consistent interface.

I don't want to give you all the answers, mostly because I don't have them. There's a wealth of people all over experimenting with Arrow in a large number of different use cases, some of which we'll cover in other chapters. Hopefully, this chapter, and the chapters to come after it, set you up with all the building blocks you need to create awesome things, either by leveraging Arrow to facilitate a new library or utility or by utilizing Arrow and those tools to analyze your data in increasingly faster ways.

The next chapter is *Chapter 4, Format and Memory Handling*. We're going to take a closer look at the various ways data is passed around and stored and discuss the relationships and use cases they are all trying to address. The goal is to see where Arrow and its IPC format can fit in the existing data ecosystem with the multitude of trade-offs, and pros and cons that exist for how something is used or implemented.

Onwards!

Section 2: Interoperability with Arrow: pandas, Parquet, Flight, and Datasets

This section of the book focuses in more depth on how Arrow interacts with or replaces other common technologies. It describes how it stacks up against data interchange formats such as Protobuf, storage formats such as Parquet, and others. It also explores the Arrow Flight RPC protocol, including examples of setting up a simple client and server. Finally, this section also covers multi-file datasets and using the Compute APIs.

This section comprises the following chapters:

- *Chapter 4, Format and Memory Handling*
- *Chapter 5, Crossing the Language Barrier with the Arrow C Data API*
- *Chapter 6, Leveraging the Arrow Compute APIs*
- *Chapter 7, Using the Arrow Datasets API*
- *Chapter 8, Exploring Apache Arrow Flight RPC*

4
Format and Memory Handling

I've continuously extolled the virtues of using Arrow as a data interchange technology for tabular data, but how does it stack up against the more common technologies that people tend to utilize for transferring data? When does it make sense to use one over the other for your **application programming interface (API)**? The answer is to know how different technologies utilize memory. Clever management of your memory can be the key to performant processes. To decide which format to use for your data, you need to understand which use cases your options were designed for. With that in mind, you can take advantage of the runtime properties of the most common data transport formats such as **Protocol Buffers (Protobuf)**, **JavaScript Object Notation (JSON)**, and **FlatBuffers** when appropriate. By understanding how to utilize memory in your program, you can process very large amounts of data with minimal memory overhead.

We're going to cover the following things in this chapter:

- Which use cases make sense for using Arrow versus using Protobuf, JSON, FlatBuffers, or storage formats such as **comma-separated values (CSV)** and Apache Parquet

- Processing huge 100-**gigabyte (GB)** files using only a few **megabytes (MB)** of physical **random-access memory (RAM)** by utilizing memory mapping

Technical requirements

As before, you'll need an internet-connected computer with the following software so that you can follow along with the code examples here:

- Python 3.7 or higher, with the `pyarrow` and `pandas` modules installed

- Go 1.16 or higher

- A C++ compiler capable of compiling C++11 or higher, with the Arrow libraries installed

- Your preferred IDE, such as Emacs, Sublime, or VS Code

- A web browser

Storage versus runtime in-memory versus message-passing formats

When we're talking about formats for representing data, there are a few different, complementary, yet competing things we typically are trying to optimize. We can generally (over-) simplify this by talking about three main components, as follows:

- **Size**—The final size of the data representation

- **Serialize/deserialize speed**—The performance for converting data between the formats and something that can be used in-memory for computations

- **Ease of use**—A catch-all category regarding readability, compatibility, features, and so on

How we choose to optimize between these components is usually going to be heavily dependent upon the use case for that format. When it comes to working with data, there are three high-level use case descriptions I tend to group most situations into: long-term storage, in-memory runtime processing, and message passing. Yes—these groupings are quite broad, but I find that every usage of data can ultimately be placed into one of these three groups.

Long-term storage formats

What makes a good storage format? Size is typically considered first, as you're often sharing files and storing large datasets in a single format. With the advent and proliferation of cloud storage, storage costs aren't the driving reason for this so much as **input-output (I/O)** costs. You can use Amazon's **Simple Storage Service (S3)** storage or Microsoft's Azure Blob Storage and get nearly limitless storage for pennies or better, but when you want to retrieve that data, you're going to pay in bandwidth costs and network latency if the data is very large.

Depending on the way the data is going to be used, you're also going to be often trading off between optimizing for reads and optimizing for writes, as optimizing for one is usually going to be sub-optimal for the other. Some examples of persistent storage formats are provided here:

- CSV

- Apache Parquet

- Avro

- **Optimized Row Columnar (ORC)**

- JSON

In almost all cases, binary formats are going to be smaller and more efficient than plain text formats simply by virtue of the ability to represent more data with fewer bytes. You just have to sacrifice some of that ease of use since we can't just read binary data with our eyes! Unless you're a robot… Anyway, this is why most of the time, it is recommended for data to be stored in compact binary formats such as Parquet instead of text formats such as CSV or JSON. When we're looking at data stored on disk, there are two ways to optimize for reads, as outlined here:

- Make the physical size of the data smaller

- Use a format that minimizes how much data needs to be read to satisfy a query

Because reading from a disk—even **solid-state disks** (**SSDs**)—is so much slower than reading from memory, the bottleneck for processing will be how much data needs to be read into memory to get the data needed. While this can make it very efficient to read the data from disk into the main memory, it still requires decompressing that data before you can work with it, making it less optimal for being an in-memory computational format, as shown in the following diagram:

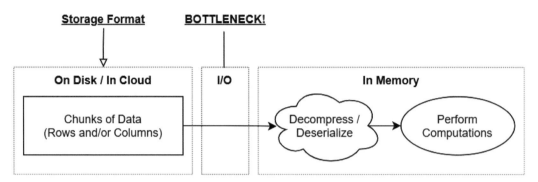

Figure 4.1 – Workflow to bring stored data into memory

Binary formats are often easier to compress based on how they store the data and can sometimes use tricks to make the data even more compressible. Parquet and ORC store the data in column-oriented forms that are generally more compressible than CSV and Avro, for example. You also have to take into account the way the data will be used. While you might be able to get a smaller file size with column-oriented storage formats, this is most beneficial if your most common workflow is to only need a subset of columns from the rows. The most common workflows for modern big data are **online transaction processing** (**OLTP**) and **online analytical processing** (**OLAP**).

OLTP systems usually process data at a record (row) level and perform **Create, Read, Update, Delete** (**CRUD**) operations on each record as a whole. The tasks performed by an OLTP system are focused on maintaining the integrity of the data when being accessed by multiple users at once and measuring their effectiveness by the number of transactions per second they can process. In the vast majority of cases, an OLTP system will want the entire record of data, not just a subset of fields. For this type of workflow, a row-based storage format such as Apache Avro would be most beneficial since you're usually going to need entire rows anyway.

OLAP systems are designed to quickly perform analytical operations such as aggregations, filtering, and statistical analysis across multiple dimensions such as time or other fields. As mentioned in previous chapters, this type of workflow benefits more from column-oriented storage so that you can minimize I/O by only reading the columns of data you need and ignoring fields that are irrelevant to the query. By aligning data of the same type next to each other, you get higher compression ratios and can optimize the representation of `null` values in sparse columns.

Once you read data from a storage format, you're going to need to convert the data into a different representation in order to work with it and perform any computations you want on it. This representation is referred to as the in-memory runtime representation or format, as shown in the following diagram:

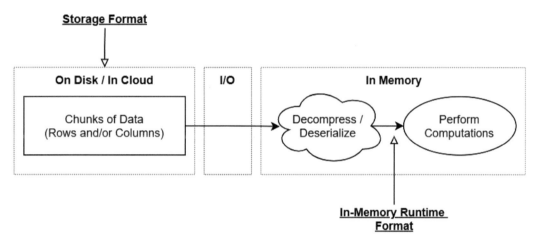

Figure 4.2 – Storage format and in-memory runtime

In the majority of cases, the I/O cost will be significantly larger than the cost to decompress or deserialize the data into a usable, in-memory representation, but this is still a cost that is proportional to the size of the data and needs to be paid before any operations can be performed. There are exceptions to this, of course. There do exist specific formats and algorithms that allow us to perform operations on compressed data without decompressing it, but they are typically uncommon and very specialized cases.

So, when we convert that data into some representation that we can perform operations on, which formats could we use? Well…

In-memory runtime formats

Formats such as Arrow and FlatBuffers have an inter-process representation that is identical to their in-memory representation, allowing developers to avoid the cost of copies when passing the data from one process to another, whether it's across a network or between processes on the same machine. The goal of formats that fall into this class is to be optimized for computation and calculation.

When working with the data in memory, the size of the data is less relevant than with on-disk formats. When performing computations and analysis in memory, the bottleneck is the **central processing unit (CPU)** itself rather than slow-moving I/O. In this situation, the major ways that modern developers speed up performance are through better algorithmic usage and optimizations such as vectorization. As such, data formats that can better take advantage of these end up being more performant for analytical computations. This is why Arrow is designed the way it is, optimizing for the most common analytical algorithms and taking advantage of **single instruction, multiple data (SIMD)** vectorization as opposed to optimizing for disk-resident data. You'll recall that we covered SIMD back in *Chapter 1, Getting Started with Apache Arrow*.

There are other concerns that can make a difference, such as byte alignment and random reads versus sequential reads, which can affect the performance of in-memory processing and disk-resident processing differently. Modern CPUs don't execute one instruction at a time but instead use a pipeline to stagger how instructions are executed through different stages. To maximize throughput, all kinds of predictions about which instructions will be next are made to keep the pipeline as full as possible. See the following screenshot for a simplified example of this pipeline concept:

Stages											
Fetch	a	b	c	d							
Decode		a	b	c	d						
Execute			a	b	c	d					
Write Back				a	b	c	d				
	1	2	3	4	5	6	7	8	9	10	**Clock Cycle**

Figure 4.3 – Ideal pipeline case

As long as the processor's predictions are correct, everything keeps chugging along smoothly as fast as it can, and *Figure 4.3* shows all four instructions completed in seven clock cycles. The hardware is going to try to predict which memory locations will be needed by the CPU and preload that data into registers before the instruction that needs it gets executed. As a result, sequential reads of contiguous chunks of memory can be extremely fast because the processor can make easy predictions and load larger chunks of data into the main memory with fewer instructions. The usage of vectorization by Arrow libraries also helps achieve this throughput, with instructions that are highly predictable for modern processors. Whenever the processor's prediction is incorrect, we get what's called a *bubble*, as seen in the following screenshot:

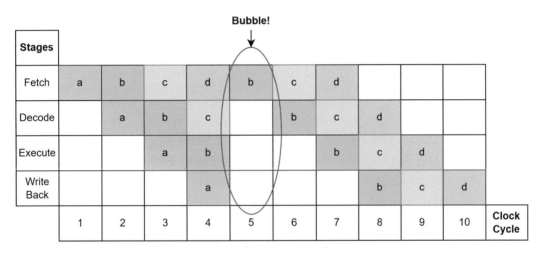

Figure 4.4 – CPU bubble misprediction

If executing instruction a results in a different branch of execution than what the processor predicted, the pipeline gets emptied and has to start over with the correct subsequent instruction. We can see in *Figure 4.4* that the result is executing the same 4 instructions, but with a misprediction, takes 10 clock cycles instead of 7. Of course, this is an oversimplified example, but over time, lots of mispredictions can result in enormous differences in runtime by preventing the processor from maximizing its throughput. Taking advantage of this sort of processor-pipelining optimization is a significant principle of the Arrow libraries.

The hardware being used can affect your execution in other ways too. Traditional spinning-disk hard drives are notoriously slow for random reads compared to sequential reads, since this requires moving to another sector of the disk instead of just continuing to read from one sector. SSDs instead have very little-to-no overhead for random reads as opposed to sequential ones. When we talk about in-memory representations, the way that the operating system loads data into the main memory is the driving bottleneck for random reads versus sequential ones, as discussed in *Chapter 1, Getting Started with Apache Arrow*.

The more an in-memory representation keeps data in contiguous chunks of memory, the faster it is to load that data into registers for the CPU. A single instruction to load a large contiguous area of memory will be significantly faster than multiple instructions to load many different areas of memory. This led to the decision to use a column-oriented representation for Arrow, making it easier for the operating system and processor to make predictions about which memory will be needed for execution. The trade-off for this is that for some OLTP workloads, record-oriented structure representations such as FlatBuffers might be more performant than column-oriented ones. The important thing to remember is the difference in trade-offs and use cases between on-disk formats and ephemeral runtime in-memory representations. This is where we get to our last type of data format—those that are optimized for structured message passing.

Message-passing formats

The last class of formats we're going to talk about are message-passing formats such as Protobuf, FlatBuffers, and JSON again. In computer science, programming interfaces designed to allow coordination and message passing between different processes are referred to as **inter-process communication** (**IPC**) interfaces. For message passing and IPC, you want to optimize for small sizes since you're frequently passing the data across a network. In addition, being able to easily stream the data without losing contextual information is also a large benefit for these. In the case of Protobuf and FlatBuffers, you specify the schema in some external file and use a code generator to generate optimized message handling code. These technologies typically optimize for small message sizes and can start to become unwieldy or less performant when working with larger message sizes. For example, the official documentation for Protobuf says that it's optimal for message sizes to be less than 1 MB.

Despite the fact that the purpose of these formats is to pass messages rather than to be an optimized format for computation, the cost of serialization and deserialization as overhead is still extremely important. The faster that the data can be serialized and deserialized, the faster it can be sent and made available in the main memory for computations. This is one of the core reasons for Arrow's IPC format being raw data buffers with no serialization overhead, but the small metadata structures are passed using FlatBuffers in order to benefit from its high performance as a message-passing format.

If we compare Arrow to Protobuf or FlatBuffers, we can see that they are designed to solve two different problems. Protobuf and FlatBuffers provide a common representation for sending messages *over the wire*. Using the utilities provided and a schema, code for your preferred language can be generated to accept this common and compressed over-the-wire representation and convert it to an in-memory representation that can then be used. For passing smaller messages, this overhead of serialization and deserialization is relatively negligible. For use cases that need even better performance, FlatBuffers allows operations to be performed on the data without needing to copy from deserialized structures.

However, it's when we're looking at very large datasets that serialization and deserialization costs add up significantly and become a bottleneck. Moreover, you can't take the raw memory bytes that make up a Protobuf structure in C++ and then give those bytes to a Java program to use as-is. The structure needs to get serialized first by C++ to that common representation and then deserialized by Java into the in-memory representation that Java understands. This is why the Arrow format specification was created to have the same internal in-memory structure regardless of the language it is implemented in.

Summing up

If it wasn't already abundantly clear, to simplify the point: Arrow is not a competing technology with formats such as Protobuf for message passing, nor is it competing as an on-disk format with formats such as ORC or Parquet (despite it having a file format). The use case that Arrow targets is, instead, complementary. On-disk formats are designed for persistent, long-term storage on disk and require non-trivial amounts of work to decode and decompress the data before you can operate on it. Message-passing formats such as Protobuf are compacted by using tricks such as packing integer values together and tags to leave out optional fields with default values. This is to cut down on message sizes for fast transmission across networks; using Arrow as a small message-passing format would likely be less efficient.

Arrow is designed as an ephemeral, runtime in-memory format for processing data on a per-array-cell basis with minimal overhead. It is not intended for long-term, persistent storage, even though it has a file format for convenience. But when you do need to pass around Arrow record batches and tables of data, you're going to want to understand the Arrow IPC format and how to utilize it.

Passing your Arrows around

Since Arrow is designed to be easily passable between processes, regardless of whether they are locally on the same machine or not, the interfaces for passing around record batches are referred to as IPC libraries for Arrow. If the processes happen to be on the same machine, then it's possible to share your data without performing any copies at all!

What is this sorcery?!

First things first. There are two types of binary formats defined for sharing record batches between processes—a **streaming format** and a **random access format**, as outlined in more detail here:

- The streaming format exists for sending a sequence of record batches of an arbitrary length. It must be processed from start to end; you can't get random access to a particular record batch in the stream without processing all of the ones before it.

- The random access—or file—format is for sharing a known number of record batches. Because it supports random access to particular record batches, it is very useful in conjunction with memory mapping.

> **Remember**
>
> It's crucial to remember what a record batch is if you want to understand the format for sending binary Arrow data. A *record batch* is simply an ordered collection of arrays that all have the same length but potentially different data types. The field names, types, and metadata are collectively referred to as a record batch's *schema*.

Arrow's IPC protocol defines three message types used for conveying information: Schema, RecordBatch, and DictionaryBatch. The series of binary payloads for these messages can be reconstructed into in-memory record batches without the need for memory copying. Each message consists of a **FlatBuffers** message for metadata and an optional message body. FlatBuffers is a highly efficient, cross-platform serialization library designed originally by Google. The design of FlatBuffers provides for the message to be interpreted and accessed *as-is* without the need to deserialize it into a different intermediate format first. (You can learn more about FlatBuffers at https://google.github.io/flatbuffers/.)

The following diagram shows the format of encapsulated messages sent along the stream. The first 8 bytes consist of 0xFFFFFFFF to indicate a valid message followed by a 4-byte, **little-endian** (**LE**) integer value that indicates the size of the FlatBuffers message and the padding combined. Finally, the message is completed by the raw bytes of an optional message body whose length is a multiple of 8 bytes.

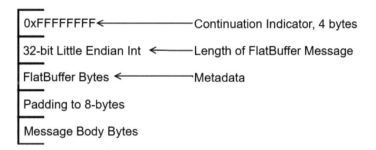

Figure 4.5 – IPC encapsulated message format

Okay; so, I know you're possibly thinking: *Hey, didn't I read that there was no deserialization cost? Don't I have to unpack the FlatBuffer data?* Well, the reason why FlatBuffers was chosen was that the binary data for fields in a FlatBuffer message can be accessed directly without having to unpack it into some other form. You only need the memory of the message itself to access the data; no additional allocations are necessary. Not only that, but it also even only requires part of the buffer to be in memory at a time if desired. Bottom line? It's *fast!* Also, keep in mind that you only have to deal with the FlatBuffer parts if you're actually implementing the specification; otherwise, all of this is just handled for you by the Arrow libraries.

So, let's take a look at the schema of a `FlatBuffer` message table, as follows:

```
table Message {
    version: org.apache.arrow.flatbuf.MetadataVersion;
    header: MessageHeader;
    bodyLength: long;
    custom_metadata: [ KeyValue ];
}
```

As you can see, the `FlatBuffer` message data contains a format version number, a specific message value (either `Schema`, `RecordBatch`, or `DictionaryBatch`), the length of the body in bytes, and a field for application-defined, key-value pairs of metadata. Generally, reading a stream of messages consists of reading the `FlatBuffer` message value first in order to obtain the size of the body, and then reading the body bytes. A typical stream will consist of a `Schema` message first, followed by some number of `DictionaryBatch` and `RecordBatch` messages. This doesn't contain any data buffers, only metadata information about the message, such as type information. We can visualize the stream of data like this:

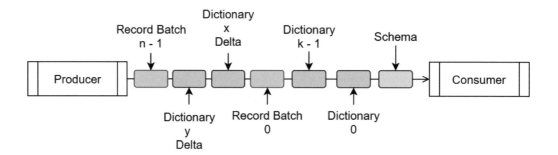

Figure 4.6 – Visualized IPC stream

Each box in the stream is an encapsulated message, as described before, containing the `FlatBuffer` data and optional body buffers. Dictionary messages would only show up in the stream if there are dictionary-encoded arrays in the schema. Each dictionary message contains an `id` field that is referenced by the schema to indicate which arrays use that dictionary, allowing optimization of using the same dictionary for multiple fields if possible, by referencing the `id` field for multiple arrays. In addition, there is an `isDelta` flag, allowing an existing dictionary to be expanded for subsequent record batches rather than having to resend the entire dictionary. `Schema` messages will contain no body data; they'll only contain the `FlatBuffer` message describing the types and metadata.

Record-batch messages contain the following:

- A header defined by the `RecordBatch FlatBuffer` message, containing the length and `null` count of each field in the record batch, along with the memory offset and length of each corresponding data buffer in the message body. To handle nested types, the fields are flattened into a pre-ordered depth-first traversal.

    - As an example, consider the following schema:

        - Col1: `Struct<a: int32, b: List<item: float32>, c: float64>`

        - Col2: `String`

    The flattened version would look like this:

    ```
    Field0:  Struct name='Col1'
    Field1:  Int32 name='a'
    Field2:  List name='b'
    Field3:  Float32 name='item'
    Field4:  Float64 name='c'
    Field5:  UTF8 name='Col2'
    ```

- Raw buffers of data that make up the record batch, end to end and padded to ensure an 8-byte alignment:

    - For each flattened field in the record batch, the data buffers that make up the array would be based on the descriptions back in *Chapter 1*, *Getting Started with Apache Arrow*, which described which buffers exist based on the type: the validity bitmap, raw data, offsets, and so on.

    - When reading the message in, there's no need to copy or transform the data buffers; they can just be referred to as-is where they are without any copies or deserialization.

After each message in the stream, the reader can read the next 8 bytes to determine whether there is more data and the size of the following `FlatBuffer` metadata message. There are two possible ways for a writer to signal that there's no more data, or **end of stream** (**EOS**), as outlined here:

- Just closing the stream

- Writing 8 bytes that contain a 4-byte continuation indicator (`0xFFFFFFFF`) and then a length of `0` as a 4-byte integer for the next message (`0x00000000`)

There's just one more thing before we get to examples of actually using the IPC streams: the random-access file format. Trust me—if you understand the streaming format, the file format is really easy. The following diagram describes the file format:

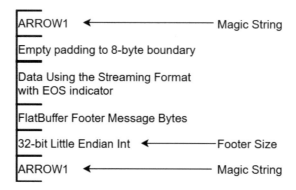

Figure 4.7 – IPC file format

The file format is really just an extension of the streaming format, with a magic string indicator to start and end the file, and a footer. The footer contains a copy of the schema (remember—the first message in the streaming format is also the schema) and the memory offsets and lengths for each block of data in the file, enabling random access to any record batch in the file. It is recommended to use the `.arrow` extension. A stream typically won't be written to a file, but if it is, the recommended extension is `.arrow`. There are also registered **Multipurpose Internet Mail Extension** (**MIME**) media types for both the streaming and file format of Apache Arrow data, as follows:

- `https://www.iana.org/assignments/media-types/application/vnd.apache.arrow.stream`

- `https://www.iana.org/assignments/media-types/application/vnd.apache.arrow.file`

> **Extra Information**
>
> There's an option in the IPC format that indicates that individual body buffers can be compressed in order to further reduce the size of the messages across the wire at the expense of some increased CPU usage. This could be very useful in cases where network latency is the bottleneck rather than CPU, or to reduce the file size if writing to a file. The two compression types supported by the IPC format are **Zstandard** (**ZSTD**) and **Lempel-Ziv 4** (**LZ4**) compression.

Okay; we've covered the protocol for communicating Arrow data, so let's see some examples.

Producing and consuming Arrows

What if you wanted to build a service that read in remote files and streamed the data back to the client? Seems simplistic, but it is the basis of a lot of data transfer use cases if you toss a variety of data manipulation in between the reading of the data files and streaming the data along. So, we're going to build something similar to this:

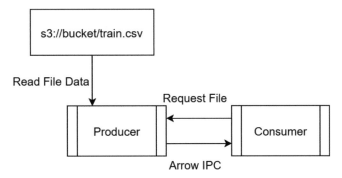

Figure 4.8 – Simple server-consumer IPC example

By following *Figure 4.8*, we see the following steps:

1. The consumer requests a file (not covered here, but will exist in GitHub samples).

2. Establishing an input stream from S3 to read the file as Arrow record batches.

3. Writing record batches to the consumer as we read them in from S3.

Should we take a stab at this, then? Here we go!

We've already covered reading files from S3 in Python and C++, so let's write the example for the producer side using Go, as follows:

1. First, we need our imports, as shown here:

```
import (
    "context"

        ...

    "github.com/apache/arrow/go/v7/arrow"
    "github.com/apache/arrow/go/v7/arrow/csv"
    "github.com/apache/arrow/go/v7/arrow/ipc"
    "github.com/aws/aws-sdk-go-v2/aws"
    "github.com/aws/aws-sdk-go-v2/service/s3"
)
```

2. Next, we can create our S3 client and establish our input stream, as follows:

```
client := s3.New(s3.Options{Region: "us-east-1"})
obj, err := client.GetObject(context.Background(),
        &s3.GetObjectInput{
                Bucket: aws.String("nyc-tlc"),
                Key: aws.String("trip data/yellow_
tripdata_2020-11.csv")})
if err != nil {
    // handle the error
}
```

Assuming there were no errors, there is a member called Body on the obj return that will be a stream to read the data for the file.

3. Now, we can set up our CSV reader, as follows:

```
schema := arrow.NewSchema([]arrow.Field{
    // put the expected schema of the CSV file
}, nil)
headerline := true // set to false if first line is not
                   // the column headers
reader := csv.NewReader(obj.Body, schema,
    csv.WithHeader(headerline))
defer reader.Release()
```

You can see the documentation to find other possible options that exist for creating a CSV reader.

4. To set up our IPC stream, we create an ipc.Writer interface and pass it a stream to write to. It could be anything that meets the io.Writer interface, whether it's a file or a **HyperText Transfer Protocol** (**HTTP**) response writer. The code is illustrated in the following snippet:

```
// assume w is our stream to write to
writer := ipc.NewWriter(w, ipc.WithSchema(reader.Schema()))
defer writer.Close()
```

5. Finally, we can just read in record batches and write them out as we go! This is what the process looks like:

```
for reader.Next() {
    if err := writer.Write(reader.Record()); err != nil {
```

```
            // handle the error
            break
        }
    }
    if reader.Err() != nil {
        // we didn't stop because we're done, we stopped
because
        // the reader had an error, handle the error!
    }
```

And that's that!

Consuming this stream is also easy to do regardless of the programming language you're using. Conceptually, all the following work in the same way as they pertain to reading and writing the IPC format:

- With Go, you'd use `ipc.Reader`.

- For Python, there is `pyarrow.RecordBatchStreamReader`, and writing would be done with `pyarrow.RecordBatchStreamWriter`.

  The reader also has a special `read_pandas` function to simplify the case where you might want to read many record batches and convert them to a single DataFrame.

- The C++ library provides `arrow::ipc::RecordBatchStreamReader::Open`, which accepts `arrow::io::InputStream` to create a reader, and `arrow::ipc::MakeStreamWriter` for creating a writer from `arrow::io::OutputStream`.

If you'd prefer to use the random-access file format, then each of the preceding functions has corresponding versions for reading and writing the file format instead. If you're storing DataFrames or Arrow tables as files, you may have come across functions or documentation mentioning the Feather file format. The Feather file format is just the Arrow IPC file format on disk and was created early on during the beginnings of the Arrow project as a **proof of concept** (**PoC**) for language-agnostic DataFrame storage for Python and R. Originally, the formats were not identical (the **version 1** (**V1**) Feather format), so there still exist functions in the `pyarrow` and `pandas` libraries for specifically reading and writing Feather files (that will default to the V2 format, which is exactly the current Arrow IPC format).

To ensure efficient memory usage when dealing with all these streams and files, the Arrow libraries all provide various utilities for memory management that are also utilized internally by them. These helper classes and utilities are what we're going to cover next so that you'll know how to take advantage of them to make your scripts and programs as lean as possible. We're also going to cover how you can share your buffers across programming language boundaries for improved performance, and why you'd want to do so.

The Arrow IPC file format, or Feather, was created to provide performance benefits through memory mapping. Because the Arrow IPC format has raw data buffers precisely in the same way they would be in memory, a technique called memory mapping can be utilized to minimize memory overhead for processing. Let's see what that is and how it works!

Learning about memory cartography

One draw of distributed systems such as Apache Spark is the ability to process very large datasets quickly. Sometimes, the dataset is so large that it can't even fit entirely in memory on a single machine! Having a distributed system that can break up the data into chunks and process them in parallel is then necessary since no individual machine would be able to load the whole dataset in memory at one time to operate on it. But what if you could process a huge, multiple-GB file while using almost no RAM at all? That's where memory mapping comes in.

Let's look to our *NYC Taxi* dataset once again for help with demonstrating this concept. The file named `yellow_tripdata_2015-01.csv` is approximately 1.8 GB in size, perfect to use as an example. By now, you should easily be able to read that CSV file in as an Arrow table and look at the schema. Now, let's say we wanted to find out and calculate the mean of the values in the `total_amount` column. For the ease and brevity of code snippets, we'll use the Python Arrow library for this example.

Acquiring the Data

You can download the sample file we're using here from the public-facing **Amazon Web Services** (**AWS**) S3 bucket at this URL: `https://s3.amazonaws.com/nyc-tlc/trip+data/yellow_tripdata_2015-01.csv`.

The base case

In order to see how much benefit we get out of memory mapping, we first need to construct our base case. We need to first calculate the mean of the values in the `total_amount` column without memory mapping so that we have a baseline for the runtime and memory usage. Using the `pyarrow` library and `pandas`, if you remember from *Chapter 3*, *Data Science with Apache Arrow*, there are two easy ways to calculate the `total_amount` column of the CSV file. One is significantly slower than the other. Do you remember what they are? Have a look at the following code snippet:

```
In [0]: import pandas as pd
In [1]: %%timeit
   ...: pd.read_csv('yellow_tripdata_2015-01.csv')['total_
amount'].mean()
   ...:
```

As usual, because we used the special `%%timeit` function, we get the time that it took to execute output below the results in IPython. On my laptop, the timing output from IPython shows it taking 20.2 seconds, give or take 400 milliseconds, to do this. This is the slow way. See if you remember the fast way; I'll still be here when you get back.

Figured it out? I hope so! But for those who didn't, here it is:

```
In [2]: import pyarrow as pa
In [3]: import pyarrow.csv
In [4]: %%timeit
   ...: df = pa.csv.read_csv('yellow_tripdata_2015-01.csv',
   ...:     convert_options=pa.csv.ConvertOptions(
   ...:     include_columns=['total_amount'])).to_pandas()
   ...: df.mean()
   ...:
```

When I run this, it takes 816 milliseconds—plus or minus 27 milliseconds—on my laptop. We now have our base-case time that it takes to get the mean value of the `total_amount` column from our 1.8 GB CSV file. The next step for our comparison is to write the data out to a Parquet file instead of a CSV file and see how it compares for us to read the single column and calculate the mean.

Parquet versus CSV

When written as a Parquet file using the default settings, the table of data from the
`yellow_tripdata_2015-01.csv` file clocks in at just over 282 MB. Just as I said
earlier, binary formats allow for higher compression ratios among the other compression
techniques that Parquet utilizes. We can then use the Parquet file to see how the
smaller file size and I/O benefits of Parquet can let us improve the performance of the
computation. Let's try calculating the same mean of the column, but this time using the
Parquet file instead of the CSV file, as follows:

```
In [5]: %%timeit
   ...: pd.read_parquet('yellow_tripdata_2015-01.parquet',
   ...: columns=['total_amount']).mean()
   ...:
```

As I mentioned before, we can take advantage of the fact that Parquet allows us to only
read the column we want rather than having to read everything, as we do with CSV.
Combining the smaller size of the compressed data and the reduction in I/O by only
having to read a single column of data, my laptop reports that this takes about 230
milliseconds. That's around 3.5 times faster than calculating it from the CSV file using
`pyarrow`, and 87 times faster than using `pandas` directly. Depending on whether you're
using an SSD, **Non-Volatile Memory Express** (**NVMe**), or spinning-disk hard drive, your
performance may vary.

Before we move on, let's look at the data we have compiled so far. Here it is:

CSV	1.8 GB	*calc mean*
	pandas read_csv	20.2 s ± 400ms
	pyarrow.csv.read_csv	816 ms ± 27ms
Parquet	**286 MB**	*calc mean*
	pandas/pyarrow	230 ms

Figure 4.9 – File size and performance numbers (CSV and Parquet)

Now let's try using a memory-mapped file.

Mapping data into memory

I'll go into the mechanics of what exactly is happening behind the scenes a little later in the chapter, but for now, we'll examine how to use memory mapping with the Arrow libraries. In order to benefit from the memory map, we need to write the file out as an Arrow IPC file. Let's use `RecordBatchFileWriter` to write out our table, as follows:

```
In [6]: table = pa.csv.read_csv('yellow_tripdata_2015-01.csv').
combine_chunks() # we want one contiguous table
In [7]: with pa.OSFile('yellow_tripdata_2015-01.arrow', 'wb')
as sink:
   ...:       with pa.RecordBatchFileWriter(sink, table.schema)
as writer:
   ...:              writer.write_table(table)
   ...:
```

Notice the use of the `.arrow` extension to denote the file. This follows the standard media types that are recognized by the **Internet Assigned Numbers Authority** (**IANA**). By default, this file is not compressed in any way, which means that it's pretty big. While the CSV file is around 1.82 GB, the Arrow IPC file ends up being around 1.77 GB, roughly only around 50 MB difference. We can then map the file into memory and do the same thing we did earlier to calculate the mean from the Arrow table, as follows:

```
In [8]: %%timeit
   ...: source = pa.memory_map('yellow_tripdata_2015-01.arrow')
   ...: table = pa.ipc.RecordBatchFileReader(source).read_
all().column('total_amount')
   ...: result = table.to_pandas().mean()
   ...:
```

This clocks in at a very speedy 200 milliseconds on my laptop, which is quite nice. The following screenshot shows an updated version of the table from *Figure 4.9*, now including our Arrow IPC file:

CSV	1.8 GB	*calc mean*
	pandas read_csv	20.2 s ± 400ms
	pyarrow.csv.read_csv	816 ms ± 27ms
Parquet	**286 MB**	*calc mean*
	pandas/pyarrow	230 ms
Arrow IPC	**1.77 GB**	*calc mean*
	pyarrow mmap	200 ms

Figure 4.10 – File size and performance, including memory mapping

To really see the benefit, we need to check how much memory is being allocated and used by the process for each of these approaches. In order to do this, we'll need to install the psutil package using pip, as follows:

```
$ pip install psutil
```

To check the memory usage of the approaches, we can just check the currently allocated memory by the process before and after each read and check the difference. We can put a script together that does this rather than using IPython or Jupyter and doing it interactively. Let's walk through the script, starting with the first line, as follows:

```
# initial memory usage in megabytes
memory_init = psutil.Process(os.getpid()).memory_info().rss >>
20
```

We check the current memory usage of the process using the psutil library and convert the value from bytes to MB for easy reading. Now, we can just read the data and get the column we wanted in various ways, storing the current memory usage after each one, first by reading the CSV file and taking just the column we want from the resulting table, as follows:

```
col_pd_csv = pd.read_csv('yellow_tripdata_2015-01.csv')['total_
amount']
memory_pd_csv = psutil.Process(os.getpid()).memory_info().rss
>> 20
```

Then, we pass the column in as an option to prune unnecessary columns earlier in the processing, as follows:

```
col_pa_csv = pa.csv.read_csv('yellow_tripdata_2015-01.csv',
                convert_options=pa.csv.ConvertOptions(
            include_columns=['total_amount'])).to_pandas()
memory_pa_csv = psutil.Process(os.getpid()).memory_info().rss
>> 20
```

Now, we use the Parquet file instead of the CSV file, as follows:

```
col_parquet = pd.read_parquet('yellow_tripdata_2015-01.
parquet', columns=['total_amount'])
memory_parquet = psutil.Process(os.getpid()).memory_info().rss
>> 20
```

Then, we use the Feather—or Arrow IPC—file, but without memory mapping, as follows:

```
with pa.OSFile('yellow_tripdata_2015-01.arrow', 'rb') as source:
    col_arrow_file = pa.ipc.open_file(source).read_all().
column(
                            'total_amount').to_pandas()
memory_arrow = psutil.Process(os.getpid()).memory_info().rss >>
20
```

It's important to note that the whole `.arrow` file needs to be loaded in via `read_all` before you can filter on a single column. This is where memory-mapping the Arrow IPC file can come in handy! Memory mapping the file allows us to reference locations in the file that contain the column data we want without having to load it in. Getting the column by memory mapping the Arrow IPC file looks like this:

```
source = pa.memory_map('yellow_tripdata_2015-01.arrow', 'r')
table_mmap = pa.ipc.RecordBatchFileReader(source).read_all().
column(
            'total_amount')
col_arrow_mmap = table_mmap.to_pandas(zero_copy_only=True)
memory_mmapped = psutil.Process(os.getpid()).memory_info().rss
>> 20
```

The highlighted lines in the preceding code snippet each show the variables we store the memory usage in after each time we read the data. If we progressively subtract the values, we can see how much memory was allocated by the process for each way of getting the data. In order of appearance in the script, this is how we get the memory usage value for each of the ways we tried reading in the column:

1. With `pandas`, read CSV: `memory_pd_csv - memory_init`
2. Read CSV using `pyarrow`: `memory_pa_csv - memory_pd_csv`
3. Read Parquet column: `memory_parquet - memory_pa_csv`
4. Read Arrow file normally: `memory_arrow - memory_parquet`
5. Read memory-mapped Arrow IPC file: `memory_mmapped - memory_arrow`

And now, the moment of truth! How much memory did each approach use? Let's take a look:

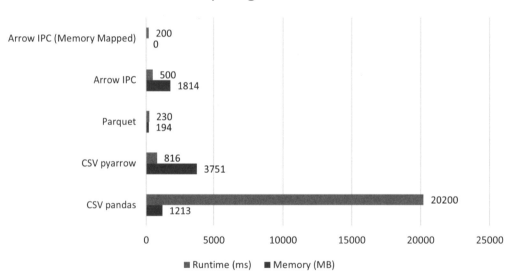

Figure 4.11 – Memory usage and runtime to calculate the mean

There we have it—by using a memory-mapped file, even though it's a 1,814 MB file, there's effectively zero physical memory allocated to read in the column. Magic! We can also see that the memory usage for reading the Arrow IPC file normally is the entire file size because it has to read the whole file into memory to process it. Meanwhile, Parquet uses a very respectable 194 MB only. The real shocking one is reading in the file using the `pyarrow` library, just over twice the size of the file used as memory. This is because the multithreaded reads don't allocate a single contiguous chunk of memory but instead multiple smaller chunks. So, when we create the `pandas` DataFrame, it needs to insert a copy of the data into a contiguous memory location. We're sacrificing memory for performance as compared to the single-threaded version of reading the file, but then have to pay the cost of allocating all that memory.

There are two reasons why the memory-mapped file approach ends up being faster than the Parquet version: not having to allocate any memory, and no decoding is necessary to access the data. We just reference the memory as-is and can work with it immediately!

If you're curious about how this magical sorcery works, then read on, my adventurous reader!

Too long; didn't read (TL;DR) – Computers are magic

Before I can explain the sorcery behind memory mapping, you have to understand how memory for a running process works. There's going to be a bit of oversimplification here, and that's okay! This is a crash course, not a college class.

Virtual and physical memory space

Most modern operating systems use the concept of virtualized memory for handling the memory used for a running process. This means that the entirety of the space of addresses that a process might reference doesn't have to be stored in the physical RAM on the device all the time. Instead, the operating system can *swap* data from the process' memory out of the main memory, and write *pages* to a pagefile or a cache, or any other way it wants to handle it. In this context, think of a *page* of data as just a chunk of memory, frequently around 4 **kilobytes** (**KB**). The operating system then maintains a mapping table, known as a *page table*, which maps the virtual addresses to physical locations in RAM where that data is stored. If a request is made to load data that isn't physically in RAM, it's called a *page fault*. The requested data is then swapped back into RAM so that it can be referenced properly by the process. This is all invisible to the process and is handled at the operating-system level. You can see an illustration of the process in the following diagram:

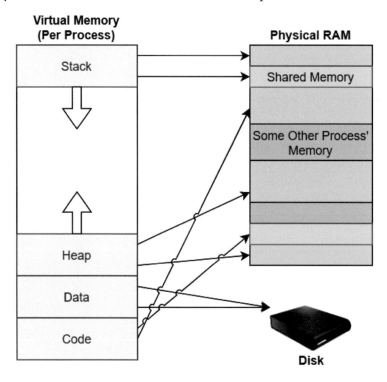

Figure 4.12 – Virtual and physical memory

Figure 4.12 shows a diagram of how a process' view of its virtual memory might map to physical memory and the disk. The process gets to see its memory as if it's a contiguous space that has its stack, heap, shared libraries, and anything else it has to reference in memory. But physically, chunks of that memory can exist in various locations on the RAM chips or even on disk in a *pagefile* or a cache somewhere. The operating system then keeps track of the mappings between the virtual-memory locations and the physical locations of the memory, updating that table as it moves data into and out of the physical RAM on-demand by processes.

There are various benefits to virtualized memory that have made it the de facto standard, some of which are listed here:

- Processes don't need to manage shared memory spaces themselves.
- The operating system can leverage shared libraries between processes to share the same memory spaces and reduce overall memory consumption.
- Increased security by isolating one process' memory from another process.
- Being able to conceptually reference and manipulate more memory than is physically available.

When you read data from a file, your process makes a system call that then has to pass through various drivers and memory managers every time you want to read or write data to the file. At many steps along the way, that data gets buffered and cached (read *copied*). Memory mapping a file allows us to bypass all those copies and treat the data of a file as if it were normal memory with *load/store* calls as opposed to system calls, which are orders of magnitude slower.

What does memory mapping do?

Memory mapping is functionality that is provided by the **Portable Operating System Interface** (**POSIX**)-defined mmap function on many operating systems. When you memory map a file, a chunk of the virtual address space for the process equivalent to the size of the file is blocked out, allowing the process to treat the file data as simple memory loading and storing. In most cases, the region of memory that is mapped is directly the kernel's page (file) cache, which means that no copies get created when accessing the data.

The following diagram shows an example of a situation when a file is memory-mapped. All accesses to a file go through the kernel's page cache so that updates to the mapped file are immediately visible to any processes that attempt to read the file, even though they won't exist physically on the device until the buffers are flushed and synced back to the physical drive. This means that multiple processes can memory map the same file and treat it as a region of shared memory, which is how dedicated shared process memory is often implemented under the hood.

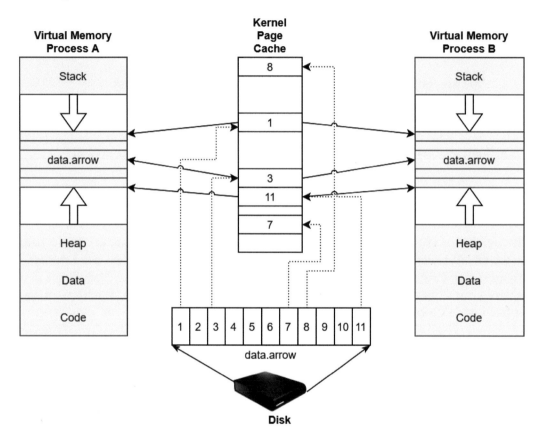

Figure 4.13 – Memory-mapped file-page cache

In our example of memory mapping, the large Arrow file to read the values and process the column, we're taking advantage of the *lazy loading* and zero-copy properties of memory mapping and the `pyarrow` library. By memory mapping the 1.77 GB file, the library is able to treat the file as if it were already in memory without having to actually allocate the entire 1.77 GB of the file. It will only read the pages from the file that it needs when the corresponding virtual memory locations are accessed. In the meantime, we can just pass references to the memory addresses around. We read a few KB of data from the bottom of the file, which, as you'll remember from *Chapter 1, Getting Started with Apache Arrow*, is where the metadata and schema will be stored, accessing only the corresponding pages. When we finally want to read the values in the column in order to perform a computation, only then will the data be materialized and pulled into RAM. The code snippet from the *Mapping data into memory* section, when we measured the memory usage, didn't perform the mean calculations; it only read the data into `pandas` DataFrame objects. Since we never tried to read the data in the column, the only data pulled into memory from the file was the few KB of metadata.

If we add the highlighted line to perform the mean calculation, then we'll see the memory usage for reading from the file, as follows:

```
source = pa.memory_map('yellow_tripdata_2015-01.arrow', 'r')
table_mmap = pa.ipc.RecordBatchFileReader(source).read_all().
column(
                'total_amount')
col_arrow_mmap = table_mmap.to_pandas(zero_copy_only=True)
result = col_arrow_mmap.mean()
memory_mmapped = psutil.Process(os.getpid()).memory_info().rss
>> 20
```

Running the script with this added line results in an output saying that it now uses 97 MB instead of 0, which is exactly what you get when you multiply the number of rows (12,748,986) by the size of a double (8 bytes). To calculate the mean of the column from the 1.77 GB file, we were able to only require as much RAM as the column itself to perform the aggregation calculation—just 97 MB. Pretty cool, right?

So, why don't we just always memory map files? Well, it's not as simple as that. Let's find out why.

Memory mapping is not a silver bullet

As we saw in the preceding sections, the primary reason to use a persistent memory-mapped file is for I/O performance. But as with everything, it's still a trade-off. While the standard approach for I/O is slow due to the overhead of system calls and the copying of memory, memory-mapped I/O also has a cost: **minor page faults**. A page fault happens when a process attempts to access a page of its virtual memory space that hasn't yet been loaded into memory. In the case of memory-mapped I/O, a *minor* page fault is when a page exists in memory, but the memory management unit of the system hasn't yet marked it as being loaded when it is accessed by the process. This would happen when a block of data has been loaded into the page cache, such as in *Figure 4.13*, but has not yet been mapped and connected to the appropriate location in the process' virtual memory space. Depending on the access pattern and hardware, in some circumstances, memory-mapped I/O can be significantly slower than standard I/O.

For very small files, in the order of KB or smaller, memory mapping them can end up causing excess memory fragmentation and result in a waste of memory space. Memory-mapped regions are always going to be aligned to the memory page size, which is frequently around 4 KB in most systems. Once the whole file is loaded into memory, mapping a 5 KB file will require 2 memory pages, or 8 KB of allocated memory. The following diagram shows how this then results in 3 KB of wasted slack space in memory:

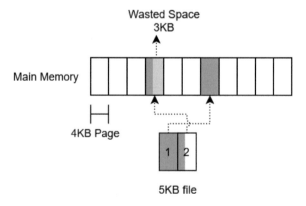

Figure 4.14 – Wasted space memory mapping small files

While 3 KB might not seem like a lot of memory space, if you memory map a large number of small files, this can add up to a lot of fragmentation and wasted memory space. Finally, when you have extremely fast devices, such as modern NVMe SSDs, you can wind up getting limited by the fact that many operating systems limit the number of CPU cores that handle page faults. The result is that memory-mapped I/O ends up being less scalable than standard I/O. With too many processes performing memory mapping, you can end up bottlenecked by this cap on cores rather than by the storage device.

There are a few other considerations that need to be kept in mind when using memory-mapped files, as outlined here:

- Any I/O error on the backing source file while accessing the mapped memory gets reported to the process as errors that wouldn't normally occur when just accessing memory. When working with memory-mapped I/O, all code accessing the mapped memory should be prepared to handle those errors.

- On hardware without a memory management unit, such as embedded or lower-power systems, the operating system can copy the entire file into memory when a request is made to map it. This obviously can only work for files that will fit in the available memory and would be slow if you only need to access a small portion of the file.

All in all, memory mapping is a crucial technique for handling very large files that you only need to read small portions of and for sharing memory between processes. Just make sure you test and benchmark frequently to ensure you're actually getting a benefit from it. Keep in mind that memory mapping things such as Parquet files is less beneficial than mapping raw Arrow IPC files. You may ask: *Why is that?* Since the data in the Parquet file still needs to be decoded and decompressed before you can use it, memory still needs to get allocated to hold the decoded data. While you might save a small amount of performance on the I/O costs of the Parquet file, on a sufficiently fast disk, the bottleneck will be the memory allocations and CPU for decoding and decompressing instead. The raw bytes of Arrow IPC files, on the contrary, can be used in memory directly as they are, as we saw earlier, bypassing the need for any additional memory allocations to use and reference the data from the file.

Summary

If you are building up data pipelines and large systems, regardless of whether you are a data scientist or a software architect, you're going to have to make a lot of decisions regarding which formats to use for various pieces of the system. You always want to choose the best format for the use case, and not just pick the latest trends and apply them everywhere. Many people hear about Arrow and either react by thinking that they need to use it everywhere for everything, or they wonder why we needed *yet another* data format. The key takeaway I want you to understand is the differences in the problems that are trying to be solved.

If you need longer-term persistent storage either on disk or in the cloud, you typically want a storage format such as Parquet, ORC, or CSV, with the primary access cost being I/O time for these use cases, so you want to optimize to reduce that based on your access patterns. If you're passing small messages around, such as metadata or control messages, then formats such as Protobuf, FlatBuffers, and JSON will potentially be optimal. You don't want to use this for large tabular datasets, though, especially if you will need to perform analytics and computations on the data. These are not hard-and-fast rules—they are guidelines. The use case that Arrow targets is to be an in-memory ephemeral runtime format for data, providing a shared-memory format so that more CPU time can be spent on performing computations rather than on having to convert large amounts of data between different formats as it passes through a system.

Hopefully, you've also picked up ideas for optimizing your memory usage when it comes to dealing with these large files and data handling, such as when it might make sense to use Arrow IPC files instead of compact Parquet files or otherwise. As I said, make sure to use the right format to solve the problem in front of you given all of the factors: the hardware, the networks, the data, and the process itself.

The next chapter is titled *Crossing the Language Barrier with the Arrow C Data API*. Up till now, we've covered a lot of the surface information, creating arrays and tables, reading and writing files in various formats, and so on. But remember: I said that Arrow is a *collection* of libraries for handling data. We're going to dive deeper and look at some of the more experimental APIs that the Arrow libraries expose, such as the Compute API. This chapter was kind of light on code; the next chapter will not be. I hope you stick around!

See you on the next page!

5
Crossing the Language Barrier with the Arrow C Data API

Not to sound like a broken record, but I've said several times already that Apache Arrow is a *collection* of libraries rather than one single library. This is an important distinction from both a technical standpoint and a logistical one. From a technical standpoint, it means that third-party projects that depend on Arrow don't need to use the entirety of the project and instead can only link against, embed, or otherwise include the portions of the project they need. This allows for smaller binaries and a smaller surface area of dependencies. From a logistical standpoint, it allows the Arrow project to pivot easily and move in potentially experimental directions without making large, project-wide changes.

As the goal of the Arrow project is to create a collection of tools and libraries that can be shared across the data analytics and data science ecosystems with a shared in-memory representation, there are lots of areas in which Arrow can become useful. First of all, there are the utilities for reading and writing data files which we've already covered (*Chapter 2*, *Working with Key Arrow Specifications*), and there are the interoperability utilities provided for integration with pandas and Spark (*Chapter 3*, *Data Science with Apache Arrow*). This chapter is going to specifically cover another area – the efficient sharing of data between different languages and runtimes in the same process:

- The Arrow C data interface for sharing both schemas and data

- The Arrow C data interface for streaming record batches of data

- Use cases where this interface is beneficial

Technical requirements

This chapter is intended to be highly technical, with various code examples and exercises diving into the usage of the different Arrow libraries. As such, like before, you need access to a computer with the following software to follow along:

- Python 3+ – the `pyarrow` module installed and importable

- Go 1.16+

- A C++ compiler supporting C++11 or better

- Your preferred IDE – Sublime, Visual Studio Code, Emacs, and so on

Using the Arrow C data interface

Back in *Chapter 2*, *Working with Key Arrow Specifications*, I mentioned the Arrow C data interfaces in regard to the communication of data between Python and Spark processes. At that point, we didn't go much into detail about the interface or what it looks like; now, we will.

Because the Arrow project is fast-moving and evolving, it can sometimes be difficult for other projects to incorporate the Arrow libraries into their work. There's also the case where there might be a lot of existing code that needs to be adapted to work with Arrow piecemeal, leading to you having to create or even re-implement adapters for interchanging data. To avoid redundant efforts across these situations, the Arrow project defines a very small, stable set of C definitions that can be *copied* into a project to allow to easily pass data across the boundaries of different languages and libraries. For languages and runtimes that aren't C or C++, it should still be easy to use whatever **Foreign Function Interface** (**FFI**) declarations correspond to your language or runtime.

The benefits of this approach are as follows:

- Developers can choose to either tightly integrate their utilities with the Arrow project and all of its facilities and libraries, or have minimal integration with just the Arrow *format*.

- A stable **Application Binary Interface** (**ABI**) for zero-copy sharing of data between different runtimes and components in the same process.

- Allows for integration of Arrow without needing an explicit compile-time or runtime dependency on the Arrow libraries.

- Avoids needing to create singular adapters for specific cases such as JPype (a bridge between Java and Python) in favor of a generalized approach that anyone can implement support for, with little investment needed.

One thing to keep in mind is that the C interface is not intended to provide a C API for the higher-level operations exposed by things such as Java, C++, or Go. It's specifically for just passing the Arrow data itself. Also, the interface is intended for sharing data between different components of the same process – if you're passing data in between distinct processes or attempting to store the data, you should use the IPC format instead (which we covered in *Chapter 4, Format and Memory Handling*).

If we compare the IPC and C data formats, we can see some important considerations.

A C data interface is superior to the IPC format in the following ways:

- Zero-copy by design.

- Customizable release callback for resource lifetime management.

- Minimal C definition that is easily copied to different code bases.

- Data is exposed in Arrow's logical format without any dependency on FlatBuffers.

The IPC format is superior to the C data interface in the following ways:

- It allows for storage and persistence or communication across different processes and machines.

- It does not require C data access.

- It has room to add other features such as compression since it is a streamable format.

Now that we've explained why the C data interface exists, let's dive into the structure definitions and how it all works. There are three structures exposed in the header file – `ArrowSchema`, `ArrowArray`, and `ArrowArrayStream`. At the time of writing, the following Arrow language libraries already provide functionality for both exporting and importing Arrow data using the C data interface:

- C++
- Python
- R
- Rust
- Go
- Java
- Ruby
- C/GLib

The first thing we're going to dive into is the `ArrowSchema` structure.

The ArrowSchema structure

When working with data frequently, either the data type or schema is fixed by the API or one schema applies to multiple batches of data of varying sizes. By separating the schema description and the data itself into two separate structures, the ABI allows producers of Arrow C data to avoid the cost of exporting and importing the schema for every single batch of data. In cases where it's just a single batch of data, the same API call can return both structures at once, providing efficiency in both situations.

> **An Interesting Tidbit**
>
> Despite the name, the `ArrowSchema` structure is actually more similar to the `arrow::Field` class in the C++ library than the `arrow::Schema` class. The C++ `Schema` class represents a collection of fields (containing a name, datatype, and potential metadata) and optional schema-level metadata. By having the `ArrowSchema` structure more closely resemble the `Field` representation, it can serve dual purposes; a full schema is represented as the `Struct` type whose `children` are the individual fields of the schema. This reuse keeps the ABI smaller and requires only the two `ArrowSchema` and `ArrowArray` structures instead of requiring another to represent fields too.

This is the definition of the `ArrowSchema` structure:

```
#define ARROW_FLAG_DICTIONARY_ORDERED 1
#define ARROW_FLAG_NULLABLE 2
#define ARROW_FLAG_MAP_KEYS_SORTED 4
struct ArrowSchema {
    // Array type description
    const char* format;
    const char* name;
    const char* metadata;
    int64_t flags;
    int64_t n_children;
    struct ArrowSchema** children;
    struct ArrowSchema* dictionary;
    // Release callback
    void (*release)(struct ArrowSchema*);
    // Opaque producer-specific data
    void* private_data;
};
```

Simple, straightforward, and easy to use, right? Let's look at the different fields.

- `const char* format` (*required*):

  - A null-terminated, UTF8-encoded string describing the data type. Child data types for nested arrays are encoded in the child structures.

- `const char* name` (*optional*):

  - A null-terminated, UTF8-encoded string containing the name of the field or array. Primarily for reconstructing child fields of nested types. If omitted, it can be NULL or an empty string.

- `const char* metadata` (*optional*):

  - A binary string containing the metadata for the type; it is not null-terminated. The format is described in *Figure 5.6*.

- `int64_t flags` (*optional*):

    - Bitfield of flags computed by performing a bitwise `OR` of the flag values. If omitted, it should be `0`. The flags available are the macros defined above the structure:

        - `ARROW_FLAG_NULLABLE`: Set if the field is allowed to be null (regardless of whether there are actually any nulls in the array).

        - `ARROW_FLAG_DICTIONARY_ORDERED`: If this is a dictionary-encoded type, set this if the order of the index is semantically meaningful.

        - `ARROW_FLAG_MAP_KEYS_SORTED`: For a map type, set this if the keys within each value are sorted.

- `int64_t n_children` (*required*):

    - The number of children for this data type if nested, or `0`

- `struct ArrowSchema** children` (*optional*):

    - There *must* be a number of pointers equal to `n_children` in this C array. If `n_children` is `0`, this *may* be null.

- `struct ArrowSchema* dictionary` (*optional*):

    - If this schema represents a dictionary-encoded type, this *must* be non-null and point to the schema for the type of the dictionary values. Otherwise, this *must* be null.

- `void (*release)(struct ArrowSchema*)` (*required*):

    - A pointer to a callback function for releasing the associated memory for this object

- `void *private_data` (*optional*):

    - A pointer to some opaque data structure provided by the producing API if necessary. Consumers *must not* process this member; the lifetime of any memory it points to is handled by the producing API.

Note that the `format` field describes the data type using a string. Let's see how to determine the data type from that string.

The data type format

The data type itself is described by a format string that only describes the top-level type's format. Nested data types will have their child types in child schema objects, and metadata will be encoded in a separate member field. All the format strings are designed to be extremely easy to parse, with the most-common primitive formats each having a single character for their format string. The primitive formats are shown in *Figure 5.1*:

Arrow Type	Null	Boolean	Int8 Uint8	Int16 Uint16	Int32 Uint32	Int64 Uint64	Float16
Format String	n	B	c C	s S	i I	l L	e

Arrow Type	Float32	Float64	Binary	Large Binary	UTF-8 String	Large UTF-8 String
Format String	f	g	z	Z	u	U

Figure 5.1 – Primitive type format strings

A couple of parameterized data types such as decimal and fixed-width binary have format strings consisting of a single character and a colon, followed by parameters, as shown in *Figure 5.2*:

Arrow Type	Format String
Decimal128 [precision 19, scale 10]	d:19,10
Decimal Bit width = NNN [precision 19, scale 10]	d:19,10,NNN
Fixed-Width Binary [42 bytes]	w:42

Figure 5.2 – Decimal and fixed-width binary format strings

Our next group of types are the temporal types, the dates and the times; these format strings are all multi-character strings that start with t, as depicted in *Figure 5.3*. For the timestamp types that may optionally contain a specified time zone, that time zone is appended as is after the colon without any quotes around it. The colon character is not omitted when the time zone is empty; it must still be included:

Arrow Type	Date32 [days]	Date64 [milliseconds]	Time32 [seconds] [milliseconds]	Time64 [microseconds] [nanoseconds]
Format String	tdD	tdm	tts ttm	ttu ttn

Arrow Type	Duration [seconds] [milliseconds]	Duration [microseconds] [nanoseconds]	Interval [months] [day, time]	Interval [month, day, nanoseconds]
Format String	tDs tDm	tDu tDn	tiM tiD	tin

Arrow Type	Timestamp with Timezone "..." [seconds] [milliseconds]	Timestamp with Timezone "..." [microseconds] [nanoseconds]
Format String	tss:... tsm:...	tsu:... tsn:...

Figure 5.3 – Temporal data type format strings

Note that dictionary-encoded types don't have a specific format string to indicate that they are encoded as such. For a dictionary-encoded array, the format string of ArrowSchema indicates the format of the *index* type with the *value* type of the dictionary described by the dictionary member field. For example, a dictionary-encoded timestamp array using milliseconds as the unit with no time zone that uses the int16 indices would have a format string of s, and the dictionary member field would have a format string of tsm:.

Finally, there are the nested types. All the nested types, shown in *Figure 5.4*, are multi-character format strings that begin with +:

Arrow Type	List	Large List	Fixed-size List [123 items]	Struct	Map	Dense Union type-ids I,J,...	Sparse Union type-ids I,J,...
Format String	+l	+L	+w:123	+s	+m	+ud:I,J,...	+us:I,J,...

Figure 5.4 – Nested-type format strings

Just like the case for dictionary-encoded arrays, the data type and name of the child fields for the nested types will be in the array of child schemas. Keep in mind when thinking about the Map data type; according to the Arrow format specification, it should always have a single child type named entries, which is itself a struct, with two child types named key and value.

The last important piece for the schema description is encoding metadata for your field or record batch.

The encoding scheme for metadata

The metadata field in our schema object needs to represent a series of pairs of keys and values in a single binary string. To do this, the metadata key-value pairs are encoded with a defined format that can be easily parsed but is still compact:

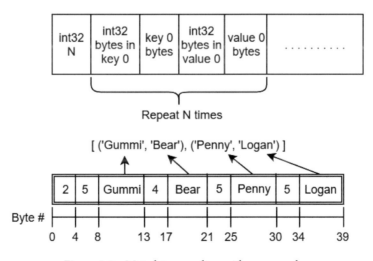

Figure 5.5 – Metadata encoding with an example

Figure 5.5 shows the format of the encoded metadata along with an example using the key-value pairs ([('**Gummi**', '**Bear**'), ('**Penny**', '**Logan**')]). The 32-bit integers being encoded in the metadata will use whatever the native endianness is for the platform, so for the same metadata, here is what it would look like on a little-endian machine:

```
\x02\x00\x00\x00\x05\x00\x00\x00Gummi\x04\x00\x00\x00Bear\x05\
x00\x00\x00Penny\x05\x00\x00\x00Logan
```

Note that the bytes for the keys and values are not null-terminated. On a big-endian machine, the same metadata would be represented like this:

```
\x00\x00\x00\x02\x00\x00\x00\x05Gummi\x00\x00\x00\x04Bear\x00\
x00\x00\x05Penny\x00\x00\x00\x05Logan
```

Look closely at the 4-byte groups that define the number of keys and the length of the strings. The difference between the endianness is the order of the bytes when specifying numbers, with the most significant byte occurring first on a big-endian machine and last on a little-endian machine.

What about the extension type?

Eagle-eyed readers may notice that one data type was missing from those data type format strings – the user-defined **extension type**. To recap a little, the extension type exists as a way for users of Arrow to define their own data types *in terms of the existing ones* by defining metadata keys. The format field of the ArrowSchema struct indicates the storage type of the array and, as such, wouldn't indicate something like an extension type. Instead, that information would get encoded in the metadata using the established ARROW:extension:name and ARROW:extension:metadata keys. Exporting an array of an extension type is merely just exporting the storage type array with those metadata key-value pairs added in.

Exercises

Before we move on to describe how the array data is described, try a couple of exercises:

1. How would the schema of a dictionary-encoded decimal128 (precision=12, scale=5) array using the uint32 indices be represented with the format strings and this struct?

2. What about a list<uint64> array?

3. Let's switch it up a bit now – try the struct<ints: int32, floats: float32> data type.

4. Try with an array with the map<string, float64> type.

Okay, let's now move on to the data itself.

The ArrowArray structure

To interpret an `ArrowArray` instance and use the data that is being described, you need to already know the schema or array type first. This is determined either by convention, such as a defined type that your API always produces, or by passing a corresponding `ArrowSchema` object along with the `ArrowArray` object. The definition of this structure is as follows:

```
struct ArrowArray {
    int64_t length;
    int64_t null_count;
    int64_t offset;
    int64_t n_buffers;
    int64_t n_children;
    const void** buffers;
    struct ArrowArray** children;
    struct ArrowArray* dictionary;
    // release callback
    void (*release)(struct ArrowArray*);
    // opaque producer related data
    void* private_data;
};
```

If you look closely, it essentially just follows the definition of how the Arrow format specification describes an array. Here's what each field is used for and whether it is required or optional:

- `int64_t length` (*required*):

  - The logical length of the array and the number of items

- `int64_t null_count` (*required*):

  - The number of null items in the array. It *may* be -1 to represent it not being computed yet.

- `int64_t offset` (*required*):

  - The number of physical items in the buffers before the start of the array. This allows buffers to get reused and sliced by setting lengths and offsets into the buffers. It *must* be 0 or a positive integer.

- `int64_t n_buffers` (*required*):

  - The number of allocated buffers that contain the data associated with this array, dependent on the data type, as described in *Chapter 1, Getting Started with the Arrow Format*. The buffers of child arrays are not included; this must match the length of the C array of buffers.

- `const void** buffers` (*required*):

  - A C array of pointers to the start of each buffer of data associated with this array. Each `void*` pointer *must* point to the start of a contiguous chunk of memory or be null. There *must* be exactly n_buffers pointers in this array. If null_count is 0, the null bitmap buffer *may* be omitted by setting its pointer to null.

- `int64_t n_children` (*required*):

  - The number of child arrays that this array has, depending on the data type. For example, a `List` array should have exactly 1 child, while a `Struct` array will have 1 child for each of its fields.

- `ArrowArray** children` (*optional*):

  - A C array of pointers to the `ArrowArray` instances for each child of this array. There *must* be exactly n_children pointers in this array. If n_children is 0, this *may* be null.

- `ArrowArray* dictionary` (*optional*):

  - A pointer to the dictionary value array if the data is dictionary-encoded. If the array is a dictionary-encoded array, this *must* be a valid pointer and *must* be null if it's not a dictionary-encoded array.

- `void (*release)(struct ArrowArray*)` (*required*):

  - A pointer to a callback function for releasing the associated memory for this object

- `void *private_data`: (*optional*):

    - A pointer to some opaque data structure provided by the producing API if necessary. Consumers *must not* process this member; the lifetime is handled by the producing API.

So, why would you use this? When would it be relevant to you? Let's see.

Example use cases

One significant proposed benefit of having the C Data API was to allow applications to implement the API without requiring a dependency on the Arrow libraries. Let's suppose there is an existing computational engine written in C++ that wants to add the ability to return data in the Arrow format without adding a new dependency or having to link with the Arrow libraries. There are many possible reasons why you might want to avoid adding a new dependency to a project. This could range from the development environment to the complexity of deployment mechanisms, but we're not going to focus on that side of it.

Using the C Data API to export Arrow-formatted data

Do you have your development environment all set up for C++? If not, go and do that and come back. You know the drill; I'll wait.

We'll start with a small function to generate a vector of random 32-bit integers, which will act as our sample data. You know how to do that? Well, good. Go and do that yourself before you look at my bare-bones random data generator code snippet, as follows:

```
#include <algorithm>
#include <limits>
#include <random>
#include <vector>
std::vector<int32_t> generate_data(size_t size) {
    static std::uniform_int_distribution<int32_t> dist(
        std::numeric_limits<int32_t>::min(),
        std::numeric_limits<int32_t>::max());
    static std::random_device rnd_device;
    std::default_random_engine generator(rnd_device());
    std::vector<int32_t> data(size);
    std::generate(data.begin(), data.end(), [&]() {
        return dist(generator); });
```

```
    return data;
}
```

Note that we use the `static` keyword in the function, so it only instantiates the random device once. However, this has the side effect of the function not being thread-safe.

Okay, now that we have our random data generator function, we can make something to utilize the C Data API and export the data:

1. First, you will need to download a copy of the C Data API from the Arrow repository. The file you want is located here: `https://github.com/apache/arrow/blob/master/cpp/src/arrow/c/abi.h`.

    Make sure you have that header file locally; it has the definitions for the `ArrowSchema` and `ArrowArray` structs I mentioned earlier.

2. Next, we need to create a function that will export the data. To simulate the idea of an engine that exports data through this C API, it will be a function that only takes a pointer to an `ArrowArray` struct. We know that we're exporting 32-bit integer data, so this example won't pass `ArrowSchema`. The following function will populate the passed-in struct with the data generated from our random generator function:

    I. The function signature will take a pointer to the `ArrowArray` object to populate:

        ```
        void export_int32_data(struct ArrowArray* array) {
        ```

    II. First, we'll create a pointer to a vector on the heap using the move constructor and our data generator:

        ```
        std::vector<int32_t>* vecptr =
            new std::vector<int32_t>(
                std::move(generate_data(1000)));
        ```

    III. Now, we can construct our object. Note the highlighted lines pointing out where we allocate the C array for the buffers and the release callback function, and maintain a pointer to the vector of data. We know the length will be the size of the vector and that we're going to have two buffers, the null bitmap and the raw data. An `ArrowArray` object is marked as released by setting its `release` callback to `null`, which we do as the last step of the `release` Lambda function:

        ```
        array = (struct ArrowArray) {
            .length = vecptr->size(),
            .null_count = 0,
        ```

```
    .offset = 0,
    .n_buffers = 2,
    .n_children = 0,
    .buffers = (const void**)malloc(sizeof(void*)*2),
    .children = nullptr,
    .dictionary = nullptr,
    .release = [](struct ArrowArray* arr) {
        free(arr->buffers);
        delete reinterpret_cast<
            std::vector<int32_t>*>(
                arr->private_data);
        arr->release = nullptr;
    },
    .private_data =
            reinterpret_cast<void*>(vecptr),
};
```

IV. Finally, since there are no nulls, we can set the first buffer (the null bitmap) to null. The highlighted line sets the second buffer to just point at the raw underlying data of the vector itself:

```
array->buffers[0] = nullptr;
array->buffers[1] = vecptr->data();
} // end of function
```

3. So far, we have a C++ file that creates a function, but we want to export it as a C-compatible API. All we have to do is add this snippet somewhere before the definition of the function we just created:

```
extern "C" {
    void export_int32_data(struct ArrowArray*);
}
```

If you're familiar with the differences between C++ linking and C linking, you'll understand why this is needed. For everyone else, the long and short of it is that C++ likes to mangle the names of your exported functions in specific ways. By declaring the function as extern "C", you're informing the compiler of your intent to keep this function name unmangled because you want it to be externally linkable by C.

4. Now, we compile this file and create a lovely little shared library that we can load to call this function. Assuming you are using g++ as your compiler, the command you would use is the following:

```
$ g++ -fPIC -shared -o libsample.so example_cdata.cc
```

    This will create a shared-object file, with the .so extension, which anything that can call a C API can use to call the export function we just made. We didn't include any Arrow C++ headers, just the copy of the C structs, and we didn't link against any Arrow libraries. This enables any caller, regardless of the language, runtime, or library, to call the function with a pointer to an ArrowArray struct and have it filled in with a chunk of data.

What can we do with this library? Well, let's write something to call it from a non-C++ runtime. Yes, I know – this is a trivial example. But you're a creative person, right? I'm sure you can take the concepts and generalized examples I've made here and adapt them for lots of creative purposes. Looking back at the earlier example in *Chapter 3, Data Science with Apache Arrow*, regarding how data was passed from Python to Java to improve performance, let's write a small script that will call the API from Python.

Importing Arrow data with Python

The common terminology for runtimes providing an interface for calling an API of another runtime or language is an FFI. In Python, we're going to use a library called cffi, which is used by the pyarrow module to implement the C Data API. Make sure that you're running the script we're about to write in the same directory as the libsample.so library file that we created in the previous exercise:

1. First, the imports – the following highlighted line represents the essential case that we're importing the already compiled ffi library that is part of the pyarrow module:

```
import pyarrow as pa
from pyarrow.cffi import ffi
```

2. There are a few different ways to integrate the FFI module, but for the purposes of this exercise, we're going to use dynamic loading of the library with the defined interface through the cdef function. Then, we load our shared object library with dlopen:

```
ffi.cdef("void export_int32_data(struct ArrowArray*);")
lib = ffi.dlopen("./libsample.so")
```

    Note that this matches our extern "C" declaration from before.

3. Now, we can create an `ArrowArray` struct and call the function we exported to populate it:

```
c_arr = ffi.new("struct ArrowArray*")
c_ptr = int(ffi.cast("uintptr_t", c_arr))
lib.export_int32_data(c_arr)
```

4. Then, we use the `pyarrow` module to import data; remember that since we're passing around pointers, there's no copying of the data buffers. So, it doesn't matter if this array has 1,000 elements or 1 million elements; we're not copying the data here. Importing the data is just hooking everything up to point to the right areas in memory:

```
arrnew = pa.Array._import_from_c(c_ptr, pa.int32())
# do stuff with the array
del arrnew # will call the release callback
           # once it is garbage collected
```

You can add a `print` statement in there if you like, to confirm that it is actually working as intended. But that's it. The library we created could create that array of data in any way we want, but as long as it properly populates the C struct, we're able to pass the data around in the Arrow format without having to copy it.

What if we wanted to work in the other direction? We can read in our data with Python and then hand it off to something faster for processing, similar to how Spark used JPype to communicate the data from Python to Java without copying. How would we go about doing that?

Exporting Arrow data with the C Data API from Python to Go

For this example, we're going to add a level here to go from Python to Go via the C Data API. As I mentioned earlier, the Arrow libraries for both Python and Go implement the C Data API directly, so you can easily export and import data to and from the libraries. So, let's get to it!

The first thing we're going to do is create the shared library in Go that will export a function for us to call. We're going to trivially import a passed-in Arrow record batch and write the schema, the number of columns, and the number of rows to the terminal. This can easily be replaced with calling some existing Go library or otherwise use the data, by performing calculations or some other operation that would be significantly faster in a compiled language such as Golang rather than Python, but I'll leave those ideas up to you. I'm just showing you how to do the connection to efficiently pass the data without having to perform any copies.

Building the Go shared library

Because of our usage of Cgo, you need to make sure you have the C and C++ compilers on your path and available in your Go development environment. If you're on a Linux or macOS machine, you probably already have gcc and g++ easily accessible already. On Windows, you must use either MSYS2 or MinGW development environments and install gcc and g++ to build this.

> **Important Note**
>
> There are a bunch of nuances and gotchas involved in using Cgo that I won't touch on much, but I highly recommend reading the documentation, which can be found here: https://pkg.go.dev/cmd/cgo.

The following steps will walk you through constructing a dynamic library using Go, which exports a function that can be called as a C-compatible API:

1. First, let's put together the function that we're going to export. We start off by initializing a go module:

   ```
   $ go mod init sample
   ```

2. When creating a dynamic library, we use the main package, similar to creating an executable binary. So, let's create our sample.go file:

   ```go
   package main
   import (
       "fmt"
       "github.com/apache/arrow/go/v7/arrow/cdata"
   )
   func processBatch(scptr, rbptr uintptr) {
       schema := cdata.SchemaFromPtr(scptr)
       arr := cdata.ArrayFromPtr(rbptr)

       rec, err := cdata.ImportCRecordBatch(arr, schema)
       if err != nil {
           panic(err) // handle the error!
       }
       // make sure we call the release callback when we're done
       defer rec.Release()
   ```

```
        fmt.Println(rec.Schema())
        fmt.Println(rec.NumCols(), rec.NumRows())
}
```

Note the highlighted lines. The function signature takes in two `uintptr` values, the pointers to our structs. We then use the `cdata` package in the Arrow module to import our record batch.

> **Remember**
>
> "But wait!" you say. "There was no format string for record batches in the C Data API." You're correct! A record batch is simply represented as a struct array whose fields match the columns of the record batch. Importing a record batch involves just flattening the struct array out into a record batch.

3. Now that we have our function to export we just need to… well, export it!

```go
package main
import (
        "fmt"
        "github.com/apache/arrow/go/v7/arrow/cdata"
)
import "C"
//export processBatch
func processBatch(scptr, rbptr uintptr) {
        ...
}
func main() {}
```

The highlighted lines are the additions that need to be made to export the function. The `import "C"` line tells the Go compiler to use the Cgo command, which will recognize the export comment. There must be no space between the double-slash and the word `export`, and it must be followed by the function name exactly. You'll get a compiler error if it doesn't match. Finally, the addition of the `main` function is necessary for the C runtime connection with Go's runtime.

4. Finally, we can build our library!

```
$ go build -buildmode=c-shared -o libsample.so .
```

Setting the `buildmode` argument to `c-shared` tells the compiler that we're creating a dynamic library. On Windows, you'd change `libsample.so` to be `libsample.dll` instead, but otherwise, everything is the same. Building the library will also create a new file, `libsample.h` – a header file for C or C++ programs to include for calling the exported function.

We can use the `cffi` Python module as we did earlier when calling our C++ dynamic library to call the function, but we're going to take a different approach in this example, just to show some variety and other options that are available to you.

Creating a Python extension from the Go library

We're going to create what's called a Python C extension using the `cffi` module. Before we start, make sure you have the same `abi.h` file that we copied from the Arrow GitHub repository earlier – when compiling the C++ dynamic library – in the same directory as the `libsample.h` and `libsample.so` files that we created when building the shared library:

1. We first create a build script that will compile our extension using the `cffi` module. Let's call this `sample_build.py`:

    ```
    import os
    from pyarrow.cffi import ffi

    ffi.set_source("_sample",
        r"""
        #include "abi.h"
        #include "libsample.h"
        """,
        library_dirs=[os.getcwd()],
        libraries=["sample"],
        extra_link_args=[f"-Wl,-rpath={os.getcwd()}"])
    ffi.cdef("""
        void processBatch(uintptr_t, uintptr_t);
    """)

    if __name__ == "__main__":
        ffi.compile(verbose=True)
    ```

    The call to the `cdef` function should look very familiar to you, as it's precisely what we did before when we were loading the C++ shared library we built earlier, only now it matches the signature of the `processBatch` function we exported.

Looking at the highlighted lines, we can see the header includes both the C API
abi.h header file and the generated header file from our build. Then, we specify
the directory that our library is in and its name; note the lack of the lib prefix,
which is handled automatically. The extra link argument that we pass containing
the rpath specification is to make it easier at runtime. The argument for the
linker informs the system of the directory to look in for dependent libraries at
runtime – in our case, telling it where the libsample.so is so that it can be
loaded when the extension is called.

2. Now, we build the extension by calling our build script!

```
$ python3 example_go_cffi.py
generating ./_sample.c
the current directory is '/home/matt/chapter5/go'
running build_ext
building '_sample' extension
x86_64-linux-gnu-gcc -pthread -Wno-unused-result
...x86_64-linux-gnu-gcc -pthread -shared -Wl,-O1 ... ./_
sample.o -L/home/matt/chapter5/go -lsample -o ./_sample.
cpython-39-x86_64-linux-gnu.so -Wl,-rpath=/home/matt/
chapter5/go
```

This will produce a file named _sample.cpython-39-x86_64-linux-gnu.
so if you're using Python 3.9 on a Linux machine. The filename will adjust based
on your version of Python and the operating system that you're building on. This
extension can now be imported and used by Python, so let's give it a try!

3. Start a Python interpreter in the same directory you built the extension in so that
we can import it:

```
>>> from _sample import ffi, lib
```

Note that there are two things we're importing from the extension, the ffi module
and the library itself.

4. We'll test out the extension by using the same Parquet file from previous examples,
yellow_tripdata_2015-01.parquet. Use the to_batches function to
create record batches from the table:

```
>>> import pyarrow.parquet as pq
>>> tbl = pq.read_table('<path to file>/yellow_
tripdata_2015-01.parquet')
>>> batches = tbl.to_batches(None)
```

Because the default reading of Parquet files will be multi-threaded, the table is read in multiple chunks. This then results in multiple record batches being created when calling `to_batches`. On my machine, I got a list of 13 record batches; we'll just use one of the batches for this example.

5. As before, we use `ffi` to create our `ArrowSchema` and `ArrowArray` objects and pointers and then cast them to be `uintptr_t`:

    ```
    >>> c_schema = ffi.new('struct ArrowSchema*')
    >>> c_array = ffi.new('struct ArrowArray*')
    >>> ptr_schema = int(ffi.cast('uintptr_t', c_schema))
    >>> ptr_array = int(ffi.cast('uintptr_t', c_array))
    ```

6. Then, we export the record batch and call our shared function:

    ```
    >>> batches[0].schema._export_to_c(ptr_schema)
    >>> batches[0]._export_to_c(ptr_array)
    >>> lib.processBatch(ptr_schema, ptr_array)
    ```

    When we wrote our Go shared library, the function ended by printing out the schema, the number of columns, and the number of rows of the record batch. Following the execution of the highlighted line, you should see all of these get printed out on your terminal. The line denoting the columns and rows should follow the schema:

    ```
    19 1048576
    ```

It might seem a bit unwieldy to call this repeatedly if you have many batches you want to pass. Perhaps it's even inefficient to pass the schema multiple times too. There's a need to be able to stream record batches through this API because, frequently, you're going to be dealing with streams of data, such as if you're working with Spark. This is why there's one more structure that exists in the header file for the C Data API, `ArrowArrayStream`.

Streaming across the C Data API

This particularly useful interface is considered experimental by the Arrow project currently, so technically, the ABI is not guaranteed to be stable but is unlikely to change unless user feedback proposes improvements to it. The C streaming API is a higher-level abstraction built on the initial `ArrowSchema` and `ArrowArray` structures to make it easier to stream data within a process across API boundaries. The design of the stream is to expose a chunk-pulling API that pulls blocks of data from the source one at a time, all with the same schema. The structure is defined as follows:

```
struct ArrowArrayStream {
```

```
  // callbacks for stream functionality
  int (*get_schema)(struct ArrowArrayStream*, struct
ArrowSchema*);
  int (*get_next)(struct ArrowArrayStream*, struct ArrowArray*);
  const char* (*get_last_error)(struct ArrowArrayStream*);
  // Release callback and private data
  void (*release)(struct ArrowArrayStream*);
  void* private_data;
};
```

The release callback and `private_data` member should be familiar to you by now, but the remaining members are as follows:

- `int (*get_schema)(struct ArrowArrayStream*, struct ArrowSchema*)` (*required*):

    - The callback function to retrieve the schema of the chunks of data. All chunks *must* have the same schema. This cannot be called after the object has been released. It *must* return 0 on success and a non-zero error code on failure.

- `int (*get_next)(struct ArrowArrayStream*, struct ArrowArray*)` (*required*):

    - The callback function to return the next chunk of data from the stream. This cannot be called after the object has been released and *must* return 0 on success and a non-zero error code on failure. On success, consumers should check whether the stream has been released. If so, the stream has ended; otherwise, the `ArrowArray` data should be valid.

- `const char* (*get_last_error)(struct ArrowArrayStream*)` (*required*):

    - The callback function that may only be called if the last called function returned an error and cannot be called on a released stream. It returns a null-terminated `UTF-8` string that is valid until the next call of a callback on the stream.

The lifetime of the schema and data chunks that are populated from the callback functions is not tied to the lifetime of the `ArrowArrayStream` object at all and must be cleaned up and released independently to avoid memory leaks. The non-zero error codes for failures should be interpreted just like you would interpret the `errno` values for your platform.

Streaming record batches from Python to Go

Now, we can update our previous example to stream the record batches from the Parquet file to the shared library. Again, this is a trivial case, given that we can just as easily read the Parquet file natively in Go, but the concept is what is important here. Reading the Parquet file in Python can just as easily be something that is receiving pandas DataFrames and then converting them to Arrow record batches and sending them:

1. First, we modify our Go file, adding a new function that accepts a single pointer for an `ArrowArrayStream` object and loops over our stream of batches. The difficult stuff has already been handled by the Arrow library when importing the `Stream` object:

    I. As before, we need to have the highlighted comment line to have Go export the function with a C-compatible interface:

        ```
        //export processStream
        func processStream(ptr uintptr) {
        ```

    II. Then, we can initialize the variables we're going to need in a `var` block:

        ```
        var (
            arrstream = (*cdata.CArrowArrayStream)(unsafe.
        Pointer(ptr))
            rec     arrow.Record
            err     error
            x       int
        )
        ```

    III.Now, we can create a stream reader object, passing `nil` for the schema argument so that it knows to pull the schema from the stream object itself, rather than us providing it.

        ```
        rdr := cdata.ImportCArrayStream(arrstream, nil)
        ```

    IV. Finally, we use a loop, calling the `Read` method of the reader until we get a non-`nil` error. When we hit the end of the stream, it should return `io.EOF`; any other error means we encountered a problem:

        ```
        for {
            rec, err = rdr.Read()
            if err != nil {
                break
        ```

```
        }
        fmt.Println("Batch: ",x, rec.NumCols(), rec.
NumRows())
        rec.Release()
        x++
    }

    if err != io.EOF {
        panic(err) // handle the error!
    }
} // end of the function
```

2. Build the library as before with the Cgo command and the buildmode option. Don't forget import "C"; otherwise, it won't generate the header file!

    ```
    $ go build -buildmode=c-shared -o libsample_stream.so .
    ```

3. Modify the Python extension build script to use the new library and new function; you can even have both functions in the same library if you didn't remove the processBatch function. If you don't update the build script, the new processStream function won't be available to call from Python:

    ```python
    import os
    from pyarrow.cffi import ffi
    ffi.set_source("_sample_stream",
        r"""
        #include "abi.h"
        #include "libsample_stream.h"
        """,
        library_dirs=[os.getcwd()],
        libraries=["sample_stream"],
        extra_link_args=[f"-Wl,-rpath={os.getcwd()}"])
    ffi.cdef("""
        void processBatch(uintptr_t, uintptr_t);
        void processStream(uintptr_t);
    """)

    if __name__ == "__main__":
        ffi.compile(verbose=True)
    ```

Then, run this to build the new _sample_stream extension as we did before.

4. Finally, let's open the Parquet file and then call our function to stream the data:

```
from _sample_stream import ffi, lib
import pyarrow as pa
import pyarrow.parquet as pq


f = pq.ParquetFile('yellow_tripdata_2015-01.parquet')
batches = f.iter_batches(1048756)
rdr = pa.ipc.RecordBatchReader.from_batches(
        f.schema_arrow, batches)
c_stream = ffi.new('struct ArrowArrayStream*')
ptr_stream = int(ffi.cast('uintptr_t', c_stream))


rdr._export_to_c(ptr_stream)
del rdr, batches
lib.processStream(ptr_stream)
```

If you run this script, you should get the following output from it, calling the shared library that we built with Go:

```
Batch: 0 19 1048756
Batch: 1 19 1048756
Batch: 2 19 1048756
Batch: 3 19 1048756
Batch: 4 19 1048756
Batch: 5 19 1048756
Batch: 6 19 1048756
Batch: 7 19 1048756
Batch: 8 19 1048756
Batch: 9 19 1048756
Batch: 10 19 1048756
Batch: 11 19 1048756
Batch: 12 19 163914
```

Look at that – not only did you create some fancy dynamic extensions to pass Arrow data around but you are also passing it through different programming languages! Pretty neat, right? The next time you're trying to interface different technologies in different languages, think back to this and see where else you can apply these techniques.

Other use cases

In addition to providing an interface for zero-copy sharing of Arrow data between components, the C Data API can also be used in cases where it may not be feasible to depend on the Arrow libraries directly.

Despite a large number of languages and runtimes sporting implementations of Arrow, there are still languages or environments that do not have Arrow implementations. This is particularly true in organizations with a lot of legacy software and/or specialized environments. A great example of this would be the fact that the dominant programming language in the astrophysical modeling of stars and galaxies is still **Fortran**! Unsurprisingly, there is not an existing Arrow implementation for Fortran. In these situations, it is often not feasible to rewrite entire code bases so that you can leverage Arrow in a supported language. But with the C Data API, data can be shared from a supported runtime to a pre-existing unsupported code base. Alternatively, you can do the reverse and easily build out the C data structures to pass data into a component that expects Arrow data.

There are potentially many other cases where tight integration and direct dependency on the Arrow libraries might not be desirable. A few of these might be the following:

- Heavily resource-constrained environments such as embedded software development. A minimal build of the Arrow core library clocked in at ~15 MB on my system, despite the available modularization. This might not seem like much, but for embedded development, even this might be too large.

- The Arrow library is very fast-moving and frequently updated. Some projects might not be able to depend on a fast-moving project such as Arrow and ensure that they stay current and updated.

- Development might be in an environment where users cannot manually install external libraries such as Arrow due to permissions or other restrictions.

The existence of the C Data API allows consuming applications and libraries to work with Arrow memory without having to directly depend on the Arrow libraries or build their own integration. They can choose between tightly coupling with the Arrow *project* or just the Arrow *format*.

Some exercises

Before moving on, see whether you can come up with any other use cases that use the C Data API to communicate between languages or runtimes in a single process, and sketch out simple implementations or rough outlines to set it up. You can either use the Arrow libraries to import/export data or build some adapter from one data format into the C structure to return data in the Arrow format easily.

Consider this – you have a database engine and you want to add an option to deliver results as Arrow-formatted data, but you don't want to impose a new dependency on the project by relying directly on the Arrow libraries. How can you provide this without linking against the Arrow libraries and including the Arrow C++ headers? What would the API look like?

Maybe try reversing the direction of some of our import/export examples to pass data to Python, C++, or some other combination of technologies, languages, or runtimes. Be creative!

Of course, I've mentioned many times already how Arrow provides high-speed analytical capabilities, but so far, we've focused mostly on just fetching data and moving it around. But you aren't left to your own devices when it comes to actually performing computations on your Arrow data. The Arrow libraries provide a Compute API that can be used to build out complex queries and computation engines.

Summary

For this foray into the Arrow libraries, we've explored the efficient sharing of data between libraries using the Arrow C data interface. Remember that the motivation for this interface was for zero-copy data sharing between components of the same running process. It's not intended for the C Data API itself to mimic the features available in higher-level languages such as C++ or Python – just to share data. In addition, if you're sharing between different processes or need persistent storage, you should be using the Arrow IPC format that we covered in *Chapter 4*, *Format and Memory Handling*.

At this point, we've covered lots of ways to read, write, and transfer Arrow data. But once you have the data in memory, you're going to want to perform operations on it and take advantage of the benefits of in-memory analytics. Rather than having to re-implement the mathematical and relational algorithms yourself, in *Chapter 6*, *Leveraging the Arrow Compute APIs*, we're going to cover… well, the compute library! The Arrow libraries include a Compute API that has a significant number of common mathematical operations (sum, mean, median, and so on), along with relational operations (such as joins and sorting) already implemented for you to easily use.

So, let's get cracking!

6
Leveraging the Arrow Compute APIs

We're halfway through this book and only *now* are we covering actually performing analytical computations directly with Arrow. Kinda strange, right? At this point, if you've been following along, you should have a solid understanding of all the concepts you'll need to be able to benefit from the compute library.

The Arrow community is working toward building open source computation and query engines built on the Arrow format. To this end, the Arrow compute library exists to facilitate various high-performance implementations of functions that operate on Arrow-formatted data. This might be to perform logical casting from one data type to another, or it might be for performing large computation and filter operations, and everything in between. Rather than consumers having to implement operations over and over, high-performance implementations can be based on the Arrow format in a generic fashion and then used by many consumers.

This chapter is going to teach you the following:

- How to execute simple computations using the Arrow compute library
- Working with **datums** and **scalars** when referencing computations
- When and why to use the Arrow compute library over implementing something yourself

Technical requirements

This is another highly technical chapter with various code examples and exercises. So, like before, you need access to a computer with the following software to follow along:

- Python 3+: The `pyarrow` module installed and importable

- A C++ compiler supporting C++11 or better

- Your preferred IDE: Sublime, VS Code, Emacs, and so on

Letting Arrow do the work for you

There are three main concepts to think about when working with the Arrow compute libraries:

- **Input shaping**: Describing the shape of your input when calling a function

- **Value casting**: Ensuring compatible data types between arguments when calling a function

- **Types of functions**: What kind of function are you looking for? Scalar? Aggregation? Or vector?

Let's quickly dig into each of these so you can see how they affect writing the code to use the computations.

> **Important!**
>
> Not all language implementations of the Arrow libraries currently provide a Compute API. The primary libraries that expose it are the C++ and Python libraries, while the level of support for the compute library varies in the other language implementations. For instance, the support for the compute functions in the Go library is currently something I am working on adding. It might even be done by the time this book is in your hands! Consider the possibility of using the Arrow C data interface to efficiently pass data to C++ to use the compute library and then pass it back to an environment or language that doesn't have an implementation of the compute functions.

Input shaping

For the compute functions to do anything worthwhile, you need to be able to supply an input to operate on. Sometimes a function takes an array, while other times a scalar value is needed. A generic `Datum` class exists to represent a union of different shapes that these inputs can take. A datum can be a scalar, an array, a chunked array, or even an entire record batch or table. Every function defines the shape of what inputs it allows or requires; for example, the `sort_indices` compute function requires a single input, which must be an array.

Value casting

Different functions may require precise typing of their arguments to properly execute and operate. As a result, many functions define implicit casting behavior to make them easier to utilize. For example, performing an arithmetic computation such as addition requires the arguments to have identical data types. Instead of failing if a consumer calls the addition function with a 32-bit integer array and a 16-bit integer array, the library might promote the second argument and cast the array to a 32-bit integer one first, and then perform the computation.

Another example where this might apply is with dictionary-encoded arrays. Comparison of dictionary-encoded arrays isn't directly supported by any of the computation functions currently implemented, but many of them will implicitly cast the array to a decoded form that it can operate on rather than emit an error.

Types of functions

There are three general types of functions that exist in the compute library. Let's discuss them one by one.

Aggregations

An aggregation function operates on an array (optionally chunked) or a scalar value and reduces the input to a single scalar output value.

Some examples are `count`, `min`, `mean`, and `sum`. See *Figure 6.1*:

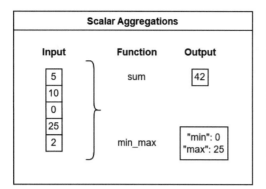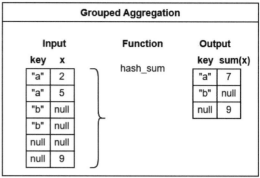

Figure 6.1 – Depiction of aggregation functions

There are also *grouped* aggregation functions, which are the equivalent of a SQL-style *group by* operation. Instead of an operation on all the values in the input, grouped aggregations first partition by a specified *key* column, and then output a single scalar value per group in the input.

Some examples are `hash_max`, `hash_product`, and `hash_any`.

Element-wise or scalar functions

Unary or single-input functions in this category operate on each element of the input separately. A scalar input produces a scalar output and array inputs produce array outputs.

Some examples are `abs`, `negate`, and `round`. See *Figure 6.2*:

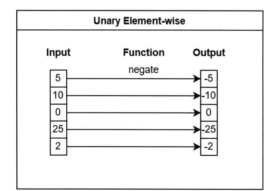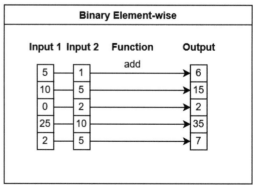

Figure 6.2 – Depiction of scalar functions

Binary functions in this category operate on aligned elements between the inputs, such as adding two arrays. Two scalar inputs produce a scalar output, while two array inputs must have the same length and produce an array output. Providing one scalar and one array input will perform the operation as if the scalar were an array of the same length, N, as the other input, with the value repeated.

Some examples are `add`, `multiply`, `shift_left`, and `equal`.

Array-wise or vector functions

Functions in this category use the entire array for their operations, frequently performing transformations or outputting a different length than the input array. See *Figure 6.3*.

Some examples are `unique`, `filter`, and `sort_indices`:

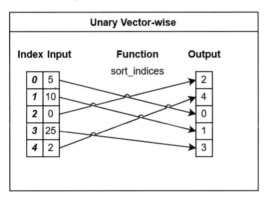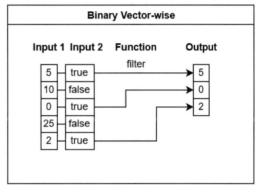

Figure 6.3 – Depiction of vector functions

Now that we've explained the concepts, let's learn how to execute the computation functions on some data!

Executing compute functions

The Arrow compute library has a global `FunctionRegistry`, which allows looking up functions by name and listing what is available to call. The list of available compute functions can also be found in the Arrow documentation at `https://arrow.apache.org/docs/cpp/compute.html#available-functions`. Let's see how to execute these functions now!

Using the C++ compute library

The compute library is managed as a separate module in the base Arrow package. If you've compiled the library yourself from source, make sure that you've used the `ARROW_COMPUTE=ON` option during configuration.

Example 1 – adding a scalar value to an array

Our first example is going to be a simple scalar function call on an array of data, using the same Parquet file as we did previously in the C Data API examples:

1. First things first, we need to read the column we want from the Parquet file. We can use the Parquet C++ library to open the file and it provides an adapter for direct conversion to Arrow objects from Parquet:

```
#include <arrow/io/file.h>
#include <arrow/status.h>
#include <parquet/arrow/reader.h>

...

constexpr auto filepath = "<path to file>/yellow_
tripdata_2015-01.parquet";
auto input = arrow::io::ReadableFile::Open(filepath).
ValueOrDie();
std::unique_ptr<parquet::arrow::FileReader> reader;
arrow::Status st = parquet::arrow::OpenFile(input,
                       arrow::default_memory_pool(),
                       &reader);
if (!st.ok()) {
    // handle the error
}
```

2. After opening the file, the easy solution would be to just read the whole file into memory as an Arrow table, which is what we will do here. Alternately, you could read only one column from the file if you prefer using the ReadColumn function:

```
std::shared_ptr<arrow::Table> table;
st = reader->ReadTable(&table);
if (!st.ok()) {
    // handle the error
}
std::shared_ptr<arrow::ChunkedArray> column =
                table->GetColumnByName("total_amount");
std::cout << column->ToString() << std::endl;
```

3. Now that we have our column, let's add the value 5.5 to each element in the array. Because addition is a commutative operation, the order of the arguments doesn't matter when passing the scalar and column objects. If we were instead performing subtraction, for example, the order would matter and be reflected in the result:

```cpp
#include <arrow/compute/api.h>
#include <arrow/scalar.h>
#include <arrow/datum.h>

...
arrow::Datum incremented =
arrow::compute::CallFunction("add",
        {column, arrow::MakeScalar(5.5)}).ValueOrDie();
std::shared_ptr<arrow::ChunkedArray> output =
        std::move(incremented).chunked_array();
std::cout << output->ToString() << std::endl;
```

4. Finally, we just need to compile this. As before, we'll use pkg-config to generate our compiler and linker flags on the command line to make life easier:

```
$ g++ compute_functions.cc -o example1 'pkg-config
--cflags --libs parquet arrow-compute'
```

5. When we run our mainprog, we can see the output to confirm that it worked. In the preceding code snippets, we printed out the column of data both before and after we added the scalar value 5.5 to it, allowing us to directly see that it worked:

```
$ ./example1
[
  [
    17.05,
    17.8,
    10.8,
    4.8,
    <values removed for brevity>
  ]
]
[
  [
    22.55,
    23.3,
```

```
    16.3,
    10.3,
    <values removed for brevity>
  ]
]
```

> **Note**
>
> Notice in the code snippets that we are using `arrow::ChunkedArray` instead of `arrow::Array`. Remember what a chunked array is from *Chapter 2, Working with Key Arrow Specifications*? Because Parquet files can be split into multiple **row groups**, we can avoid copying data by using a chunked array to treat the collection of one or more discrete arrays as a single contiguous array. Arrow table objects allow each individual column to also be chunked, potentially with different chunk sizes between them. Not all compute functions can operate on both chunked and non-chunked arrays, but most can. If your input is a chunked array, your output will be chunked also.

While we used `arrow::compute::CallFunction` in the preceding example, many functions also have convenient concrete APIs that are available to call. In this case, we could have used `arrow::compute::Add(column, arrow::MakeScalar(5.5))` instead.

Example 2 – min-max aggregation function

For our second example, we're going to compute the minimum and maximum values of the `total_amount` column from the file. Instead of outputting a single scalar number, this will produce a scalar structure that contains two fields. Always look at the documentation to see what the return value looks like for the compute functions:

1. Open the Parquet file and retrieve the `total_amount` column as before. Consult the previous example's *steps 1* and *2* if you need to. I trust you.

2. Some functions, such as the `min_max` function, accept or require an `options` object, which can affect the behavior of the function. The return value is a scalar struct containing fields named `min` and `max`. We just need to cast the `Datum` object to `StructScalar` to access it:

```
arrow::compute::ScalarAggregateOptions scalar_agg_opts;
scalar_agg_opts.skip_nulls = false;
arrow::Datum minmax = arrow::compute::CallFunction("min_
max",
        {column}, &scalar_agg_opts).ValueOrDie();
```

```
std::cout <<
    minmax.scalar_as<arrow::StructScalar>().ToString()
        << std::endl;
```

3. Compile with the same options as before and you should get the following output when running it:

```
$ g++ examples.cc -o example2 'pkg-config --cflags --libs
parquet arrow-compute'
$ ./example2
{min:double = -450.3, max:double = 3950611.6}
```

Did you get the same output I did? Getting the hang of calling different functions by name and using the documentation to determine the data types yet? Let's keep going!

Example 3 – sorting a table of data

Our last example is of a vector compute function, sorting the entire table of data by the total_amount column:

1. Once again, open the file and read it into arrow::Table like we did in the previous two examples.

2. Create the sort options object to define what column we want to sort the table by and the direction to sort:

```
arrow::compute::SortOptions sort_opts;
sort_opts.sort_keys = { // one or more key objects
    arrow::compute::SortKey{"total_amount",
        arrow::compute::SortOrder::Descending}};
arrow::Datum indices = arrow::compute::CallFunction(
        "sort_indices", {table},
        &sort_opts).ValueOrDie();
```

3. The sort_indices function on its own doesn't do any copying of data; however, the output is an array of the row indices of the table, which define the sorted order. We could take the array of indices and build our new sorted version of the table if we wanted, but we can instead let the Compute API do that for us!

```
arrow::Datum sorted = arrow::compute::Take(table,
indices).ValueOrDie();
// or you can use CallFunction("take", {table, indices})
auto output = std::move(sorted).table();
```

The `take` function takes an array, chunked array, record batch, or table for the first argument and an array of numeric indices as the second argument. For each element in the array of indices, the value at that index in the first argument is added to the output. In our example, it's using the generated list of sorted indices to output the data in sorted order. Since we gave it a table as input, it outputs a table. The same would happen for a record batch, array, or chunked array.

Try playing around with different functions and compute functionality to see what the outputs look like and what options are available for customizing the behavior, such as whether `null` values should be placed at the beginning or end when sorting. As an exercise, try sorting a table of data by multiple keys in different directions or performing different transformations of the data, such as filtering or producing derived computations. Then, we can move on to performing the same examples but using Python.

Using the compute library in Python

The compute library is also made available to Python as part of the `pyarrow` module. Python's syntax and ease of use make it even simpler to utilize than the C++ library. Many of the functions that you may convert to `pandas` DataFrames or use NumPy for are made accessible directly on the Arrow data using the compute library, saving you precious CPU cycles from having to convert between formats.

Example 1 – adding a scalar value to an array

Just like the C++ examples, we'll start with adding a scalar value to the `total_amount` column from the NYC trip data Parquet file:

1. Do you remember how to read a column from a Parquet file using Python? I'll recap it here just in case you don't:

    ```
    >>> import pyarrow.parquet as pq
    >>> filepath = '<path to file>/yellow_tripdata_2015-01.
    parquet'
    >>> tbl = pq.read_table(filepath) # read the entire file
    in
    >>> tbl = pq.read_table(filepath, columns=['total_
    amount']) # read just the one column
    >>> column = tbl['total_amount']
    ```

2. The `pyarrow` library will perform a lot of the necessary type casting for you, making it very easy to use the Compute API with it:

```
>>> import pyarrow.compute as pc
>>> pc.add(column, 5.5)
<pyarrow.lib.ChunkedArray object at 0x7fdd2a3719a0>
[
  [
    22.55,
    23.3,
    16.3,
    10.3,
  ...
```

The arguments can be native Python values, `pyarrow.Scalar` objects, arrays, or chunked arrays. The library will cast accordingly as best it can if necessary.

Example 2 – min-max aggregation function

Continuing the tour, we can find the minimum and maximum values just like we did in C++:

Get our column of data from the Parquet file just like in the previous example. Try to figure it out yourself before looking at the following code snippet. I promise you that it's very easy:

```
>>> pc.min_max(column)
<pyarrow.StructScalar: [('min', -450.3), ('max', 3950611.6)]>
```

As expected, the values match those that were computed in the C++ version.

Example 3 – sorting a table of data

To complete our examples, we will sort the entire table of data in the Parquet file. Try figuring it out yourself before following the steps, then see whether you're right:

1. Once again, read the whole Parquet file in using the `read_table` function.

2. Are you ready for this? While the compute library has a `take` function, there's one directly exposed on the `Table` object itself in the Python library, making this easier:

```
>>> sort_keys = [('total_amount', 'descending')]
>>> out = tbl.take(pc.sort_indices(tbl, sort_keys=sort_
keys)
```

That's it! The sort keys are defined similarly to the C++ as a tuple of the column name and the direction to sort in. Other options can be passed by instead using the full `pc.SortOptions` object and passing that to `sort_indices` using the `options` keyword instead of `sort_keys`.

Given the ease of use and convenience of the compute library, you might wonder how it stacks up against just performing simple computations yourself. For instance, does it make more sense to manually write a loop to add a constant to an Arrow array or should you always use the compute library? Well, let's take a look…

Picking the right tools

The Arrow compute libraries provide an extremely easy-to-use interface, but what about performance? Do they exist just for ease of use? Let's try it out and compare!

Adding a constant value to an array

For our first test, let's try adding a constant value to a sample array we construct. It doesn't need to be anything extravagant, so we can create a simple 32-bit integer Arrow array and then add 2 to each element and create a new array. We're going to create arrays of various sizes and then see how long it takes to add a constant value of 2 to the Arrow array using different methods.

> **Remember!**
>
> Semantically, an Arrow array is supposed to be *immutable*, so adding a constant produces a new array. This property of immutability is often used to create optimizations and reusability of memory depending on the particular Arrow implementation. While it is possible to potentially achieve greater performance by modifying a buffer in place, care must be taken if you choose to do that. Ensure that there are no other Arrow array objects that also share the same buffers of memory; otherwise, you can end up shooting yourself in the foot.

First thing's first: we need to create our test array. Let's do that!

```
#include <numeric> // for std::iota
std::vector<int32_t> testvalues(N);
std::iota(std::begin(testvalues), std::end(testvalues), 0);
arrow::Int32Builder nb;
nb.AppendValues(testvalues);
std::shared_ptr<arrow::Array> numarr;
```

```
nb.Finish(&numarr);
auto arr = std::static_pointer_cast<arrow::Int32Array>(numarr);
```

Pretty simple, right? In the first highlighted line, we utilize `std::iota` to fill the vector with the range of values between `0` and `N`. Then, we append these values to an `Int32Builder` object in the second highlighted line to create our test array.

There are four cases we're going to test:

- Using the `arrow::compute::Add` function
- A simple `for` loop with `arrow::Int32Builder`
- Using `std::for_each` with `arrow::Int32Builder`, calling `Reserve` on the builder to pre-allocate the memory
- Treating the raw buffer as a C-style array, pre-allocating a new buffer, and constructing the resulting Arrow array from the buffers

We're going to walk through the code for each of these first, then we'll run each of them with different length arrays by changing the value of `N`. We'll use our trusty `timer` class from previous examples, like in *Chapter 3*, *Data Science with Apache Arrow*, to time how long it takes. (You can find the `timer.h` file in this book's GitHub repository: `https://github.com/PacktPublishing/In-Memory-Analytics-with-Apache-Arrow-/blob/main/chapter6/cpp/timer.h`.) Let's see what patterns we can observe!

Compute Add function

This is our simplest case, showcasing the ease of use of the compute library. Give it a try yourself before looking at the code snippet:

```
arrow::Datum res1;
{
    timer t;
    res1 = cp::Add(arr, arrow::Datum{(int32_t)2}).
MoveValueUnsafe();
}
```

What do you think? Short and sweet! We declare `arrow::Datum` outside of the scope so that we can hold onto it and verify that our other approaches produce the same result.

A simple for loop

For this case, we'll just create an `Int32Builder` object and iterate the array, calling `Append` and `AppendNull`. This is the naive solution that someone would likely come up with if asked to perform the addition of a constant to an Arrow array:

```
arrow::Datum res2;
{
    timer t;
    arrow::Int32Builder b;
    for (size_t i = 0; i < arr->length(); ++i) {
        if (arr->IsValid(i)) {
            b.Append(arr->Value(i)+2);
        } else {
            b.AppendNull();
        }
    }
    std::shared_ptr<arrow::Array> output;
    b.Finish(&output);
    res2 = arrow::Datum{std::move(output)};
}
std::cout << std::boolalpha << (res1 == res2) << std::endl;
```

Not too bad, right? That final highlighted line will output `true` if the result generated is equal to our previous result and `false` if it is not. Onward!

Using std::for_each and reserve space

This implementation is mostly a variation on the previous `for` loop solution, with some pre-allocation of memory. We're just going to utilize `std::for_each` and a lambda function instead. For this solution, we're going to need a couple of extra headers:

```
#include <arrow/util/optional.h>
#include <algorithm>
```

Now, the implementation:

```
arrow::Datum res3;
{
    timer t;
    arrow::Int32Builder b;
```

```
      b.Reserve(arr->length());
      std::for_each(std::begin(*arr), std::end(*arr),
          [&b](const arrow::util::optional<int32_t>& v) {
              if (v) { b.Append(*v + 2); }
              else { b.AppendNull(); }
          });
      std::shared_ptr<arrow::Array> output;
      b.Finish(&output);
      res3 = arrow::Datum{std::move(output)};
  }
  std::cout << std::boolalpha << (res1 == res3) << std::endl;
```

Notice that the highlighted lines are pretty much the only changes (outside of assigning to res3 instead of res2). Here, we're taking advantage of the fact that Arrow arrays provide stl-compatible iterators, using arrow::util::optional<T> as value_type they return. This is convenient because the optional class can be coerced to be a Boolean to check whether it is null, and overloads the * operator to retrieve the actual value. Now the last one…

Divide and conquer

For this implementation, we take advantage of a few elements of the Arrow specification. Consider these premises:

- For indexes that are null, the value in the raw data buffer can be literally anything.

- A primitive numeric array contains two buffers, a bitmap and a buffer containing the raw data.

- When adding a constant to an Arrow array, the resulting array's null bitmap would be identical to the original array.

Given these three premises, we can divide and process the array's null bitmap and data buffer separately. Since this example is a bit more complex, we'll break it up more to make it easier to explain:

1. We start the same as the previous examples, creating Datum and a timer inside of a nested scope:

    ```
    arrow::Datum res4;
    {
        timer t;
    ```

2. Next, we allocate a buffer to hold the resulting data. Since we know the length of the array, we can multiply it by the size of a 32-bit integer to determine the total number of bytes to allocate. Then, we use `reinterpret_cast` to acquire a pointer to the allocated memory, which we can treat as a C-style array:

```cpp
std::shared_ptr<arrow::Buffer> new_buffer =
    arrow::AllocateBuffer(sizeof(int32_t)*arr->length())
        .MoveValueUnsafe();
auto output = reinterpret_cast<int32_t*>(
    new_buffer->mutable_data());
```

3. Now, we just use `std::transform` to add a constant of 2 to every element in the array, regardless of whether or not it is `null`:

```cpp
std::transform(arr->raw_values(),
               arr->raw_values() + arr->length(),
               output,
               [] (const int32_t v) {
                   return v + 2;
               });
```

4. Finally, we reference the existing `null` bitmap and create our new array using the new buffer:

```cpp
    res4 = arrow::Datum{arrow::MakeArray(
      arrow::ArrayData::Make(
        arr->type(), arr->length(),
        std::vector<std::shared_ptr<arrow::Buffer>>{
                arr->null_bitmap(), new_buffer},
        arr->null_count()))};
}
std::cout << std::boolalpha << (res1 == res4) <<
std::endl;
```

Did you follow all that? If not, have a look at *Figure 6.4*:

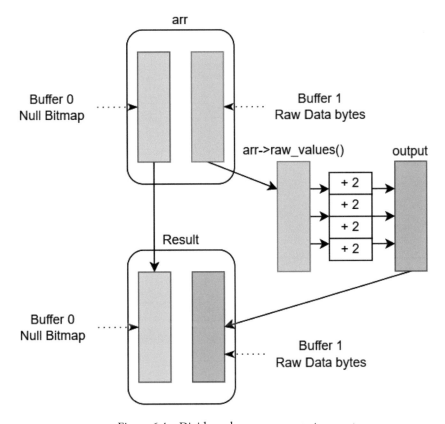

Figure 6.4 – Divide and conquer compute

You can see in *Figure 6.4* where each of the variables fits in the diagram, hopefully painting a clear picture of how we split up and processed the two buffers separately to create the new array.

Now, the moment of truth. Let's compare the performance of these approaches! *Figure 6.5* is a graph showing the performance of each one:

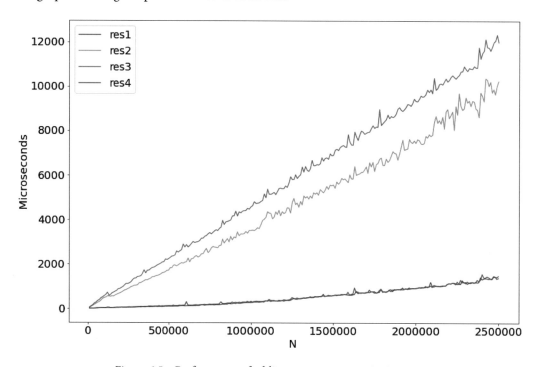

Figure 6.5 – Performance of adding a constant to an int32 array

To create this chart, I smoothed any outliers by running each approach in a loop numerous times and then dividing the time it took by the number of iterations. This is a standard benchmarking approach. It's pretty clear that not only does the compute library provide an easy-to-use interface, but it's also extremely performant. Of the different methods we tried, the only one that was on par with just calling the Add function of the compute library was our *divide and conquer* approach. This makes sense because it's actually the same underlying strategy that the compute library uses! This is awesome when dealing with a single table of data, but most modern datasets aren't quite so simple. When you're dealing with multifile datasets of tabular data, you'll need some extra utilities.

Summary

The compute APIs aren't just a convenient interface for performing functions on Arrow-formatted data but are also highly performant. The goal of the library is to expose highly optimized computational functions for as many use cases as possible in an easy-to-use way. The functions that it exposes are also highly composable as we saw with the examples for sorting a table.

Between this chapter and the previous one, *Chapter 5, Crossing the Language Barrier with the Arrow C Data API*, we've explored the building blocks of any analytical engine. Both the Arrow C data interface and the compute APIs are extremely useful in different use cases and even in conjunction with one another. For example, let's say you're using Arrow in a language that doesn't yet expose the compute APIs. By using the C Data API, you can efficiently share the data with another component that has access to the compute APIs.

Now, if you're dealing with multifile datasets of tabular data, which might be larger than the available memory on a single machine, you can still use the compute libraries. This is what we're going to cover next in *Chapter 7, Using the Arrow Datasets API*. The datasets library can do a lot of the heavy lifting for you in reading, selecting, filtering, and performing computations on data in a streaming fashion.

Onward and upward! To the cloud!

7
Using the Arrow Datasets API

In the current ecosystem of **data lakes** and **lakehouses**, many datasets are now huge collections of files in partitioned directory structures rather than a single file. To facilitate this workflow, the Arrow libraries provide an API for easily interacting with these types of structured and unstructured data. This is called the **Datasets API** and is designed to perform a lot of the heavy lifting for querying these types of datasets for you.

The Datasets API provides a series of utilities for easily interacting with large, distributed, and possibly partitioned datasets that are spread across multiple files. It also integrates very easily with the Compute APIs we covered previously, in *Chapter 6, Leveraging the Arrow Compute APIs*.

In this chapter, we will learn how to use the Arrow Datasets API for efficient querying of multifile, tabular datasets regardless of their location or format. We will also understand how to use the dataset classes and methods to easily filter or perform computations on arbitrarily large datasets.

Here are the topics that we will cover:

- Querying multifile datasets
- Filtering data programmatically
- Using the Datasets API in Python
- Streaming results

Technical requirements

As before, this chapter has a lot of code examples and exercises to drive home an understanding of using these libraries. You'll need an internet-connected computer with the following to try out the examples and follow along:

- Python 3+: With the `pyarrow` module installed and the `dataset` submodule.
- A C++ compiler supporting C++11 or higher: With the Arrow libraries installed and able to be included and linked against.
- Your preferred coding IDE, such as Emacs, Vim, Sublime, or VS Code.
- As before, you can find the full sample code in the accompanying GitHub repository at `https://github.com/PacktPublishing/In-Memory-Analytics-with-Apache-Arrow-`.
- We're also going to utilize the NYC taxi dataset located in the public AWS S3 bucket at `s3://ursa-labs-taxi-data/`.

Querying multifile datasets

> **Note**
>
> While this section details the Datasets API in the Arrow libraries, it's important to note that this API is still considered experimental as of the time of writing. As a result, the APIs described are not yet guaranteed to be stable between version upgrades of Arrow and may change in some ways. Always check the documentation for the version of Arrow you're using. That said, the API is unlikely to change drastically unless requested by users, so it's being included due to its extreme utility.

To facilitate the very quick querying of data, modern datasets are often partitioned into multiple files across multiple directories. Many engines and utilities take advantage of this or read and write data in this format, such as Apache Hive, Dremio Sonar, Presto, and many AWS services. The Arrow datasets library provides functionality as a library for working with these sorts of tabular datasets, such as the following:

- Providing a single, unified interface that supports different data formats and filesystems. As of version 7.0.0 of Arrow, this includes Parquet, ORC, Feather (or Arrow IPC), and CSV files that are either local or stored in the cloud, such as S3 or HDFS.

- Discovering sources by crawling partitioned directories and providing some simple normalizing of schemas between different partitions.

- Predicate pushdown for filtering rows efficiently along with optimized column projection and parallel reading.

Using the trusty NYC taxi dataset again, let's see an example of how you might partition this data for easier querying. The most obvious, and most likely, way that this data would get partitioned is by date, specifically, by year and then by month. *Figure 7.1* shows what this might look like:

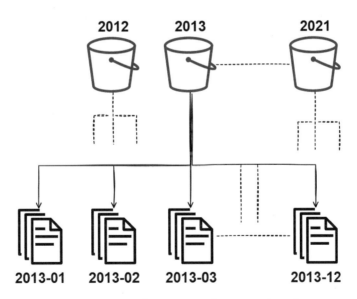

Figure 7.1 – Sample partition scheme, year/month

Partitioning the data in this way allows us to utilize the directories and files to minimize the number of files we actually have to read to satisfy a query that is requesting a particular time frame. For example, if a query is requesting information about the data for the entire year of 2015, we're able to skip reading any files that aren't in the 2015 bucket. The same would go for a query about data from year to year but only in January; we'd be able to simply read only the 01 file in each year's bucket.

In the case of the NYC taxi dataset, another potential way to partition the data would be to partition it by the source type first and then by year and month. Whether or not it makes sense to do this depends on the query pattern that you're expecting to serve. If the majority of the time you're only querying one type (yellow, green, fhv, and so on), then it would be highly beneficial to partition the dataset in this way, as shown in *Figure 7.2*. If instead the queries will often mix the data between the dataset types, it might be better to keep the data only partitioned by year and month to minimize the I/O communication:

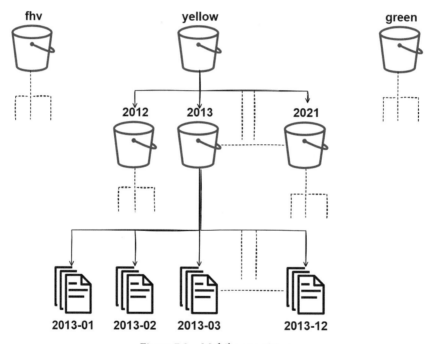

Figure 7.2 – Multikey partition

This partitioning technique can be applied for any columns that are frequently filtered on, not just the obvious ones, such as date and dataset type. It's making a trade-off between improving the filtering by reducing the number of files to read in and having potentially more files to read when not filtering on that column.

But we're getting ahead of ourselves here. Let's start with a simple example and work from there.

Creating a sample dataset

The first thing we're going to do is to create a sample dataset consisting of a directory containing two Parquet files. For simplicity, we can just have three `int64` columns named a, b, and c. Our whole dataset can look like *Figure 7.3*, which shows the two Parquet files. Before looking at the code snippet, try coding up something to write the two files yourself in the language of your choice:

data1.parquet				data2.parquet		
a	b	c		a	b	c
0	9	1		5	4	2
1	8	2		6	3	1
2	7	1		7	2	2
3	6	2		8	1	1
4	5	1		9	0	2

Figure 7.3 – Sample dataset

Here's a code snippet that will produce those two files just as we want them. I'll use C++ for this example but you can use whichever language you want. There are also Python versions of these in the accompanying GitHub repository for you to peruse:

1. First, here's a small helper macro to abort on an error:

```
#include <arrow/api.h>
#include <iostream>

#define ABORT_ON_FAIL(expr) \
    do {                                    \
        arrow::Status status_ = (expr);     \
        if (!status_.ok()) {                \
            std::cerr << status_.message() \
                      << std::endl;         \
            abort();                        \
        }                                   \
    } while(0);
```

2. We'll make a `create_table` function next for simplicity:

```
#include <memory>
std::shared_ptr<arrow::Table> create_table() {
```

```
    auto schema =
        arrow::schema({arrow::field("a", arrow::int64()),
                       arrow::field("b", arrow::int64()),
                       arrow::field("c", arrow::int64())});
    std::shared_ptr<arrow::Array> array_a, array_b,
array_c;
    arrow::NumericBuilder<arrow::Int64Type> builder;
    builder.AppendValues({0, 1, 2, 3, 4, 5, 6, 7, 8, 9});
    ABORT_ON_FAIL(builder.Finish(&array_a));
    builder.Reset();
    builder.AppendValues({9, 8, 7, 6, 5, 4, 3, 2, 1, 0});
    ABORT_ON_FAIL(builder.Finish(&array_b));
    builder.Reset();
    builder.AppendValues({1, 2, 1, 2, 1, 2, 1, 2, 1, 2});
    ABORT_ON_FAIL(builder.Finish(&array_c));
    builder.Reset();
    return arrow::Table::Make(schema,
                              {array_a, array_b, array_c});
}
```

3. Then, add a function to write the Parquet files from the table we create:

```
#include <arrow/filesystem/api.h>
#include <parquet/arrow/writer.h>

namespace fs = arrow::fs;
std::string create_sample_dataset(
            const std::shared_ptr<fs::FileSystem>&
filesystem,
            const std::string& root_path) {
    auto base_path = root_path + "/parquet_dataset";
    ABORT_ON_FAIL(filesystem->CreateDir(base_path));
    auto table = create_table();
    auto output =
            filesystem->OpenOutputStream(base_path +
                    "/data1.parquet").ValueOrDie();
    ABORT_ON_FAIL(parquet::arrow::WriteTable(
            *table->Slice(0, 5),
```

```
                arrow::default_memory_pool(),
                output, /*chunk_size*/2048));
        output = filesystem->OpenOutputStream(base_path +
                "/data2.parquet").ValueOrDie();
        ABORT_ON_FAIL(parquet::arrow::WriteTable(
                *table->Slice(5),
                arrow::default_memory_pool(),
                output, /*chunk_size*/2048));
        return base_path;
    }
```

4. Finally, we add a `main` function to initialize the filesystem and set a root path:

```
int main() {
    std::shared_ptr<fs::FileSystem> filesystem =
            std::make_shared<fs::LocalFileSystem>();
    auto path = create_sample_dataset(filesystem,
                            "/home/matt/sample");
    std::cout << path << std::endl;
}
```

Of course, replace the root path to write to with the relevant path for you.

Discovering dataset fragments

The Arrow Dataset library is capable of discovering the files that exist for a filesystem-based dataset for you, without requiring you to describe every single file path that is part of it. The current concrete dataset implementations as of version 7.0.0 of the Arrow library are as follows:

- `FileSystemDataset`: Dataset constructed of various files in a directory structure

- `InMemoryDataset`: Dataset consisting of a bunch of record batches that already exist in memory

- `UnionDataset`: Dataset that consists of one or more other datasets as children

When we talk about fragments of a dataset, we're referring to the units of parallelization that exist for the dataset. For `InMemoryDataset`, this would be the individual record batches. Most often, for a filesystem-based dataset, the "fragments" would be the individual files. But in the case of something such as Parquet files, a fragment could also be a single row group from a single file too. Let's use the factory functions that exist in the library to create a dataset of our two sample Parquet files:

1. Let's get our `include` directive and function signature set up first:

    ```cpp
    #include <arrow/dataset/api.h>


    namespace ds = arrow::dataset; // convenient
    std::shared_ptr<arrow::Table> scan_dataset(
        const std::shared_ptr<fs::FileSystem>& filesystem,
        const std::shared_ptr<ds::FileFormat>& format,
        const std::string& base_dir) {
    ```

2. Inside of the function, we first set up a `FileSelector` and create a `factory`:

    ```cpp
    fs::FileSelector selector;
    selector.base_dir = base_dir;
    auto factory = ds::FileSystemDatasetFactory::Make(
        filesystem, selector, format,
        ds::FileSystemFactoryOptions()).ValueOrDie();
    ```

3. For now, we're not going to do anything interesting with `factory`, just get the dataset from it. With the dataset, we can loop over all the fragments and print them out:

    ```cpp
    auto dataset = factory->Finish().ValueOrDie();
    auto fragments = dataset->GetFragments()
                                    .ValueOrDie();
    for (const auto& fragment : fragments) {
        std::cout << "Found Fragment: "
                    << (*fragment)->ToString()
                    << std::endl;
    }
    ```

4. Finally, we create a scanner and get a table from the dataset by scanning it:

    ```cpp
    auto scan_builder = dataset->NewScan()
    ```

```
                                              .ValueOrDie();
    auto scanner = scan_builder->Finish().ValueOrDie();
    return scanner->ToTable().ValueOrDie();
} // end of function scan_dataset
```

To compile this function, make sure you have installed the `arrow-dataset` library since it is packaged separately in most package managers. Then, you can use the following command:

```
$ g++ -o sampledataset dataset.cc 'pkg-config --cflags --libs
arrow-dataset'
```

Using `pkg-config` will append the necessary `include` and `linker` flags for compiling the file, which would include the `arrow`, `parquet`, and `arrow-dataset` libraries. Also, keep in mind that as written, the code snippet will read the whole dataset into memory as a single table. This is fine for our sample dataset, but if you're trying this on a very large dataset, you'd probably instead prefer to stream batches rather than read the whole thing into memory.

The function also takes the file format in as a parameter. In this case, we would use `ParquetFileFormat`, like so:

```
auto format = std::make_shared<ds::ParquetFileFormat>();
```

From there, you can customize the format with whatever specific options you want to set before passing it into the function and using it with the `Dataset` class. We're doing the same thing to pass the filesystem to use, in this case, the local filesystem, as seen in the `main` function when we created the dataset. This could be swapped out with an S3 filesystem object if desired, or another `FileSystem` instance, without having to change anything else. The other available formats are as follows:

- `arrow::dataset::CsvFileFormat`
- `arrow::dataset::IpcFileFormat`
- `arrow::dataset::OrcFileFormat`

The last thing to remember is that creating the `arrow::dataset::Dataset` object doesn't automatically begin reading the data itself. It will only crawl through the directories based on the provided options to find all the files it needs, if applicable. It will also infer the schema of the dataset by looking at the metadata of the first file it finds by default. You can instead either supply a schema to use or tell the object to check and resolve the schema across all the files based on the desired `arrow::dataset::InspectOptions` passed to the call to `Finish` on the `factory`.

Okay. So now that we have our dataset object, we can benefit from the optimized filtering and projection of rows and columns.

Filtering data programmatically

In the previous example, we created a scanner and then read the entire dataset. This time, we're going to muck around with the builder first to give it a filter to use before it starts reading the data. We'll also use the `Project` function to control what columns get read. Since we're using Parquet files, we can reduce the IO and memory usage by only reading the columns we want rather than reading all of them; we just need to tell the scanner that that's what we want.

In the previous section, we learned about the Arrow Compute API as a library for performing various operations and computations on Arrow-formatted data. It also includes objects and functionality for defining complex expressions referencing fields and calling functions. These expression objects can then be used in conjunction with the scanners to define simple or complex filters for our data. Before we dig into the scanner, let's take a quick detour to cover the `Expression` class.

Expressing yourself – a quick detour

In terms of working with datasets, an **expression** is one of the following:

- A literal value or datum, which could be a scalar, an array, or even an entire record batch or table of data

- A reference to a single, possibly nested, field of an input datum

- A compute function call containing arguments that are defined by other expressions

With just those three building blocks, consumers have the flexibility to customize their logic and computations for whatever input they have. It also allows for static analysis of expressions to simplify them before execution for optimizing calculations. The sample dataset we constructed before will be our input datum, meaning the fields we can refer to are named a, b, and c. Here are a couple of examples:

- First, *Figure 7.4* shows a simple field reference from the input. We reference the column named b, so our output is just that column itself:

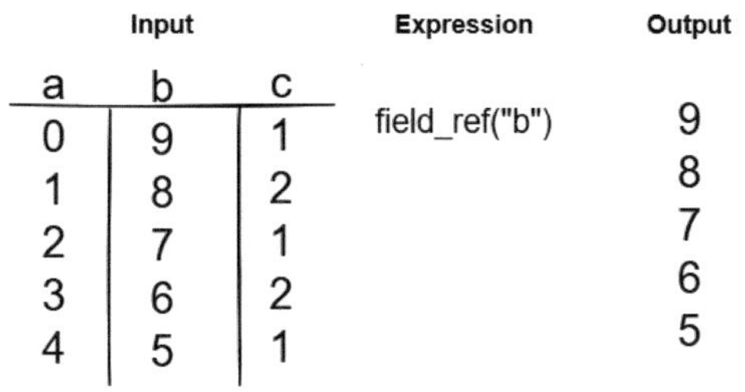

Input			Expression	Output
a	b	c		
0	9	1	field_ref("b")	9
1	8	2		8
2	7	1		7
3	6	2		6
4	5	1		5

Figure 7.4 – Basic field reference expression

- Something a little tougher, *Figure 7.5* shows the expression a < 4. Notice this is constructed using a compute function call named less, a field reference, and a literal value as the arguments. Because the expression is a Boolean expression, the output is a Boolean array of true or false, with each element being the corresponding result for that index in the input of column a:

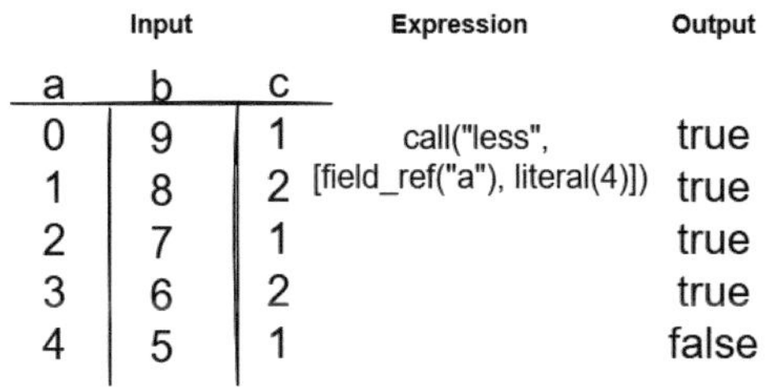

Input			Expression	Output
a	b	c		
0	9	1	call("less",	true
1	8	2	[field_ref("a"), literal(4)])	true
2	7	1		true
3	6	2		true
4	5	1		false

Figure 7.5 – Expression with function call and arguments

To make it easier to read and interact with, some of the most common compute functions have direct API calls for creating expressions with them. This includes your standard binary comparisons, such as less, greater, and equal, along with Boolean logic such as and, or, and not.

Using expressions for filtering data

We're going to build on the function we used for scanning the entire dataset by adding a filter to it. Let's create a new function with the same signature as the previous scan_dataset function; we can call it filter_and_select. Instead of just scanning the entire dataset like before, we're going to only read one column and then filter out some rows:

1. Add these include directives to the file first. We need them for using Expression objects and compute options:

    ```
    #include <arrow/compute/api.h> // general compute
    #include <arrow/compute/exec/expression.h>
    ```

2. For convenience, we aliased the `arrow::dataset` namespace to just `ds` previously. Now, we'll do a similar alias for the `arrow::compute` namespace:

    ```
    namespace cp = arrow::compute;
    ```

3. Our function signature is identical to the previous function, just using the new name:

    ```
    std::shared_ptr<arrow::Table> filter_and_select(
        const std::shared_ptr<fs::FileSystem>& filesystem,
        const std::shared_ptr<ds::FileFormat>& format,
        const std::string& base_dir) {
    ```

4. The beginning of the function is the same for constructing the `factory` and `dataset` objects, so I won't repeat those lines here. Just do the same thing we did in the `scan_dataset` function. (See *Step 2* under the *Discovering dataset fragments* section.)

5. Where things change is after we create `scan_builder`. Instead of getting all of the columns in the dataset, we can tell the scanner to only materialize one column. In this case, we'll only retrieve column b:

    ```
    auto factory = ...
    auto dataset = ...
    auto scan_builder = dataset->NewScan().ValueOrDie();
    ABORT_ON_FAIL(scan_builder->Project({"b"}));
    ```

6. Alternatively, instead of providing a list of columns, we could provide a list of expressions and names for the output columns, similar to a SQL `SELECT` query. The previous line would be equivalent to running `SELECT b FROM dataset`. This next line is the equivalent of adding a `WHERE` clause to the SQL query. What do you think that would look like?

    ```
    ABORT_ON_FAIL(scan_builder->Filter(
        cp::less(cp::field_ref("b"), cp::literal(4))));
    ```

    Can you figure out what the query would look like if we were using SQL? Adding this call to `Filter` on the scan builder tells the scanner to use this expression to filter the data as it scans. Therefore, it's equivalent to executing something similar to this SQL query on our dataset: `SELECT b FROM dataset WHERE b < 4`.

7. Then, just as before, we can retrieve and return a table of our results from the scan:

    ```
    auto scanner = scan_builder->Finish()
                                    .ValueOrDie();
    ```

```
        return scanner->ToTable().ValueOrDie();
    } // end of filter_and_select function
```

If we use the same sample dataset from back in *Figure 7.5*, what should our new output look like? If you run the new `filter_and_select` function, does it match what you'd expect? Look over the following output and double-check that your output matches!

```
b: int64
----
b:
  [
    [
      3,
      2,
      1,
      0,
    ]
  ]
```

Try playing around with different expressions when calling the filter function and seeing whether the output matches what you'd expect. If the filter expression references a column that isn't in the project list, the scanner still knows to read that column in addition to any it needs for the results. Next, we'll throw in some more modifications for manipulating the result columns.

Deriving and renaming columns (projecting)

Building further on our function, we can throw in some extra complexity to read the three columns, rename a column, and get a derived column using expressions. Once again, keep the same function signature and structure for the function; we're only modifying the lines that utilize `scan_builder`:

1. First, we'll use the schema of the dataset to add a field reference for each column of the data. By getting the field list from the schema, we don't have to hardcode the whole list:

    ```
    std::vector<std::string> names;
    std::vector<cp::Expression> exprs;
    for (const auto& field : dataset->schema()->fields()) {
        names.push_back(field->name());
    ```

```
                  exprs.push_back(cp::field_ref(field->name()));
      }
```

2. Then, we add a new output column named b_as_float32, which is just the column named b casted to a 32-bit float data type. Note the structure: we are creating an expression consisting of a call to a function named cast, passing it a field reference as the only argument, and setting the options to tell it what data type it should cast to:

```
names.emplace_back("b_as_float32");
exprs.push_back(cp::call("cast", {cp::field_ref("b")},
      cp::CastOptions::Safe(arrow::float32())));
```

3. Next, we create another derived column named b_large, which will be a Boolean column computed by returning whether or not the value of field b is greater than 1:

```
names.emplace_back("b_large");
// b > 1
exprs.push_back(cp::greater(cp::field_ref("b"),
                               cp::literal(1)));
```

4. Finally, we just pass the two lists of expressions and names to the scanner by calling the Project function:

```
ABORT_ON_FAIL(scan_builder->Project(exprs, names));
```

5. After this, the rest of the function is identical to what it's been in the previous examples for performing the scan and retrieving the table of results.

Did you follow all of that? Can you think of what an equivalent SQL-style query would look like compared to what the code does? I mention SQL because much of the Datasets API is designed to be semantically similar to performing SQL queries on the dataset, and can even be used to implement a SQL engine!

Don't read ahead until you try it!

Seriously, try it first.

Okay, here's the answer:

```
SELECT
              a, b, c,
              FLOAT(b) AS b_as_float32,
              b > 1 AS b_large
```

```
FROM
            dataset
```

This only scratches the surface of what is possible with the Datasets and Compute APIs, but should be a useful starting point for experimentation. Play around with different types of filtering, column deriving and renaming, and so on. Maybe you have some use cases where these APIs could be used to simplify existing code. Try it out!

We've covered C++, so now, let's shift back to Python!

Using the Datasets API in Python

Before you ask: yes, the datasets API is available in Python too! Let's do a quick rundown of all the same features we just covered, but using the `pyarrow` Python module instead of C++. Since the majority of data scientists utilize Python for their work, it makes sense to show off how to use these APIs in Python for easy integration with existing workflows and utilities. Since Python's syntax is simpler than C++, the code is much more concise, so we can run through everything really quickly in the following sections.

Creating our sample dataset

We can start by creating a similar sample dataset to what we were using for the C++ examples with three columns, but using Python:

```python
>>> import pyarrow as pa
>>> import pyarrow.parquet as pq
>>> import pathlib
>>> import numpy as np
>>> import os
>>> base = pathlib.Path(os.getcwd())
>>> (base / "parquet_dataset").mkdir(exist_ok=True)
>>> table = pa.table({'a': range(10), 'b': np.random.randn(10),
'c': [1, 2] * 5})
>>> pq.write_table(table.slice(0, 5), base / "parquet_dataset/
data1.parquet")
>>> pq.write_table(table.slice(5, 10), base / "parquet_dataset/
data2.parquet")
```

After we've got our imports squared away and set up a path to write the Parquet files to, the highlighted lines are where we actually construct the sample dataset. We create a table with 10 rows and 3 columns, then split the table into 2 Parquet files that each have 5 rows in them. Using the Python `pathlib` library makes the code very portable since it will handle the proper formatting of file paths based on the operating system you're running it under.

Discovering the dataset

Just like with the C++ library, the `dataset` library for Python is able to perform a discovery of file fragments by passing the base directory to start searching from. Alternatively, you could pass the path of a single file or a list of file paths instead of a base directory to search:

```
>>> import pyarrow.dataset as ds
>>> dataset = ds.dataset(base / "parquet_dataset",
format="parquet")
>>> dataset.files
['<path>/parquet_dataset/data1.parquet', '<path>/parquet_
dataset/data2.parquet']
```

<path> should be replaced by the path to the directory you created for the sample dataset in the previous section.

This will also infer the schema of the dataset just like the C++ library. By default, it will do this by reading the first file in the dataset. You could also manually supply a schema to use as an argument to the `dataset` function instead:

```
>>> print(dataset.schema.to_string(show_field_metadata=False))
a: int64
b: double
c: int64
```

Finally, we also have a method to load the entire dataset (or a portion of it) into an Arrow table just like the `ToTable` method in C++:

```
>>> dataset.to_table()
pyarrow.Table
a: int64
b: double
c: int64
----
```

```
a: [[0,1,2,3,4],[5,6,7,8,9]]
b: [[[[0.4496826452924734,0.8187826910251114,0.293394262192757,-
0.9355403104276471,-0.19315460805569024],[1.3384156936773497,-
0.6000310181068441,0.16303489615416472,-1.4502901450565746,-
0.5973093999335979]]]
c: [[1,2,1,2,1],[2,1,2,1,2]]
```

While we used Parquet files for the preceding examples, the `dataset` module does allow specifying the file format of your dataset during discovery.

Using different file formats

Currently, the Python version supports the following formats, providing a consistent interface regardless of the underlying data file format:

- Parquet
- ORC
- Feather/Arrow IPC
- CSV

More file formats are planned to be supported over time. The `format` keyword argument to the `dataset` function allows specifying the format of the data.

Filtering and projecting columns with Python

Like the C++ interface, the `pyarrow` library provides an `Expression` object type for configuring filters and projections of the data columns. These can be passed to the dataset as arguments to the `to_table` function. For convenience, operator overloads and helper functions are provided to help with constructing filters and expressions. Let's give it a try:

- Selecting a subset of columns for the dataset will only read the columns requested from the files:

    ```
    >>> dataset.to_table(columns=['a', 'c'])
    pyarrow.Table
    a: int64
    c: int64
    ----
    a: [[0,1,2,3,4],[5,6,7,8,9]]
    c: [[1,2,1,2,1],[2,1,2,1,2]]
    ```

- The `filter` keyword argument can take a Boolean expression that defines a predicate to match rows against. Any row that doesn't match will be excluded from the returned data. Using the `field` helper function allows specifying any column in the table, regardless of whether or not it's a partition column or in the list of projected columns:

```
>>> dataset.to_table(columns=['a', 'b'], filter=ds.
field('c') == 2)
pyarrow.Table
a: int64
b: double
----
a: [[1,3],[5,7,9]]
b: [[0.8187826910251114,-0.9355403104276471],
[1.3384156936773497,0.16303489615416472,
-0.5973093999335979]]
```

- You can also use function calls and Boolean combinations with the expressions to create complex filters and perform set membership testing:

```
>>> dataset.to_table(filter=(ds.field('a') >
ds.field('b')) & (ds.field('a').isin([4,5])))
pyarrow.Table
a: int64
b: double
c: int64
----
a: [[4],[5]]
b: [[-0.19315460805569024],[1.3384156936773497]]
c: [[1],[2]]
```

- Column projection can be defined using expressions by passing a Python dictionary that maps column names to the expressions to execute for deriving columns:

```
>>> projection = {
... 'a_renamed': ds.field('a'),
... 'b_as_float32': ds.field('b').cast('float32'),
... 'c_1': ds.field('c') == 1,
... }
>>> dataset.to_table(columns=projection)
```

```
pyarrow.Table
a_renamed: int64
b_as_float32: float
c_1: bool
----
a_renamed: [[0,1,2,3,4],[5,6,7,8,9]]
b_as_float32: [[0.44968265,0.8187827,0.29339427,
-0.9355403,-0.1931546],[1.3384157,-0.600031,0.1630349,
-1.4502902,-0.5973094]]
c_1: [[true,false,true,false,true],
[false,true,false,true,false]]
```

All of the examples so far have involved reading the entire dataset and performing the projections or filters, but we wanted to be able to handle very large datasets that potentially won't fit in memory, right? Both the C++ and Python dataset APIs support streaming, iterative reads for these types of workflows, and allowing processing of data without loading the entire dataset at once. We're going to cover working with the streaming APIs next.

Streaming results

You'll recall from the beginning of this chapter, in the *Querying multifile datasets* section, that I mentioned this was the solution for when you had multiple files and the dataset was potentially too large to fit in memory all at one time. So far, the examples we've seen used the ToTable function to completely materialize the results in memory as a single Arrow table. If your results are too large to fit into memory all at one time, this obviously won't work. Even if your results could fit into memory, it's not the most efficient way to perform the query anyway. In addition to the ToTable (C++) or to_table (Python) function we've been calling, the scanner also exposes functions that return iterators for streaming record batches from the query.

To demonstrate the streaming, let's use a public AWS S3 bucket hosted by Ursa Labs, which contains about 10 years of NYC taxi trip record data in Parquet format. The URI for the dataset is s3://ursa-labs-taxi-data/. Even in Parquet format, the total size of the data there is around 37 GB, significantly larger than the memory available on most people's computers. We're going to play around with this dataset with both C++ and Python, so let's have some fun!

First, let's see how many files and rows are in this very large dataset. We'll try Python first. Let's use Jupyter or IPython so that we can time the operations using %time:

```
In [0]: import pyarrow.dataset as ds
In [1]: %%time
   ...: dataset = ds.dataset('s3://ursa-labs-taxi-data/')
   ...: print(len(dataset.files))
   ...: print(len(dataset.count_rows())
   ...:
   ...:
125
1547741381
Wall Time: 5.63 s
```

Using the Python dataset library, we can see that there are 125 files in that dataset and were able to count the number of rows (over 1.5 billion) across those 37 gigabytes of 125 files in around 5.6 seconds. Not bad, not bad. Now, using C++, first we'll time the dataset discovery in finding all the files. Let's get the include directives out of the way first:

```
#include <arrow/filesystem/api.h>
#include <arrow/dataset/api.h>
#include "timer.h" // located in this book's GitHub Repository
#include <memory>
#include <iostream>
```

Then, we have the namespace aliases for convenience:

```
namespace fs = arrow::fs;
namespace ds = arrow::dataset;
```

Before we can utilize the interfaces for S3, we need to initialize the AWS S3 libraries by calling the aptly named InitializeS3 function:

```
fs::InitializeS3(fs::S3GlobalOptions{});
auto opts = fs::S3Options::Anonymous();
opts.region = "us-east-2";
```

Working with S3FileSystem works just like using the local filesystem in the previous examples, making this really easy to work with:

```
std::shared_ptr<ds::FileFormat> format =
```

```
        std::make_shared<ds::ParquetFileFormat>();
std::shared_ptr<fs::FileSystem> filesystem =
        fs::S3FileSystem::Make(opts).ValueOrDie();
fs::FileSelector selector;
selector.base_dir = "ursa-labs-taxi-data";
selector.recursive = true; // check all the subdirectories
```

By setting the `recursive` flag to `true`, the discovery mechanisms of the Datasets API will properly iterate through the keys in the S3 bucket and find the various Parquet files. Let's create our dataset and time how long it takes:

```
std::shared_ptr<ds::DatasetFactory> factory;
std::shared_ptr<ds::Dataset> dataset;

{
    timer t; // see timer.h,
             // will print elapsed time on destruction
    factory =
        ds::FileSystemDatasetFactory::Make(filesystem,
                selector, format,
                ds::FileSystemFactoryOptions()).ValueOrDie();
    dataset = factory->Finish().ValueOrDie();
}
```

Remember, the handy `timer` object you see in the code snippet will output the amount of time between its construction and when it goes out of scope, writing directly to the terminal. Compiling and running this code shows, in the output, that it took 1,518 milliseconds to discover the 125 files of the dataset. Then, we can add a call to count the rows, as we did in Python:

```
auto scan_builder = dataset->NewScan().ValueOrDie();
auto scanner = scan_builder->Finish().ValueOrDie();

{
    timer t;
    std::cout << scanner->CountRows().ValueOrDie()
                << std::endl;
}
```

We get the same 1.54-billion-row count, only this time it took just 2,970 milliseconds, or 2.9 seconds, compared to the 5.6 seconds that Python took. Granted, this is an easy one. It just needs to check the metadata in each Parquet file for the number of rows in it and then sum them all together. The amount of data it needs to read is actually very little.

Let's try something a bit more interesting than just listing the total number of rows. How about getting the average number of passengers across the entire dataset? OK, it's not a complex expression to compute. But the point is to show how easy it is to do something like this and how quickly it can execute. How long do you think it would take to perform this computation across the entire dataset using just my laptop? No compute cluster or anything, just a single laptop on my home network. Remember, this isn't just a simple "calculate the mean of a column." Look at *Figure 7.6*, a visual representation of what we're going to do. It's basically a pipeline:

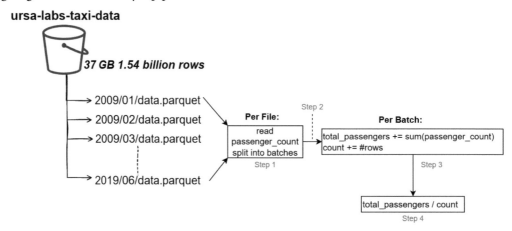

Figure 7.6 – Dataset accumulation

Let's go through this step by step:

1. The dataset scanner will read only the `passenger_count` column from each file asynchronously and split the data into configurable batches.

2. The batches will be streamed so that we never load the entire dataset in memory at one time.

3. For each batch we get in the stream, we'll use the `compute` library to calculate the sum of the data and add it to a running total. We'll also keep track of the total number of rows we see.

4. Once there are no more batches, we can just compute the mean using the values we computed.

How complex do you think this will be to write? How long do you think it'll take to run? Ready to be surprised?

First, we'll do it in Python using the `dataset` object we created earlier:

```
In [2]: import pyarrow.compute as pc
In [3]: scanner = dataset.scanner(columns=['passenger_count'],
use_async=True)
In [4]: total_passengers = 0
In [5]: total_count = 0
In [6]: %%time
   ...: for batch in scanner.to_batches():
   ...:         passengers += pc.sum(batch.column('passenger_
count')).as_py()
   ...:         count += batch.num_rows
   ...: mean = passengers/count
   ...:
   ...:
Wall time: 2min 37s
In [7]: mean
1.669097621032076
```

Simple enough! And it only took around 2.5 minutes to run on a single laptop, to calculate the mean across over 1.5 billion rows. Not bad, if I say so myself. After a bit of testing, it turns out that the bottleneck here is the connection with S3 to transfer the gigabytes of data being requested across the network, rather than the computation.

Anyway, now the C++ version. It's just a matter of using a different function on the scanner object. Creating the factory and the dataset objects works the same as in all the previous C++ examples, so let's create our scanner:

```
#include <atomic> // new header
...
// creating the factory and dataset is the same as before
{
    timer t;
    auto scan_builder = dataset->NewScan().ValueOrDie();
    scan_builder->BatchSize(1 << 28); // default is 1 << 20
    scan_builder->UseThreads(true);
    scan_builder->Project({"passenger_count"});
    auto scanner = scan_builder->Finish().ValueOrDie();
```

With our scanner all set up, we then pass a lambda function to the `Scan` method of the scanner, which will asynchronously call it as record batches are received. Because this is done in a thread pool, potentially at the same time, we use `std::atomic<int64_t>` to avoid any race conditions:

```
std::atomic<int64_t> passengers(0), count(0);
ABORT_ON_FAIL(scanner->Scan(
  [&](ds::TaggedRecordBatch batch) -> arrow::Status {
    ARROW_ASSIGN_OR_RAISE(auto result,
    cp::Sum(batch.record_batch->
             GetColumnByName("passenger_count")));
    passengers +=
        result.scalar_as<arrow::Int64Scalar>().value;
    count += batch.record_batch->num_rows();
    return arrow::Status::OK();
  }));
```

If we look back at the Python version we wrote, you might be wondering why we didn't need any synchronization there. This is because `scanner.to_batches` is a Python generator producing a stream of record batches. There's never the potential that we're processing more than one record batch at a time. In the preceding C++ code snippet, we pass a callback lambda to the scanner, which can potentially call it from multiple threads simultaneously. With this multithreaded approach, and the potential that we might process more than one record batch simultaneously, `std::atomic` ensures that everything is processed correctly.

Finally, we can just calculate our result and output it once the scan has completed:

```
double mean =
        double(passengers.load())
        / double(count.load());
std::cout << mean << std::endl;
} // end of the timer block
```

Running this locally on my laptop, it runs on average for about 1 minute and 53 seconds, or roughly 26% faster than the Python version.

If you look back at *Figure 7.6*, you'll see the structure of the keys in the AWS S3 bucket and how they are partitioned into folders by year and month. Well, we can take advantage of that to super-charge any filtering we want to do by those fields! All you have to do is use the partitioning settings that are included with the Arrow Datasets API, which is, of course, the next thing we're going to do.

Working with partitioned datasets

In the previous example, we shifted from files in a flat directory to files that were partitioned into directories. If we were to place filter expressions into the scanner, it would have to open up each file and potentially read the whole file first, and then filter the data. By organizing the data into partitioned, nested subdirectories, we can define a partitioning layout where the names of the subdirectories provide information about which subset of the data is stored there. Doing this allows us to completely skip loading files that we know won't match a filter.

Let's look at the partitioning structure used by the taxi dataset on S3 again:

```
2009/
    01/data.parquet
    02/data.parquet
    ...
2010/
    01/data.parquet
    02/data.parquet
    ...
...
```

It may be obvious, but using this structure means that we can assume by convention that the file located at `2009/01/data.parquet` will only contain data where `year == 2009` and `month == 1`. By using the configurations, we can even provide pseudo-columns for our data that represent the year and month, even though those columns don't exist in the files. Let's give it a try, first in C++, initializing the S3 filesystem and creating the `selector` object as before:

```cpp
ds::FileSystemFactoryOptions options;
options.partitioning =
  ds::DirectoryPartitioning::MakeFactory({"year", "month"});

auto factory = ds::FileSystemDatasetFactory::Make(
    filesystem, selector, format, options).ValueOrDie();
auto dataset = factory->Finish().ValueOrDie();
auto fragments = dataset->GetFragments().ValueOrDie();

for (const auto& fragment : fragments) {
    std::cout << "Found Fragment: "
```

```
                        << (*fragment)->ToString() << std::endl;
        std::cout << "Partition Expression: "
                  << (*fragment)->partition_expression().ToString()
                  << std::endl;
}
```

The highlighted lines are the additions made as compared to the way we constructed the dataset in the previous examples. The `DirectoryPartitioning` factory object is used to add the `partitioning` option to the factory denoting the order of the pieces of the file paths and what they should be called. This even adds columns to the schema of the created dataset named `year` and `month`, inferring the types of those columns from the values. If we print out the schema, we can confirm this; just add a line to print out the schema:

```
std::cout << dataset->schema()->ToString() << std::endl;
```

We see it reflected in the output:

```
vendor_id: string
...
year: int32
month: int32
```

In this case, the dataset inferred from the values that our `year` and `month` columns were 32-bit integer fields. If you prefer, you could instead specify the types directly with the partitioning options by providing a full Arrow schema object:

```
options.partitioning = std::make_
shared<ds::DirectoryPartitioning>(
    arrow::schema({arrow::field("year", arrow::uint16()),
                   arrow::field("month", arrow::int8())})
);
```

Of course, we can do exactly the same thing with Python, like so:

```
In [3]: part = ds.partitioning(field_names=["year", "month"])
In [4]: part = ds.partitioning(pa.schema([("year",
pa.uint16()), ("month", pa.int8())])) # or specify the types
In [5]: dataset = ds.dataset('s3://ursa-labs-taxi-data/',
partitioning=part, format='parquet')
In [6]: for fragment in dataset.get_fragments():
```

```
    ...:         print("Found Fragment:", fragment.path)
    ...:         print("Partition Expression:", fragment.partition_
expression)
    ...:
```

In both cases, C++ or Python, our code snippets provide the same output list of files and partition expressions:

```
Found Fragment: ursa-labs-taxi-data/2009/01/data.parquet
Partition Expression: ((year == 2009) and (month == 1))
Found Fragment: ursa-labs-taxi-data/2009/02/data.parquet
Partition Expression: ((year == 2009) and (month == 2))
...
```

A common partitioning scheme that is frequently seen is the partitioning scheme used by Apache Hive, a SQL-like interface for files and data that integrates with Hadoop. The Hive partitioning scheme includes the name of the field in the path along with the value, instead of just the value. For example, with the taxi data we were just using, instead of a file path of /2009/01/data.parquet, it would be /year=2009/month=1/ data.parquet. Because this scheme is very common due to the proliferation and use of Apache Hive, the Arrow library already provides convenient classes for specifying the Hive partition scheme, regardless of whether you're using C++, as follows:

```
options.partitioning = ds::HivePartitioning::MakeFactory();
// or specify the schema to define the types
options.partitioning = std::make_shared<ds::HivePartitioning>(
    arrow::schema({arrow::field("year", arrow::uint16()),
                   arrow::field("month", arrow::int8())})
);
```

Or if you're using Python, as follows:

```
In [7]: dataset = ds.dataset('s3://ursa-labs-taxi-data/',
partitioning='hive', format='parquet') # infer the types
In [8]: part = ds.partitioning( # or specify the schema
    ...: pa.schema([("year", pa.uint16()), ("month", pa.int8())]),
    ...: flavor='hive') # and denote it is using the hive style
```

If we scan the dataset after defining the partitioning using a filter on either or both of the fields that we partition on, we won't even read the files whose partition expressions don't match the filter. We can confirm that by using filters and checking how long things take. Let's count the rows based on a filter so we can confirm this:

```
In [9]: dataset = ds.dataset('s3://ursa-labs-taxi-data',
partitioning=part, format='parquet')
In [10]: %time dataset.count_rows(filter=ds.field('year') ==
2012)
Wall time: 421 ms
Out[10]: 178544324
In [11]: import datetime
In [12]: start = pa.scalar(datetime.datetime(2012, 1, 1, 0, 0, 0))
In [13]: end = pa.scalar(datetime.datetime(2013, 1, 1, 0, 0, 0))
In [14]: %%time
    ... : dataset.count_rows(filter=
    ... : (ds.field('pickup_at') >= start) &
    ... : (ds.field('pickup_at') < end))
    ... :
    ... :
Wall time 20.9 s
Out[14]: 178544324
```

In the first highlighted section, we count the number of rows that meet the filter where the year field is equal to the value 2012. This turns out to be very quick and easy despite the size of the dataset because of the partitioning. We just need to read the Parquet metadata of each file under the 2012 directory and its subdirectories and add up the number of rows in each one, taking only *421 milliseconds*.

In the second highlighted section, we use two timestamp scalar values to create a filter expression. We then count the rows where the pickup_at field is *greater than or equal to January 1, 2012, and less than January 1, 2013*. Because it's not a partition field, we have to open and read *every file* in the dataset to check the rows to find out what rows match the filter. Granted, because Parquet files can maintain statistics on their columns, such as the minimum and maximum value, this isn't as expensive as having to check every single last row. We don't have to read all 1.5 billion rows to get the answer but can instead use the statistics to skip large groups of rows. Unfortunately, this still means we have to at least read the metadata from every single file in the dataset, instead of being able to skip files entirely as we did with the partition field. That extra work leads to the almost *21 seconds* it takes to get the same answer, almost *49 times slower* than using the partition field.

Try doing the same experiment with the C++ library!

Now, that's all fine and helpful when reading data, but what about when you have to write data? The Datasets API also simplifies writing data, even partitioning it for you if you desire.

Writing partitioned data

There are two sides to working with data: querying data that exists and writing new data. Both are heavily important workflows and so we want to simplify both. In the previous sections, we were looking solely at reading and querying a dataset that existed. Writing a dataset is just as easy as writing a single table. (Remember? We did that back in *Chapter 2, Working with Key Arrow Specifications*.)

If you have a table or record batch already in memory, then you can easily write your dataset. Instead of providing a filename, you provide a directory and a template for what the files will get named. As usual, Python has a simpler syntax for you to use. Have a look:

```
In [15]: base = pathlib.Path(...) # use base path for your
datasets
In [16]: root = base / "sample_dataset"
In [17]: root.mkdir(exit_ok=True)
In [18]: ds.write_dataset(table, root, format='parquet')
```

This will write a single file named part-0.parquet to the directory specified. If you want to name it differently, then you can pass the basename_template keyword argument with a string describing the template for the filenames. The syntax for this template is pretty simple; it's just a string containing {i} in it. The {i} characters will be replaced by an integer that will increment automatically as files get written based on the other options, such as the partition configuration and maximum file sizes. The write_dataset function will automatically partition data for you if you pass the same partitioning option as we did for reading:

```
In [19]: part = ds.partitioning(pa.schema([('foobar', pa.int16())]),
    ... : flavor='hive')
In [20]: ds.write_dataset(table, root, format='parquet',
    ... : partitioning=part)
```

It will automatically create directories for the partitions and write the data, accordingly, using the same `basename_template` option that can be passed when writing a single table to name the individual files of each partition. All of this functionality is, of course, also available from the C++ library:

```cpp
auto dataset = std::make_shared<ds::InMemoryDataset>(table);
auto scanner_builder = dataset->NewScan().ValueOrDie();
auto scanner = scanner_builder->Finish().ValueOrDie();
auto format = std::make_shared<ds::ParquetFileFormat>();


ds::FileSystemDatasetWriteOptions write_opts;
write_opts.file_write_options = format->DefaultWriteOptions();
write_opts.filesystem = filesystem;
write_opts.base_dir = base_path;
write_opts.partitioning = std::make_
shared<ds::HivePartitioning>(
    arrow::schema({arrow::field("year", arrow::uint16()),
                   arrow::field("month", arrow::int8())})
);


write_opts.basename_template = "part{i}.parquet";
ABORT_ON_FAIL(ds::FileSystemDataset::Write(write_opts,
scanner));
```

Did you notice that the `Write` function takes a `scanner`? Can you think of why that might be the case?

We're talking about potentially very large datasets, larger than can fit into memory at one time. Because the `Write` function takes `scanner` as a parameter, you can very easily stream data to the writer from a scanner. That scanner could be configured using filters and projection to customize the record batch stream that you're writing. The Python version of the dataset writer can also take a scanner as the first argument instead of a table.

We can also write our dataset in different formats than just Parquet and combine it with filtering our data. For example, we could write out a portion of the taxi dataset as CSV files with just the following code changes from the previous example.

Just like before, we call `fs::InitializeS3` and create `FilesystemDatasetFactory` with the partition options, file selector, and format. However, this time we're going to add some options to control how it infers the schema. We mentioned `InspectOptions` back in the *Discovering dataset fragments* section, talking about discovering the schema. By default, the factory will only read one fragment to determine the schema of the dataset.

At the start of this *Working with partitioned datasets* section, we printed out the schema to see the addition of the `year` and `month` fields. If you run that code snippet again, take note of the type of the field named `rate_code_id`:

```
...
rate_code_id: null
...
```

This is the schema that was inferred by only reading the first fragment. Now, let's add the necessary options to inspect all the fragments and validate the schemas by adding the highlighted lines:

```
auto factory = ds::FileSystemDatasetFactory::Make(
        filesystem, selector,
        format, options).ValueOrDie();
ds::FinishOptions finish_options;
finish_options.validate_fragments = true;
finish_options.inspect_options.fragments =
            ds::InspectOptions::kInspectAllFragments;
auto dataset = factory->Finish(finish_options);
```

By setting the options to both inspect all the fragments and validate them, the factory will compose a common schema if it is possible. When we now print out the dataset's schema, note the `rate_code_id` field again:

```
...
rate_code_id: string
...
```

`DatasetFactory` inspected all the fragments and created a combined schema. Some of the fragments have the `rate_code_id` field as type `null`, and others have it as type `string`. Since we can trivially cast from a `null` type to a `string` array consisting of only `null` values, it's a valid combined schema to identify it as a `string` column. If you tried processing this dataset in its entirety before this, you may have encountered an error that looks like this:

Unsupported cast from string to null using function cast_null

This makes sense if you think about it. If our dataset's schema has a `null` type for the column, when we encounter a fragment with type `string` for this column, it attempts to cast the values. While we can easily cast a `null` array to a `string` array consisting entirely of `null` values, it's invalid to do the reverse: casting a `string` array with values to a `null` array. By taking the time to inspect our fragments and generate the combined schema, we fix this problem! Now, to write our data out as CSV files, all we need to do is use `CsvFileFormat`:

```
auto format = std::make_shared<ds::CsvFileFormat>();
ds::FileSystemDatasetWriteOptions write_opts;
auto csv_write_options =
    std::static_pointer_cast<ds::CsvFileWriteOptions>(
        format->DefaultWriteOptions());
csv_write_options->write_options->delimiter = '|';
write_opts.file_write_options = csv_write_options;
...
ABORT_ON_FAIL(ds::FileSystemDataset::Write(write_opts,
scanner));
```

Note the highlighted lines. After we create our default options using the `CsvFileFormat` class, we can set various options, such as the delimiter to use when writing. In this case, we write our data as pipe-delimited files. The same holds true for using `IpcFileFormat` or `OrcFileFormat` to write data in those respective data formats.

> **An Exercise for You**
>
> Write a function that repartitions a large dataset without pulling the entirety of the data into memory at one time. Try it in C++ and/or in Python to familiarize yourself with writing datasets. Play around with the batch sizes and other options to see how you can tweak it for performance.

Finally, the dataset writer also provides hooks that can be customized to allow inspecting and customizing the files that are written. In Python, you can provide a `file_visitor` function that takes in the written file as an argument to the `write_dataset` function. In C++, the `FileSystemDatasetWriteOptions` object has two members, `writer_pre_finish` and `writer_post_finish`, which are each a lambda function that takes a pointer to `FileWriter` and is called before and after each `FileWriter` finalizes a file.

> **Another Exercise for You to Try**
>
> Try writing a partitioned dataset and constructing an index of the files written and some metadata about them using the exposed `write` hooks via the `file_visitor` or `writer_pre_finish`/`writer_post_finish` functions.

There's a wealth of options that exist for datasets, ranging from the different file formats to using `UnionDataset` to interact with multiple physical datasets compiled into one interface. You can also manipulate the file format objects to set format-specific options for your reads and writes. Whether you're reading, writing, or using partitioned or non-partitioned data, the Datasets API is an extremely useful building block for many use cases. It's also particularly nice for ad hoc exploration of very large datasets, providing a huge amount of flexibility in how you can choose to interact with it and combine it with the Compute API and other Arrow usage. Go try out combining different ways of computing and manipulating data in huge datasets using these APIs before you move on. Seriously, do it! It's fun!

Summary

By composing these various pieces together (the C Data API, Compute API, and Datasets API), and gluing infrastructure on top, anyone should be able to create a rudimentary query and analysis engine that is fairly performant right away. The functionality provided allows for abstracting away a lot of the tedious work for interacting with different file formats and handling different location sources of data, to provide a single interface that allows you to get right to work in building the specific logic you need. Once again, it's the fact that all these things are built on top of Arrow as an underlying format, which is particularly efficient for these operations, that allows them to all be so easily interoperable.

So, where do we go from here?

Well, you might remember in *Chapter 3, Data Science with Apache Arrow*, when discussing **Open Database Connectivity** (**ODBC**), I alluded to the idea of something that might be able to replace ODBC and JDBC as universal protocols for interacting with databases. Armed with everything you've learned so far, we're going to look at building distributed systems using Apache Arrow next.

The next chapter is *Chapter 8, Exploring Apache Arrow Flight RPC*. The Arrow Flight protocol is a highly efficient way to pass data across the network, utilizing Arrow's IPC format as the primary data format. Over the course of the next chapter, we're going to build a Flight server and client for passing data back and forth in a customizable way. Hold on to your keyboards, this is going to be fun…

OK, well at least I think it's fun. Hopefully, you do too!

8
Exploring Apache Arrow Flight RPC

Distributed systems have always interested me. A distributed system is like a really good puzzle – immensely satisfying once you figure out how all the pieces fit together to achieve your goal. If you're not familiar with the term, a distributed system is simply a situation where you have various components of a system spread across multiple machines on a network. The idea is to split up the work and coordinate efforts among the components to complete tasks more efficiently. A great example would be **Apache Spark**, which we covered back in *Chapter 3, Data Science with Apache Arrow*.

The goal of distributed systems is generally to provide a robust, scalable, and reliable conglomeration of components that efficiently perform operations by distributing work across a system. This often means large amounts of data flowing between various components so that the data can get processed, manipulated or otherwise operated on. When it comes to Apache Arrow-formatted data, the Arrow project provides a **Remote Procedure Call** (**RPC**) framework for creating high-performance services that accept and return Arrow data called **Arrow Flight**.

By the end of this chapter, you will be able to do the following:

- Understand the technologies that Arrow Flight is built on top of and why they were chosen

- Understand the basic structure of the Flight protocol and how data flows when using it

- Create a simple Arrow Flight server and client for sending/requesting data

- Understand what **Flight SQL** is and why **ODBC** and **JDBC** were superseded by Arrow

Technical requirements

After we go through the explanations and definitions, we're going to create an Arrow Flight server and client together. You might also want to try replicating the results of some performance testing too. To do this, you'll need the following:

- An internet-connected computer

- The usual suspects for your language of choice:

  - Go 1.16+

  - Python 3.x with the `pyarrow` module installed

  - Your preferred IDE

- (Optionally) Docker installed on your machine:

  - Docker Desktop if on Windows.

  - See the Apache Spark section of *Chapter 3*, *Data Science with Apache Arrow*, for instructions on installing Docker.

The basics and complications of gRPC

Arrow Flight is built on two things:

- The Arrow IPC format (which we covered in *Chapter 4*, *Format and Memory Handling*)

- **gRPC** (`https://grpc.io`), an open source **remote procedure call** (RPC) framework built on top of Protocol Buffers for high-performance services

Since we've already covered the Arrow IPC format, let's first quickly look at what gRPC is and how to use it. To do that, we need to talk about APIs.

Building modern APIs for data

We've used the word API a lot already in this book, and most of you are likely at least already conceptually familiar with the idea of an API, but let's quickly define what we're talking about.

While the term **Application Programming Interface** (**API**) has been around since at least the 1960s, the scope of what it refers to has broadened considerably. Initially, it was used solely to describe an end user-facing interface, at the time just called *application programs* – hence the meaning, *application programming interface*. Over time, it began to refer to interfaces for all types of software, not just end user applications. At its core, an API is a contract of abstractions that hide underlying implementations and only exposes what is necessary to interact with a system, library, or otherwise.

As computer networks became more ubiquitous, engineers wanted to call functions not only on their local machine but on other computers located somewhere else. The term *remote procedure call* is generally seen as being coined in the early 1980s, even though the concept itself had been around for quite some time at that point. A **remote procedure call** is simply calling a procedure (function) that will execute outside of a process. An RPC framework allows the call to be made without an engineer having to code all the details of the remote interaction. *Figure 8.1* shows a model of a simple RPC server and client with the request<->response style acting as function calls:

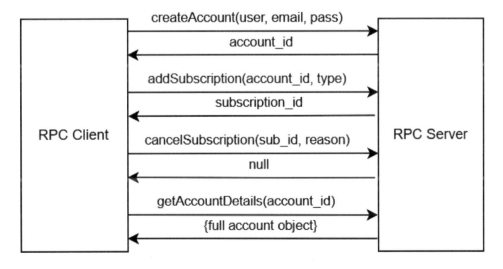

Figure 8.1 – An RPC model

Yay, history! Anyway, in 2000, one of the primary authors of the **Hypertext Transfer Protocol** (**HTTP**) specification, Roy Fielding, outlined the concept of *"network-based"* APIs as a different type of interface from traditional *"library-based"* APIs. He coined the term **Representational State Transfer** (**REST**) to describe this type of interface. REST would go on to become the dominant style of building web-based APIs across the industry and is still the most common type of service API you'll come across at the time of writing. An API that meets the constraints defined by REST is colloquially referred to as being a *RESTful* API. As with almost everything when it comes to software, there are continuous debates over the question of whether a RESTful-style API is better than a gRPC API. *Figure 8.2* shows a model of a RESTful API, using the HTTP request verbs for semantic meaning:

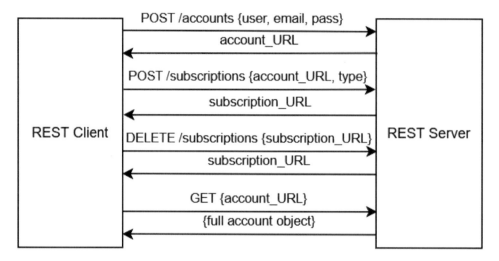

Figure 8.2 – A RESTful model

The answer is, of course, *it depends*. But what's important to understand is why Arrow Flight uses gRPC as its framework. Let's look at what makes gRPC different from *traditional* RESTful APIs.

Efficiency and streaming are important

When it comes to the mechanics and usage of RESTful APIs versus using gRPC, there are a few significant differences that had an impact on the development and usage of APIs. These differences explain why gRPC was chosen for Arrow Flight:

- The message format
- Code generation
- Network usage and support

Message formats

When choosing a message format for their API, most RESTful services end up opting to use JSON or XML. This is because these formats are flexible, human-readable, and platform-agnostic, and almost every programming language has libraries for reading and writing both formats. The problem is that these formats are very verbose, and if you're trying to transfer a large amount of data between systems, you get bogged down by the size of the messages and the cost to serialize and deserialize them.

> **Remember**
>
> This isn't the first time we've mentioned Protocol Buffers! We also talked about it briefly back in *Chapter 4, Format and Memory Handling*.

By contrast, gRPC uses Protocol Buffers as its message format. Like JSON or XML, Protocol Buffers is platform- and language-agnostic. Being a binary format though, it trades human readability for being much more compressed, resulting in significantly smaller messages. Protobuf is a lightweight messaging format consisting of an **Interface Description Language** (**IDL**) and a compiler that generates code for serialization and deserialization of messages in a chosen language. Unlike JSON or XML, the message definitions for Protobuf are strictly typed, so it can focus strictly on serialization and deserialization. This results in making data transmission much faster, as you have much fewer bytes you need to send across the network. In addition, being a binary format, it is much easier to pass Arrow-formatted data as part of a request or response using Protobuf. For JSON or XML, you would have to encode data using `base64` encoding to make it safe, or you'd need to send the Arrow data as an entirely separate message.

Code generation

Okay, let's say you're a developer and you're presented with an API specification and are told that you need to use it to request the data you need. How does the choice of framework affect this task?

If the service you're requesting from is a RESTful service, you will likely use an external utility such as **Swagger** to generate some boilerplate client code in your language of choice. In a polyglot environment that has utilities, clients, and services in multiple different programming languages, you'd have to rely on these external tools or build your own to reduce the boilerplate necessary for creating services and clients.

When creating a server or client using gRPC, you use the same `protoc` compiler that is used to generate code for utilizing Protocol Buffer messages in the first place. Even if there isn't a ready-made Arrow Flight server or client for your particular language or environment, you can easily use the protocol specification to generate bindings and get something usable up and running very quickly.

Network usage and support

This is where things get complicated. Typically, most REST APIs are built on the HTTP/1.0 or HTTP/1.1 protocols, while gRPC boosts its efficiency by using the HTTP/2 protocol. Even though version 2.0 of the HTTP specification was standardized and released in 2015, with more than 95% of browsers currently supporting it, it's not as prevalent as it could be when it comes to service infrastructure. There are two big features of HTTP/2 that gRPC takes advantage of that make it advantageous – multiplexing and bidirectional streaming connections.

With HTTP version 1, it was only possible to parallelize requests by making simultaneous, separate requests to a server. This creates two problems – resource usage and the head-of-line blocking problem. The resource usage problem is obvious; since parallelizing requires multiple simultaneous requests, multiple connections are needed to perform this. The head-of-line blocking issue happens when the maximum number of parallel requests that the browser (or any HTTP client) can handle are in use, and subsequent requests need to wait for the previous ones to complete before they can run. It can also happen on the server side when the maximum number of simultaneous connections is reached, and subsequent requests must wait for the server to complete current requests before they can be processed. HTTP version 2 uses multiplexing of multiple requests across the same connection to address this problem. With multiplexing, a single client can make many parallel requests using only a single connection.

HTTP version 2 also introduced new streaming mechanisms using the bidirectional communication it provides. As a result, gRPC provides four types of requests:

- **Unary**: Similar to traditional HTTP 1.1, the client sends one request and the server sends one response.

- **Server-side streaming**: The client sends one request, and the server sends back a stream of responses. After sending the last response, the server sends a status message and, possibly, trailing metadata, completing the request.

- **Client-side streaming**: The client sends a stream of messages to the server, and the server sends one response back to the client, usually after receiving all of the request messages from the client, along with a status message and, possibly, trailing metadata.

- **Bidirectional streaming**: The server and client send messages to each other in no special order. The client initiates this connection and is also the one that ends the connection.

With gRPC explained, we can move on to explaining the Arrow Flight protocol now. Because of the usage of Protocol Buffers with gRPC, this isn't too difficult; we can just walk through the definitions in the `.proto` file!

Arrow Flight's building blocks

Because the methods and message wire format of Arrow Flight are both defined by Protocol Buffers, clients that may support gRPC and Arrow but not Flight are able to easily still interact with, and communicate with, Arrow Flight servers. There are also specific Flight implementations provided by the Apache Arrow project for some languages. These implementations include optimizations to avoid overhead, such as reducing excessive memory copying when using Protocol Buffers. Because the Protocol Buffer objects are only used for passing metadata, Flight still maintains the benefits of Arrow's IPC protocol, allowing zero-deserialization to ensure fast delivery of data.

Here are the basic types of requests that a Flight server implements:

- `Handshake`: A simple request allowing for custom authentication logic and an implementation-defined session token if desired.
- `ListFlights`: Gets a list of the available data streams on the server.
- `GetSchema`: Retrieves the schema for a specific data stream.
- `GetFlightInfo`: Retrieves a *"plan"* for a specific dataset, potentially describing the consumption of multiple streams of data. This request allows for custom serialized commands and metadata such as a server's particular application parameters.
- `DoGet`: Retrieves a data stream.
- `DoPut`: Receives a data stream from the client to do something with.
- `ListActions`: Retrieves the list of available implementation-defined action types.
- `DoAction`: Performs a specified implementation-defined action and returns any results, such as general RPC function calls.
- `DoExchange`: Opens a bidirectional stream between the server and client for both sending and receiving Arrow data along with metadata. This is particularly useful for offloading computation.

Using the basic requests, a simple flight request pattern might look like *Figure 8.3*, optionally preceded by a call using the Handshake method:

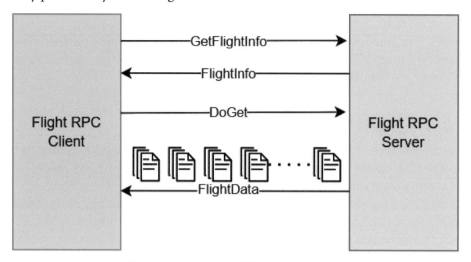

Figure 8.3 – A simple flight request pattern

For a simple dataset, or a simple request, this is really straightforward and simple to understand. But what about scalability?

Horizontal scalability with Arrow Flight

Dealing with distributed database-like systems has become increasingly common with modern data workflows. The majority of these distributed systems utilize a similar architectural pattern:

1. Requests are first routed through a coordinator node and then distributed out to worker nodes.

2. The coordinator node then gathers up all the fragments of the results from the worker nodes and sends them back to the client.

If you're trying to access a very large dataset, the data is ultimately being transported multiple times between different nodes on its way to the client. In addition, you're going to be limited by the throughput of that coordinator node in terms of how fast you can get access to all of the data. This is why the GetFlightInfo method returns a list of endpoint objects. Each endpoint object contains a location and a Ticket object, describing the server to send a DoGet request with Ticket in order to retrieve a portion of the dataset. To get the whole dataset, you just need to consume all of the endpoints.

This pattern allows you to potentially split up and delegate the responsibilities of nodes in a service. *Figure 8.4* shows a potential architecture for this kind of service:

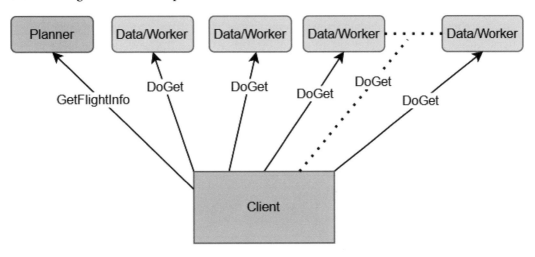

Figure 8.4 – A split-role flight architecture

In addition to having a distributed server for delegating the responsibility of serving data, we can also have a distributed client! For example, Spark can use Arrow Flight to request data from a server and then consume the results in parallel from multiple server nodes to multiple Spark workers. This is shown in *Figure 8.5*:

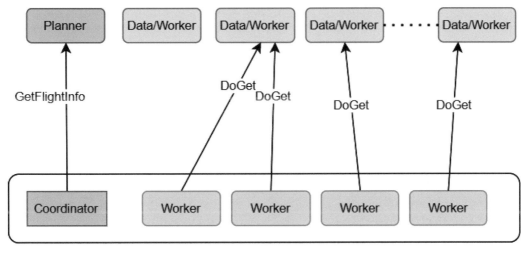

Figure 8.5 – The distributed client and server

One other use for this pattern of using `GetFlightInfo` to return a list of endpoints to consume data is handling geographically distributed servers. As is often the case with modern data networks, the same data might be available in multiple locations to enable lower-latency access to the data from different areas of the world or a caching layer. In this situation, the coordinator can return endpoints with multiple locations to allow a consumer to choose the location that is most suitable. In *Figure 8.6*, the server offers the client locations in a US region and a region in Germany, and the client chooses their preferred location:

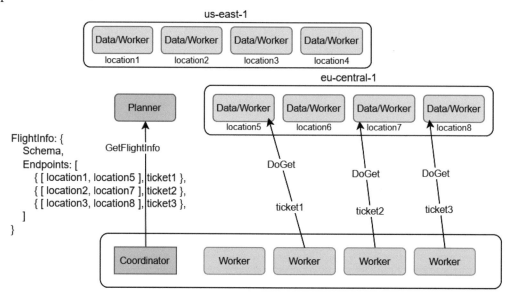

Figure 8.6 – Geographical distribution

So, we've covered the data transfer portion. But what about arbitrary business logic? Most services aren't just simple data retrieval via some serialized request, but also often need to expose other information or functionality beyond just the data fetching. Arrow Flight provides `Action` messages for this, along with adding application-defined metadata to the data messages.

Adding your business logic to Flight

Maybe a client wants to set some kind of session-specific parameter, or maybe they want to request a particular dataset to be kept in memory as a cache for future requests. Either way, there will be a need for logic above and beyond the serialized request itself. The easiest way this is exposed and managed using Arrow Flight is through the `DoAction` method. This method accepts an arbitrarily named action and optional binary data that can be interpreted in any way you want when implementing the server. This data can be strings, serialized in some way, or even the raw binary of an amusing image – whatever you want.

> **Note**
>
> It is not required for Flight servers to implement any actions, nor is it required for an action to return any results. This is all application-defined and customizable as needed. Just ensure that your Flight server exposes the actions it supports with the `ListActions` method; it's just good design.

When data is returned from a Flight server with the `FlightData` structure, there is an attribute set aside for opaque application-defined metadata. This means that every individual data message, typically a whole record batch, can potentially include arbitrary information with it that your application can define the format of. This data is exposed by the Flight objects but is otherwise ignored by the Flight implementations, allowing for it to be used in whatever fashion you want when building a client or server. When we get to the examples and exercises later in the *Using Flight, choose your language!* section, you'll see this in action.

With all this complexity, you might be wondering why you would use Flight instead of just building your own Arrow-based client and server. Ultimately, the answer is *interoperability*. By using Flight, you can leverage the existing Arrow libraries and utilities built on top, instead of having to build things yourself. Not only that, but you don't have to necessarily construct custom clients for your API! It makes your service easily interoperable with all existing Arrow Flight libraries and utilities. Using Arrow Flight, you can build out a series of microservices, all communicating using Flight RPC, and easily integrate them with other existing Flight services – essentially, all of the benefits of using a standardized API and infrastructure.

By using gRPC as the underlying technology, Flight also inherits several nice benefits by way of various useful features that are already implemented in gRPC, such as encryption, middleware, and tracing. We will discuss these features in the following section.

Other bells and whistles

Out of the box, gRPC supports TLS/OpenSSL for encryption. As a result, Flight gets all of that support for free by just using gRPC's implementations of encryption. Because the `Handshake` function is generalized as a bidirectional streaming function, it's easy to implement custom authentication schemes with Flight and most of the libraries provide extensible authentication handlers. For simple cases, the Flight Protocol Buffer definition already comes with a `BasicAuth` object, for implementing simple user and password authentication without much custom development needed.

You can also instrument "middleware" for custom wrapping and logic surrounding incoming and outgoing messages in gRPC using the existing concept of "interceptors." A common usage of this is to implement frameworks for distributed tracing such as **OpenTracing**, which has become so common that many languages that support gRPC already have open source interceptors for supporting the `OpenTracing` protocol. Once again, since this is something built-in for gRPC, Flight servers and clients can benefit from this automatically.

Musings on Handling State

Authentication is tricky to do properly. While the `Handshake` protocol with Flight is an easy way to implement custom authentication handshakes, it is likely more scalable to utilize header-based authentication methods. Because gRPC is built on HTTP/2, it allows you to use HTTP headers such as **bearer tokens** and **cookies**. This means that all the current stateless header-based authentication approaches can still be used with Arrow Flight. Why stateless? Because it scales better! Since the Flight server itself doesn't need to retain state information between calls, any request can hit any instance of the service without issue. For cases where state can be important or otherwise useful, headers and middleware can be leveraged. For example, middleware can be built that converts local state into headers that can be injected into requests. Even if you do utilize the `Handshake` method to perform authentication, do your best to ensure that the resulting authentication token can be validated in a stateless manner.

Before we start doing some examples and exercises, let's just quickly run through the Protocol Buffer definitions for Flight. It's significantly easier to work with Flight when you understand the objects and pieces that make it up first.

Understanding the Flight Protocol Buffer definitions

Let's look at the various message types in the Arrow Flight protocol. For readability purposes, I'm going to use pseudo-code, leaving out some of the Protocol Buffer trappings to better explain the object types. Feel free to go to the Arrow GitHub repository (`https://github.com/apache/arrow`) to look at the full `.proto` file yourself if you like:

- For performing handshakes, we have the `HandshakeRequest`, `HandshakeResponse`, and `BasicAuth` objects. The protocol version can be application-defined to enable progressive evolution of authentication schemes and backward compatibility for your service:

```
message HandshakeRequest {
    // some defined protocol version
```

```
        uint64 protocol_version
        // arbitrary data for authentication/handshake
        bytes payload
    }

    message HandshakeResponse {
        // some defined protocol version
        uint64 protocol_version
        // arbitrary data for authentication/handshake
        bytes payload
    }

    message BasicAuth {
        string username
        string password
    }
```

Note that the request and response objects use an arbitrary `payload` attribute, which is just an array of bytes. Because the `Handshake` method is a bidirectional streaming method, it allows you to implement any arbitrary authentication scheme as needed.

- For the `ListActions` and `DoAction` methods, we have objects named `Empty`, `Action`, `Result`, and `ActionType`. The accurately named `Empty` object is a placeholder parameter in the `ListActions` method, as it doesn't currently take any parameters, so it has no attributes:

```
    message Empty {}

    // describes an available Action
    message ActionType {
        string type
        string description
    }

    // A request to perform an action
    message Action {
        string type
        // arbitrary bytes for using this action
```

```
        bytes body
    }


    // Result from performing an action
    message Result {
        bytes body
    }
```

Once again, note that data used to call an action and data that is returned from an action are both arbitrary byte arrays. The data used is going to be application-defined, allowing for whatever functionality is needed.

- To identify particular datasets using `ListFlights` and `GetFlightInfo`, we have two other object types – `Criteria` and `FlightDescriptor`:

```
    // used for ListFlights to filter the list of flights
    returned
    message Criteria {
        // service specified arbitrary bytes
        bytes expression
    }


    // a way to identify a specific dataset
    message FlightDescriptor {
        enum DescriptorType {
            // Protobuf Pattern, Not used
            UNKNOWN
            // named path to identify a dataset, conceptually
            // similar to a file system path
            PATH
            // arbitrary command bytes
            CMD
        }

        DescriptorType type
        // if using CMD, place opaque command bytes here
        bytes cmd
        // if using PATH, provide list of strings to identify
        // the dataset
```

```
        string[] path
    }
```

- Part of describing datasets also includes retrieving the schema of those datasets via the GetSchema method. This returns a SchemaResult object, defined like so:

```
message SchemaResult {
    // The schema of the dataset in the IPC form
    //   4 bytes - optional IPC_CONTINUATION_TOKEN prefix
    //   4 bytes - 32-bit integer representing the
    //      byte length of the payload
    //   a flatbuffer Message whose header is the Schema
    // equivalent of a recordbatch with no rows in IPC form
    bytes schema
}
```

- When calling the GetFlightInfo method, the message returned explains how to retrieve data by providing a FlightInfo object:

```
// provides enough information to retrieve a dataset
message FlightInfo {
    // format is the same as in SchemaResult
    bytes schema
    // list of endpoints for the dataset. All endpoints
    // must be consumed to get the entire dataset
    FlightEndpoint[] endpoint
    // if unknown, value will be -1
    int64 total_records
    int64 total_bytes
}
```

- Next is the FlightEndpoint message definition, containing Location and Ticket, used for sending a DoGet request:

```
message FlightEndpoint {
    // token used to retrieve the stream
    Ticket ticket
    // a list of URIs where this ticket can be redeemed
    // via DoGet.
```

```
        // If the list is empty, it's expected this can only
        // be redeemed at the service where the ticket was
    generated.
        // if the list is not empty, the ticket can be
        // redeemed at any of the locations. Essentially
        // an application can use multiple locations to
        // represent redundant and/or load balanced services
        Location[] location
    }


    // full URI including the scheme of the server to
    // send a DoGet or DoPut request to
    message Location {
        string uri
    }


    // Opaque arbitrary bytes for the service to use for
    // identifying a particular stream of data to send
    message Ticket {
        bytes ticket
    }
```

- Finally, we have the data itself for use with the DoGet, DoPut, and DoExchange methods. The objects used are FlightData and PutResult:

```
    // a single batch of Arrow data from a stream of batches
    message FlightData {
        // descriptor, only relevant for DoPut
        FlightDescriptor flight_descriptor
        // flatbuffer message header for data
        bytes data_header
        // application-defined arbitrary metadata
        bytes app_metadata
        // raw body buffer bytes of Arrow data
        bytes data_body
    }

    message PutResult {
```

```
                    // arbitrary application-defined metadata
                    bytes app_metadata
        }
```

The message objects referenced in the preceding section are all the primitive objects for defining the Flight RPC interface. It might seem like a lot, but these primitives make Flight very versatile for a multitude of use cases. With that out of the way, we can start crafting some clients and servers to get a feel for how Flight works.

Using Flight, choose your language!

All three of the languages we've been using in this book, Python, C++, and Go, provide implementations of Arrow Flight servers and clients. The examples we're going to walk through here are a great way to flex your chops on the different languages and see the similarities and differences between the different languages and the interfaces of their implementations. The Arrow project takes advantage of this interoperability between languages for Flight to run automated integration tests between the different language libraries and ensure that they are all compatible with each other.

So, let's get right down to it and have some fun!

Building a Python Flight Server

The `flight` module of the `pyarrow` library provides a base implementation of a Flight server; all that needs to be done is to override the functions for the desired Flight RPC methods you want to implement on your server, and away you go. Let's give it a shot and write a Python script we can run:

1. First, let's get our imports:

    ```
    import pyarrow as pa
    from pyarrow import fs
    import pyarrow.parquet as pq
    import pyarrow.flight as flight
    ```

2. Let's implement the `ListFlights` function and have it return the files from the public `ursa-labs-taxi-data` S3 bucket that we were using previously for the exercises with the Dataset API:

    I. First, we make a class definition and initialize our `S3FileSystem` object:

    ```
    class Server(flight.FlightServerBase):
        def __init__(self, *args, **kwargs):
    ```

```
# forward any arguments for now
super().__init__(*args, **kwargs)
self._s3 = fs.S3FileSystem(region='us-east-2',
                            anonymous=True)
```

II. We'll start the `list_flights` method by checking any criteria to filter the files by and then getting the details about the files from S3:

```
def list_flights(self, context, criteria):
    path = 'ursa-labs-taxi-data'
    if len(criteria) > 0: # use criteria as start path
        path += '/' + criteria.decode('utf8')
    flist = self._s3.get_file_info(
                fs.FileSelector(path, recursive=True))
```

III. Then, we loop through the file list, reading the metadata of each Parquet file and using the Python `yield` keyword to iteratively stream the `FlightInfo` objects to the caller:

```
for finfo in flist:
    if finfo.type == fs.FileType.Directory:
        continue
    with self._s3.open_input_file(finfo.path) as
f:
        data = pq.ParquetFile(f, pre_buffer=True)
        yield flight.FlightInfo(
            data.schema_arrow, # the arrow schema
            flight.FlightDescriptor.for_
path(finfo.path),
            [], # no endpoints provided
            data.metadata.num_rows,
            -1
        )
```

What do you think? Not too bad, right? I've highlighted the key relevant lines of code for setting the server up – first, inheriting from the base server implementation and creating the __init__ function, which calls the base implementation's __init__ function. The base server implementation allows a few arguments such as the location to serve on, defaulting to a localhost and a random port, an authentication handler, middleware, and security certificates. These can all be investigated in the official documentation; for now, we're just going to pass the arguments through.

The library infrastructure handles the serialization and deserialization of the Protocol Buffer objects, so the criteria parameter is an instance of a Python bytes object. Therefore, we can decide that our protocol will be to have the criteria as a string path, and we decode it as a UTF-8 string. In a production setting, we'd probably want some more error checking though.

We use the same code we've used before to get a list of the files, and for each one, we yield a FlightInfo object.

3. At this point, we have a fully functional Flight server; all we need to do is create an instance of our Server class and call the serve function. We can easily add some simple code to construct a client and test our server:

```
if __name__ == '__main__':
    with Server() as server:
        client = flight.connect(('localhost', 'server.port'))
        for f in client.list_flights(b'2009'):
            print(f.descriptor.path, f.total_records)
```

Then, we can just run this file and see it in action:

```
$ python server.py
```

Let's make our server a bit more useful; let's implement a DoGet method for retrieving streams of record batches for some of these files. Starting with what we wrote for the previous example, we're just going to add a new function:

```
def do_get(self, context, ticket):
    in = self._s3.open_input_file(ticket.ticket.
decode('utf8'))
    pf = pq.ParquetFile(in, pre_buffer=True)
    def gen():
        try:
            for batch in pf.iter_batches():
```

```
        yield batch
    finally:
        in.close() # make sure we always close the file
return flight.GeneratorStream(pf.schema_arrow, gen())
```

Are you able to figure out what's going on here? It's not too bad, right? Remember, since the ticket is an arbitrary byte array, we need to manually decode it back to a string, since we decided to just use the path as the ticket. Then, we open the file in S3 and create a generator to iterate the record batches, passing them to the stream as we read them in. We could have instead just read the whole file in and returned that table using `flight.RecordBatchStream`, but that would require us to have the entire file in memory at one time.

Also, because we're reading entirely from S3 each time, we are limiting our potential performance. S3 becomes a bottleneck for this very simple implementation, so while it's a useful toy, it's not really indicative of Flight's performance just yet. In a production scenario, you'd have various layers of caching involved so that we wouldn't be going back to S3 for every read.

To verify that it works, we just want to add a couple of other lines:

1. First, let's modify our `list_flights` function from earlier and send back the ticket with our `FlightInfo` objects:

    ```
        . . .
                    yield flight.FlightInfo(
                        data.schema_arrow, # the arrow schema
                        flight.FlightDescriptor.for_
    path(finfo.path),
                        [flight.FlightEndpoint(finfo.path,
    [])],
                        data.metadata.num_rows,
                        -1
                    )
        . . .
    ```

2. Then, we modify our main function to pick a flight from the list and request it with the `do_get` method:

    ```
        . . .
            flights = list(client.list_flights(b'2009'))
            data = client.do_get(flights[0].endpoints[0].
    ```

```
    ticket)
            print(data.read_all())
```

In this case, we're reading in the whole table of data using the `read_all` method on the stream reader. Instead, we could iterate the stream by calling the `read_chunk` method in a loop, which would raise a `StopIteration` exception when you hit the end of the stream. Alternatively, we could call the `to_reader` method and convert the stream to a regular `RecordBatchReader` to pass it to other functions or workflows. It's very versatile.

As you can also see, managing a Flight client wasn't difficult at all either. We just fed it the hostname and port to connect to, and then we were able to call the methods we wanted. Try playing around with other implementations or ways to pass information through the various methods before moving on to the next section! Experiment! Now, let's move on to the next language!

Building a Go Flight server

My assumption was that Python would likely be the most common and well known of the languages I'm covering among the readers of this book. Now that we've got that out of the way, when considering an Arrow Flight server, let's take a look at creating a Flight server using Go. This is something near and dear to me, as I've contributed quite a lot to the official Apache Arrow Go library. We'll create the same functionality that we built using Python for our Go example.

Sketching out the skeleton

For handling the interactions with S3, I've provided a small wrapper object in the GitHub repository under the `utils` directory. It's not a complex piece of code; it just simplifies the usage of the AWS SDK, wrapping the S3 client to provide the `Reader`, `Seeker`, and `ReaderAt` interfaces. With that said, let's put together all of our imports:

```
package main

import (
    ...
    "github.com/apache/arrow/go/v8/arrow"
    "github.com/apache/arrow/go/v8/arrow/flight"
    "github.com/apache/arrow/go/v8/arrow/memory"
    "github.com/apache/arrow/go/v8/arrow/ipc"
    "github.com/apache/arrow/go/v8/parquet/file"
```

```
    "github.com/apache/arrow/go/v8/parquet/pqarrow"
    "github.com/aws/aws-sdk-go-v2/service/s3"
    "google.golang.org/grpc"
    "google.golang.org/grpc/credentials/insecure"
    "github.com/PacktPublishing/In-Memory-Analytics-with-
Apache-Arrow-/utils"

    . . .

)
```

Your Eyes Don't Deceive You!

Yes, the imports in the Go code snippet do indeed say v8 on them instead of v7. While writing this chapter, I decided that I would improve and simplify the Arrow Flight interfaces for the Go version of the Arrow libraries. As a result, I made new contributions to the library that were released with v8 of the module. We're going to use the v8 import paths from now on.

As we continue to build the server, more imports will get utilized and added. If you're using an IDE such as Visual Studio Code, it can automatically add those imports for you. However, I'll still mention it whenever we're going to need to add an import I didn't mention previously. For now, let's create the skeleton of our server. We need `struct`, which embeds the `flight.BaseFlightServer` object and implements the functions we want to provide:

```
type server struct {
    flight.BaseFlightServer
    s3Client *s3.Client
    bucket string
}


func NewServer() *server {
    return &server{
        s3Client: s3.New(s3.Options{Region: "us-east-2"},
        bucket: "ursa-labs-taxi-data",
    }
}
```

```
func (s *server) ListFlights(c *flight.Criteria, fs flight.
FlightService_ListFlightsServer) error {

    ...

    return nil
}


func (s *server) DoGet(tkt *flight.Ticket, fs flight.
FlightService_DoGetServer) error {

    ...

    return nil
}
```

I've helpfully highlighted the embedded base server, the call to create a client for S3, and the function signatures for our ListFlights and DoGet functions. Currently, the functions don't do anything, so they just return nil. With our new server object, let's create a main function to establish the server and run it:

```
func main() {
    srv := flight.NewServerWithMiddleware(nil)
    srv.Init("0.0.0.0:0")
    srv.RegisterFlightService(NewServer())
    // the Serve function doesn't return until the server
    // shuts down. For now we'll start it running in a goroutine
    // and shut the server down when our main ends.
    go srv.Serve()
    defer srv.Shutdown()

    ...
}
```

The highlighted line is where you specify the address that the server should be running on. In this case, we told the server to run locally on a random port it chooses by passing a 0 as the port number. Now that we have a server that can run, we can implement the methods for it to operate.

Implementing the ListFlights method

Since we're replicating the same logic we used for the Python server, we can implement the `ListFlights` function first. Just like before, we're going to get the list of Parquet files from S3 and then return a `FlightInfo` object for each one. We also want to use the expression from the `Criteria` argument if they passed one in, which we will assume is a string, as we did with the Python version:

1. First things first – let's get our list of files from S3 using the bucket and prefix we have:

    ```go
    func (s *server) ListFlights(c *flight.Criteria, fs
    flight.FlightService_ListFlightsServer) error {
        var prefix string
        if len(c.Expression) > 0 {
            prefix = string(c.Expression)
        }
        list, err := s.s3Client.ListObjectsV2(fs.Context(),
            &s3.ListObjectsV2Input{
                    Bucket: &s.bucket,
                    Prefix: &prefix,
            })
        if err != nil {
            return err
        }
        for _, f := range list.Contents {
            if !strings.HasSuffix(*f.Key, ".parquet") {
                continue
            }
            // do something with the file!
        }
        return nil
    }
    ```

    The first highlighted section is the call to the S3 library to get the list of objects in the bucket we wanted, using the prefix the user passed in (or an empty string if they did not). The second highlighted portion is where we're going to place the code to read the metadata from the file and get the equivalent Arrow schema to the Parquet file.

2. Now, let's make a helper function to get `FlightInfo` from the S3 filename. We could just put this code right in line, but it's better design and more readable if we make a small helper function instead. Remember, we need to return the `FlightInfo` objects to the caller as per the Flight RPC protocol:

```go
func (s *server) getFlightInfo(ctx context.Context, key
string, filesize int64) (*flight.FlightInfo, error) {
    s3file, err := utils.NewS3File(ctx, s.s3Client,
            s.bucket, key, filesize)
    if err != nil {
        return nil, err
    }


    pr, err := file.NewParquetReader(s3file)
    if err != nil {
        return nil, err
    }
    defer pr.Close()


    sc, err := pqarrow.FromParquet(pr.MetaData().Schema,
    nil, nil)
    if err != nil {
        return nil, err
    }


    return &flight.FlightInfo{
        Schema: flight.SerializeSchema(sc, memory.
        DefaultAllocator),
        FlightDescriptor: &flight.FlightDescriptor{
                Type: flight.DescriptorPATH,
                Path: []string{key},
        },
        Endpoint: []*flight.FlightEndpoint{{
            Ticket: &flight.Ticket{Ticket: []byte(key)},
        }},
        TotalRecords: pr.NumRows(),
        TotalBytes: -1,
    }, nil
}
```

Let's break this code down:

I. The first highlighted piece is where we use the S3 file utility to create a reader for the Parquet file in S3 using the server's S3 client.

II. Next, we pass that reader to the Parquet library to open the file, using `defer` to ensure that we close it after we're done.

III. Finally, we convert the Parquet schema to an equivalent Arrow schema so that we can construct the `FlightInfo` object.

3. Now, we can insert a call to our helper function into the `ListFlights` function to send the objects back as a stream:

```go
    ...
    for _, f := range list.Contents {
        if !strings.HasSuffix(*f.Key, ".parquet") {
            continue
        }
        info, err := s.getFlightInfo(fs.Context(), *f.Key,
        f.Size)
        if err != nil {
            return err
        }
        if err := fs.Send(info); err != nil {
            return err
        }
    }
    return nil
}
```

The highlighted code is the new code added to the `ListFlights` function to call our helper. Now, we can create a client and test it out!

4. In our `main` function, we can construct `FlightClient` and call our newly working `ListFlights`:

```go
func main() {
    ...
    client, err := flight.NewClientWithMiddleware(
        srv.Addr().String(), nil, nil,
        grpc.WithTransportCredentials(
            insecure.NewCredentials()))
```

```go
        if err != nil {
            panic(err) // handle the error
        }
        defer client.Close()

        infoStream, err := client.ListFlights(context.TODO(),
                &flight.Criteria{Expression: []byte("2009")})
        if err != nil {
            panic(err) // handle the error
        }

        for {
            info, err := infoStream.Recv()
            if err != nil {
                if err == io.EOF { // we hit the end of the
                stream
                        break
                }
                panic(err) // we got an error!
            }
            fmt.Println(info.GetFlightDescriptor().GetPath())
        }
```

Let's break this code down:

I.   We can interrogate the server object we created to get a string containing the address to connect to since we didn't give it a specific port number but let it choose one itself. This isn't a gRPC-specific thing but rather because using port 0 has special significance in most operating systems. It indicates that a suitable available port number should be searched for and used dynamically.

II. We're not using an authentication handler or any middleware, so all we need to do is pass a gRPC option that we're not using SSL and we can connect. Any desired gRPC options are able to be passed when constructing the client.

III. When we call ListFlights, it returns a stream that we can then use to retrieve each one of our FlightInfo objects.

IV. The last highlighted sections show that we just call the Recv method repeatedly in a loop until we get io.EOF, which indicates we hit the end of the stream.

That wasn't too complicated, right? Easy peasy! With the `ListFlights` method implemented and our main function updated to call and process the response, we can move on to fetching the actual data.

Implementing the DoGet method

Now, let's implement the `DoGet` function that will return the record batches of data from the Parquet files and have the client read them:

1. You already know how to open the file and get a reader for the Parquet file, so now, we just need to get the data from it in Arrow format. We create `pqarrow.FileReader`, which will provide a way to read the Parquet data directly into Arrow records, and then get `RecordReader` from it:

    ```go
    func (s *Server) DoGet(tkt *flight.Ticket, fs flight.
    FlightService_DoGetServer) error {
        path := string(tkt.Ticket)
        // open the file just like we did in ListFlights
        // pr will be the name of the file reader
        arrowRdr, err := pqarrow.NewFileReader(pr,
            pqarrow.ArrowReadProperties{
                Parallel: true, BatchSize: 100000,
            }, memory.DefaultAllocator)
        if err != nil {
            return err
        }
        rr, err := arrowRdr.GetRecordReader(fs.Context(), nil,
        nil)
        if err != nil {
            return err
        }
        defer rr.Release()
    ```

    When creating the file reader, we pass a set of properties to control how the data is read. We tell it to read the columns in parallel and give it a row batch size to use, reading 100,000 rows per record batch. Creating `RecordReader` allows you to fetch only a subset of the columns or row groups if desired, but since we want everything, we can pass `nil` for the default.

2. Now that we have something to read record batches from the Parquet file, we need something to write those record batches out to the client. We can create `RecordWriter` and then just copy all of the records from the reader to the writer by adding an import:

```
. . .
    // add these imports
    "fmt"
    "github.com/apache/arrow/go/v8/arrow/arrio"
. . .
```

Back inside the `DoGet` function, we just add the following:

```
    wr := flight.NewRecordWriter(fs,
                    ipc.WithSchema(rr.Schema()))
    defer wr.Close()

    n, err := arrio.Copy(wr, rr)
    fmt.Println("wrote", n, "record batches")
    return err
}
```

3. So now, we just need to have the client call the `DoGet` function and gather the record batches. Add the following to the `main` function:

```
stream, err := client.DoGet(context.TODO(), &flight.
Ticket{Ticket: []byte("2009/01/data.parquet")})
if err != nil {
    panic(err) // handle error
}

rr, err := flight.NewRecordReader(stream)
if err != nil {
    panic(err)
}
defer rr.Release()

records := make([]arrow.Record, 0)
for rr.Next() {
```

```
        rec := rr.Record()
        rec.Retain()
        defer rec.Release()
        records = append(records, rec)
    }


    fmt.Println("received", len(records), "record batches"))


    tbl := array.NewTableFromRecords(records[0].Schema(),
    records)
    defer tbl.Release()


    fmt.Println("total rows:", tbl.NumRows())
```

Let's break down the code snippet and explain the pieces:

I.   First, we call the `DoGet` function on the client. If your batch size on the server side is too large, it might end up trying to send messages that are too large. If that happens, you can add a gRPC option to the function call to set the maximum size to 10 megabytes: `grpc.MaxRecvMsgSizeCallOption{MaxRecvMsgSize: 1024 Gi '* 1024 * 10}`.

II. We then construct `RecordReader` from the stream for us to read the incoming record batches from. Don't forget to add `defer` to release it!

III. We can then create a slice to hold the records as they come in. When you get a reference to `Record` from the reader, if you want it to survive past the call to `Next`, you have to call `Retain`. Otherwise, the reader releases the memory every time a new `Record` comes in.

IV. Finally, for convenience, we construct `Table` from the records so that we can treat the whole response as one large table. If you prefer, you can instead do something with the results as they come in rather than keeping the whole table in memory.

And there we go! I have the finished code sample for the same functions in C++ in the GitHub repository, but you should try writing it yourself first before looking at the solution! Here's some exercises you could try:

•   Stand up a Flight server using one of the languages, and then use the client from another one to make requests to it. For example, use the server we wrote in Go and request the data from it using the Python Flight client or vice versa.

- Instead of fetching the data from S3, maybe return data from a local Parquet file and see how much faster it is. Maybe use CSV, JSON, or ORC files instead of Parquet, or provide some way to request a subset of the data.

- Implement something to cache portions of the Parquet files from S3 so that subsequent calls to `DoGet` don't need to fetch the data all the way from S3 each time.

So far, we've just seen examples of fetching data from raw files with Flight, but there's quite a lot more you can do with it. One thing we're going to look closer at is using Arrow Flight to request data using SQL, providing something that could replace the usage of ODBC and JDBC.

What is Flight SQL?

We've talked about Arrow Flight a lot in this chapter so far and learned how to create a simple Flight client and server. Back in *Chapter 3, Data Science with Apache Arrow*, we also talked about ODBC and JDBC as the standard way to connect to most databases currently. If you haven't guessed yet, that *something better* I was alluding to there was indeed Arrow Flight! Before we get into it, let's have a quick refresher on what ODBC and JDBC are.

ODBC and JDBC were created in 1992 and 1997, respectively, as a technology to help databases expose a common API. By creating a common abstraction layer that all database vendors could implement a driver for, application developers could simply build code to use this common interface with databases. They wouldn't have to create custom/bespoke objects for all the different database software they wanted to use. These technologies quickly became the de facto standard in the enterprise world, and then the open source world, for interacting with data.

The problem at the core of these technologies still being the de facto standard is that they were built during a very different era of computing. Data was significantly smaller than it is now, systems were much more monolithic instead of distributed, and CPUs didn't have dozens of cores to utilize. This brings us back to our discussion on column-oriented data versus row-oriented data in *Chapter 1, Getting Started with Apache Arrow*. ODBC forces a row-oriented structure to data, whereas Flight SQL allows all the performance and memory usage benefits we discussed regarding the column-oriented nature of Arrow data. The result is that ODBC and JDBC don't scale well enough for an expanding big data world and the needs of today's data scientists or data analysts.

If you don't believe me, let's prove it. We'll put Flight and ODBC head to head against each other and see which one wins.

Setting up a performance test

To have an apples-to-apples comparison, we need something that provides both an ODBC interface and an Arrow Flight interface that we can use. For this exercise, we're going to use an open source lakehouse query engine called **Dremio Sonar**. Dremio Sonar also provides a Flight SQL interface, but for this exercise, we're just going to use the Arrow Flight API, not the Flight SQL one. I've mentioned it a couple of times before in various contexts, but Dremio is one of the original creators of Arrow and created Arrow Flight and Arrow Flight SQL before they donated them to the Apache Foundation.

Once again, we're also going to utilize Docker to run a container for our examples. We are also going to need to install the ODBC driver for Dremio Sonar. To install Docker, refer to the instructions from early in *Chapter 3*, *Data Science with Apache Arrow*, when we launched the Spark/Jupyter server image. To install the Dremio Sonar ODBC driver, follow these instructions:

- Go to `https://www.dremio.com/drivers/odbc/` and download the appropriate package for your operating system:

  - For Windows, follow the instructions here: `https://docs.dremio.com/drivers/dremio-connector/`.

  - For Mac, follow the instructions here: `https://docs.dremio.com/drivers/mac-odbc/`.

  - For Linux, first ensure you install the `unixODBC` package for your distribution. Then, if you are using CentOS or Red Hat (or any distribution that uses the `yum` package manager), you can follow these instructions: `https://docs.dremio.com/drivers/odbc-linux/`.

  - For any other distribution, you can install a utility called `rpm2cpio`, which will unpack the compressed `rpm` package that you download from Dremio. Once you've downloaded the package, you can run this command:

    ```
    $ rpm2cpio dremio-odbc-<version>.x86_64.rpm | cpio -idum
    ```

    This will unpack the driver to the local directory, creating a subdirectory named `opt`. There are ODBC configuration files in the `opt/dremio-odbc/conf/` directory of the unpacked folder.

With the ODBC driver installed, let's get the Docker image up and running. The command to start up Dremio Sonar using Docker is as follows:

```
$ docker run -p 9047:9047 -p 31010:31010 -p 32010:32010 -e
DREMIO_JAVA_EXTRA_OPTS="-Ddebug.addDefaultUser=true" dremio/
dremio-oss:latest
```

Let's explain the options:

- The -p options define the ports that Docker should forward to the running image – in this case, for the UI, ODBC connections, and Flight connections.

- The -e option sets an environment variable to use a default user upon launching Dremio Sonar, rather than having to add one ourselves. This default user will have a username of dremio and a password of dremio123.

Wait a few minutes after the Docker image starts as the output scrolls across the screen. You'll know that it's up and running as soon as you see this line in the output:

```
Dremio Daemon Started as master
```

At this point, you can open up your browser and go to the address http://localhost:9047. If everything proceeded correctly, you should be greeted by the login screen, as shown in *Figure 8.7*:

Figure 8.7 – The Dremio login screen

Use the default username and password, `dremio` and `dremio123`, respectively, to log in. For our data exercise, we're going to use one of the sample data sources Dremio Sonar provides. On the left side of the screen, look for the **Add Sample Source** button, as highlighted in *Figure 8.8*:

Figure 8.8 – The Add Sample Source button on the Dremio Sonar sidebar

This will add a folder named `Samples` under the **Data Lakes** heading, which will have a folder, `samples.dremio.com`, when you click on it. You want to go to the folder labeled `NYC-taxi-trips`. For a shortcut, you can just use this link: `http://localhost:9047/source/Samples/folder/samples.dremio.com/NYC-taxi-trips`.

You should be looking at a group of Parquet files now. We're going to convert this folder so that Dremio Sonar treats all of those files as a single large table by clicking the **Convert Folder** button at the top right, as indicated in *Figure 8.9*:

Samples.samples.dremio.com.NYC-taxi-trips	
Name ⌄	Action
1_0_0.parquet	
1_1_0.parquet	
1_2_0.parquet	
1_3_0.parquet	
1_4_0.parquet	
1_5_0.parquet	
1_5_1.parquet	

Figure 8.9 – The NYC-taxi-trips file list and Convert Folder button

After clicking the button, you'll have a window pop open; click the **Save** button at the bottom-right corner. You'll finally be greeted with a **SQL Editor** window and the data (*Figure 8.10*):

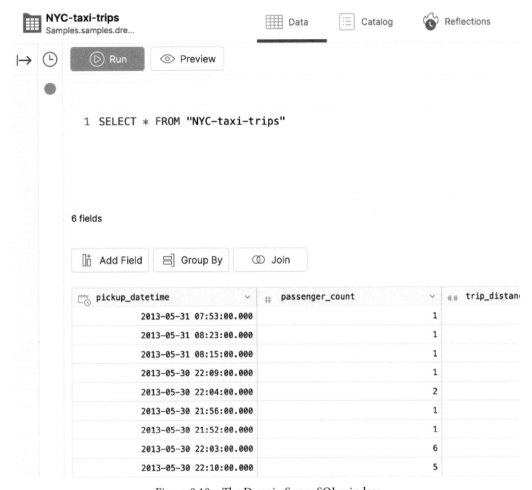

Figure 8.10 – The Dremio Sonar SQL window

At this point, we're all set to run our test! Let's get to it!

Running the performance test

To make this very simple, we're going to use Python so that we have very small and easily repeatable examples that we can time. Before we can get started, you'll need to install the pyodbc Python module. As with previous examples, you can just use pip to do this:

```
$ pip install pyodbc
```

> **Note**
>
> On Linux machines, `pyodbc` does some compiling of the C extensions it uses. Make sure you have the `unixODBC` development package installed on your computer along with a C++ compiler.

Now, we can launch IPython as we've done before, so we can use the magic `%timeit` expression. Let's open our ODBC connection first:

```
In [1]: import pyodbc
In [2]: cnxn = pyodbc.connect('DSN={};Host={};Port={};
ConnectionType={};AuthenticationType={};UID=dremio;
PWD=dremio123'.format('Dremio Connector', 'localhost',
'31010', 'Direct', 'Plain'), autocommit=True)
```

Take note of the **Data Source Name (DSN)** that we're using. The Windows ODBC driver for Dremio Sonar installs with the name `Dremio Connector`, but on Linux, it installs as `Dremio ODBC 64-bit`. Make sure to check the configuration instructions from when you installed the driver so that you have the correct name. The rest of the arguments are simple:

- It's running locally, so the host is `localhost`.

- The standard port for ODBC is `31010`.

- We're connecting directly to the running instance with plain authentication for a username and password of `dremio` and `dremio123`, respectively.

As long as you didn't get any errors there, you now have your ODBC connection. Let's use `%timeit` and make a request for 1 million rows and see how long it takes:

```
In [3]: %timeit data = cnxn.execute('SELECT * FROM
Samples."samples.dremio.com"."NYC-taxi-trips" LIMIT 1000000').
fetchall()
3.85 s ± 294 ms per loop (mean ± std. dev. of 7 runs, 1 loop
each)
```

On my laptop, we see it took roughly 3.85 seconds to transfer the 1 million rows of data using ODBC. That's a respectable time, but a little slow. Let's try doing the same thing with Flight. Since Dremio Sonar uses authentication, we're going to need to also get authentication for our Flight client, which we haven't done before. It's pretty easy though; let's create our client and authenticate:

```
In [4]: import pyarrow.flight as flight
In [5]: client = flight.FlightClient('grpc+tcp://localhost:32010')
```

```
In [6]: token = client.authenticate_basic_token('dremio',
'dremio123')
In [7]: options = flight.FlightCallOptions(headers=[token])
```

Dremio Sonar, by default, uses what's referred to as *basic authentication*, which means that after we authenticate ourselves, we receive an authorization token. We add that as a header to pass with all of our subsequent calls, showing that we're authenticated, and that's it! Now, we can request our 1 million rows and time it:

```
In [8]: %%timeit
    ...: info = client.get_flight_info(flight.FlightDescriptor
    ...: .for_command('SELECT * FROM Samples."samples.dremio.com".
    ...: "NYC-taxi-trips" LIMIT 1000000'), options)
    ...: reader = client.do_get(info.endpoints[0].ticket, options)
    ...: b = reader.read_all()
    ...:
    ...:
  596 ms ± 39.4 ms per loop (mean ± std. dev. of 7 runs, 1 loop
each)
```

Well, that's a significant difference, right? 3.85 seconds versus 596 milliseconds? What if we bumped it up to 5 million rows? Remember to run it multiple times so that you can factor out any slowness from S3 and instead ensure Dremio Sonar is serving from its cache. When I run the same test using 5 million records, I get around 1.84 seconds for Flight and 17.1 seconds for ODBC. When running the test using 1 billion records, Arrow Flight takes 3.3 minutes, while ODBC takes 150 minutes, making Arrow Flight 45x faster than ODBC at that scale (see https://www.dremio.com/blog/is-time-to-replace-odbc-jdbc/#performance-benchmarks).

You can try it with varying amounts of records, but one thing to be careful of is that these tests are keeping the whole result sets in memory rather than grabbing the rows and throwing them away. If you request too many rows, you'll likely make Python run out of memory! See if you can modify these tests to just fetch the rows and throw them away so that you can try it with arbitrary numbers of rows. The sample dataset we're using has little more than 300 million rows, but if you bring your fetch up to that number of rows, you'll probably get bottlenecked more by the communication with S3 than by ODBC versus Flight.

Okay, so now that we've established the performance benefit of Arrow Flight over ODBC, what exactly is Flight SQL? Well, I'm glad you asked…

Flight SQL, the new kid on the block

The ODBC standard has a significant number of different operations that exist in it above and beyond just executing a query and fetching data rows. It includes requests for metadata about the database, such as the following:

- The available database tables

- Schemas and catalogs of databases and tables

- What style of SQL the database uses

- What words are considered "keywords" or are reserved by the database during execution

- What SQL functions are available during execution for the database

- What SQL features the database supports

Because Arrow Flight is so general-purpose, none of these things are standardized in it. Even execution of SQL queries wasn't standardized before Flight SQL; any service that used Flight had a different way of communicating the query. They aren't that difficult to add via available metadata and functionality, but there are benefits to standardizing the protocol for the discovery of this metadata. Without supporting these types of metadata and information fetching, it would be difficult for Flight to truly replace ODBC and JDBC in every use case.

To facilitate this idea, Dremio proposed a new extension of Flight to (and which was later accepted by) the Arrow community – **Flight SQL**. Flight SQL provides a series of pre-defined objects, messages, and types to enable the same type of metadata and command information that are available through ODBC. One thing to keep in mind is that Flight SQL is a framework for managing SQL queries and metadata using the Flight protocol, while ODBC is an API that has many implementations, which all utilize different protocols.

At the time of writing this chapter, Flight SQL is still very new, and C++ and Java implementations were only recently created for it. The goal of this proposal is to be able to map all available ODBC functionality to equivalent functionality through Arrow Flight SQL, enabling it to fully and completely replace ODBC and JDBC for any use case.

Another proposal is to create a generic adapter that will allow ODBC drivers or consumers to use Flight SQL as their underlying implementation while still providing a full ODBC interface. This would allow the shifting of existing applications and workflows from ODBC to Flight SQL without requiring much engineering effort. It would let legacy software gain the performance and distribution benefits of Arrow Flight without needing to rewrite it! That said, this wouldn't provide all of the benefits of Flight to such a piece of software.

While it would gain some benefits, some features, such as streaming, that aren't supported by the ODBC API wouldn't be available. There's also the slight drawback that it does end up having the cost of serializing Arrow data to ODBC primitives, but overall, that still works out to be more performant than ODBC as-is.

I'm not going to go into the implementation details of Flight SQL here; the point was more to explain its existence and the reasoning behind it. It's still in heavy development, so maybe by the time this book is in your hands, it will be more widespread or further expanded. Keep an eye out in the Arrow documentation for updates to Flight SQL functionality!

Summary

If you need to transport data from one place to another, you should consider Arrow Flight as a possible solution for your server. Even without taking advantage of the parallelism it provides, it still shows that it is a significant improvement over most current ways to transport tabular data. Because it leverages Arrow's IPC format, it gains the benefits of avoiding serialization and deserialization costs. While it is currently built on gRPC using HTTP/2, there are many proposals to enable it to more easily support other networking configurations that may get traction.

During the course of this chapter, if you followed along, you created some simple Flight servers and clients. Let those serve as boilerplates for you. Build on them. Add more functionality to them. Explore the features and abilities that Flight provides and supports. If you work more on the data science side than on the developer side, try using Flight as a client to fetch data from engines such as Dremio Sonar. The key here is experimentation! Arrow Flight is a toolbox – a really fancy toolbox with a lot of bells and whistles – but it's still a toolbox. It's up to you to figure out how to best leverage it for your needs, and the prelude to that is experimenting with what it can do.

At this point, we're going to steer away from direct development using Arrow for a bit and instead focus on examples of Arrow being used out in the wild. The next chapter is called *Powered by Apache Arrow*, where we are going to look at already existing applications and use cases that are powered by Apache Arrow and how they are using it. I want to shed a spotlight on some innovative software that is taking Arrow and using it in creative ways. Maybe you'll be familiar with one or more of the use cases I'm going to cover, or maybe I'll introduce you to your new favorite tool.

There's only one way to find out… turn the page and keep on reading!

Section 3: Real-World Examples, Use Cases, and Future Development

This last section focuses on examples of real-world usage of Arrow and an analysis of products that embed or otherwise utilize Apache Arrow. We wrap up the book with some advice for anyone who wants to get more involved in contributing to the Apache Arrow project and other upcoming features to look forward to.

This section comprises the following chapters:

9
Powered by Apache Arrow

Apache Arrow is becoming the industry standard as more and more projects adopt and/or support it for their internal and external communication formats. In this chapter, we're going to take a look at a few projects that are using Arrow in different ways. With the flexibility that Arrow provides, it is able to serve a variety of use cases in different environments, and many developers are taking advantage of that. Of course, Arrow is used in many different analytical engine projects, but it is also used in other contexts ranging from **machine learning** (**ML**) to data visualization in the browser.

With new projects and uses popping up all the time, it only makes sense to give a small overview of a selection of some of those projects. In this chapter, you're going to see a couple of different use cases for how Arrow is being used in the wild. These include the following:

- A distributed SQL query engine named **Dremio Sonar**, which we just used to demonstrate Arrow Flight in *Chapter 8, Exploring Apache Arrow Flight RPC*

- Building applications that rely on **Artificial Intelligence** (**AI**) and **ML** techniques with **Spice AI**

- Several projects using the Arrow JavaScript library to perform super-fast computations right inside the browser

Swimming in data with Dremio Sonar

The roots of Arrow can be found in the `ValueVector` objects from the **Apache Drill** project, a SQL query engine for Hadoop, NoSQL, and cloud storage. Dremio Sonar was originally built out of Apache Drill and Dremio's founders co-created Arrow. Arrow is used by Dremio Sonar as the internal memory representation for its query and calculation engine, which helps power its performance. Since its inception, Dremio's engineers have made many contributions to the Arrow project resulting in significant innovations. First, let's look at the architecture used and where Arrow fits in.

Clarifying Dremio Sonar's architecture

As a distributed query engine, Dremio Sonar can be deployed in many different environments and scenarios. However, at its core, it has a pretty simple architecture, as shown in *Figure 9.1*. Being distributed, it can scale horizontally by increasing the number of Coordinators and Executors that handle the planning and execution of queries, respectively. Cluster coordination is handled by an Apache **ZooKeeper** cluster that is communicated with by both the **Coordinator** node and all the **Executor** nodes. While the metadata storage used by the **Coordinator** node(s) can be local to it, the executors need to all share a distributed storage mechanism. The **Executor** nodes need to share a **Distributed Storage** location so that we can ensure the raw data, configuration data, and cached data is in sync:

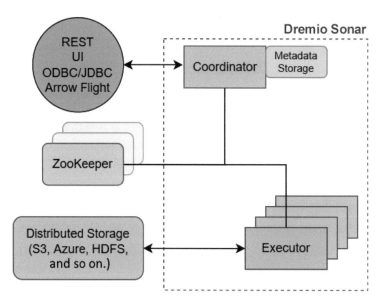

Figure 9.1 – The basic Dremio Sonar cluster architecture

So, I mentioned that Dremio Sonar uses Arrow as its internal memory representation of data for computation. Since Dremio Sonar can connect to various sources of data, this means that any raw data has to be converted into the Arrow format after it has been retrieved from its physical storage location. If your raw data simply consists of Parquet files in a distributed storage service such as S3, this can be very easy and performant because Parquet has a fast conversion to and from Arrow. But if your raw data is stored in, say, a PostgreSQL database connected with ODBC, that conversion can potentially be slower due to PostgreSQL and ODBC often becoming bottlenecks for transferring large amounts of data.

At a certain point, even the fastest execution engine cannot provide sub-second response times when hitting the limits of physics when dealing with very large datasets. To combat that, Dremio Sonar uses a technique it calls **reflections**. A reflection is a hybrid between a materialized view and an index which is stored as simply a collection of Parquet files. Each reflection may be partitioned and/or sorted in order to minimize the number of files that need to be read to service a query. That said, when aiming to achieve super-fast query times, even converting this data from Parquet to Arrow while highly optimized, can still take time for a lot of data. To address those situations, Dremio Sonar provides the option to store the data of a reflection in raw Arrow IPC format, allowing the cached Arrow data to be pulled directly into memory without any conversion required. All of this translates into super-fast query executions and computations.

With Dremio's usage of Arrow and involvement in the community, its engineers have contributed significantly to the libraries. They were involved in the creation and development of **Arrow Flight**, with Dremio being the first system with an Arrow Flight connector (which showed a 20x–50x improvement over their ODBC/JDBC connectors). They were also heavily involved in the development of Arrow Flight SQL, being part of the contributors that provided the initial official implementations of it. However, one significant contribution Dremio has made that we haven't already covered in this book is the **Gandiva Initiative**. This is an execution kernel for Arrow that provides enormous performance improvements for low-level operations on Arrow's data buffers. Initially developed to improve the performance of analytical workloads being serviced by Dremio Sonar, the *Gandiva library* was donated to the Arrow Project in 2018.

The library of the Gods...of data analysis

Gandiva is a mythical, divine bow from the Hindu epic story, the *Mahābhārata*. In the story, Gandiva is indestructible, and any arrow that is fired from it becomes 1,000 times more powerful. Given the performance benefits of the Arrow-based execution that this library provides, it seems to be an extremely fitting name.

Like many big data query engines, Dremio Sonar is implemented using Java. Before the development of Gandiva, the execution of a SQL query by Dremio Sonar involved dynamically compiling that query into an efficient byte code format that could be executed by the **Java Virtual Machine** (**JVM**). Dynamically compiling queries into a byte code representation provides significant performance benefits over simply interpreting and evaluating a SQL expression; however, Gandiva takes this approach just one step further. By leveraging the capabilities of the **LLVM** compiler, many low-level in-memory operations on Arrow data, such as sorting or filtering, can have highly optimized assembly code generated on the fly. This results in better resource utilization and faster operations.

> **What Is LLVM?**
>
> LLVM is an open source project that provides a set of compiler and toolchain utilities; it was originally developed around 2000. In addition to providing many utilities for being a general-purpose compiler for a multitude of programming languages, it also provides libraries for performing **Just-In-Time** compilation. As opposed to compiling source code to machine code before execution, just-in-time compilation occurs at runtime, allowing a program to dynamically translate operations into machine code and then execute that code. This provides extra flexibility, while still being able to leverage the execution performance of highly optimized, compiled code. This capability is what Gandiva is leveraging!

To ensure the fastest possible execution, Gandiva is a C++ library, and it provides Java APIs utilizing the Java Native Interface bridge to talk to the C++ code. Since Dremio Sonar is written in Java, it then leverages those APIs for generating code and evaluating expressions. *Figure 9.2* shows a high-level representation of how the Gandiva library is utilized:

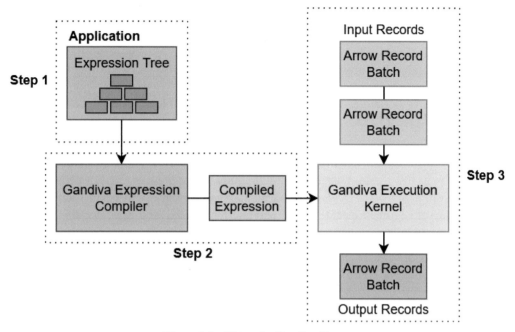

Figure 9.2 – Using the Gandiva library

The basic steps for using Gandiva are labeled and listed as follows:

- **Step 1**: First, the application creates an expression tree to represent the operation that it desires to compute. Gandiva supports filter and projection operations along with a wide variety of mathematic, Boolean, and string manipulation operations.

- **Step 2**: The expression tree is passed to the **Gandiva Expression Compiler**, which returns an object containing a reference to the compiled module. The compilation step also utilizes caches of precompiled expressions to ensure it is fast.

- **Step 3**: The compiled expression can then be passed to the **Gandiva Execution Kernel** and given a stream of Arrow record batches as input for it to operate on, returning Arrow record batches as output.

At the time of writing, in addition to the C++ API and Java bindings, there are also Python bindings for the Gandiva library. Hopefully, as time goes on, the community will continue to build bindings for using the Gandiva library with other languages, including Ruby, Go, and more. The continued adoption of Gandiva builds on Arrow's adoption, making processing data in Arrow format ever more efficient. Utilizing and embedding Gandiva prevents the need for applications to have to reinvent the wheel and implement this work on their own.

In addition to the analytics pipelines and SQL evaluations, there are other use cases where using Arrow can provide significant benefits. The next use case we're going to talk about is how to utilize Arrow as an in-memory data representation for sequence alignment/map objects for genomics data processing.

Spicing up your ML workflows

Among the various fields of engineering that work with very large sets of data, one field that deals with processing some of the largest datasets would be ML and AI workflows. However, if your full-time job isn't ML, and you don't have the support of a dedicated ML team, it can often be very difficult to create an application that can learn and adapt. This is where a group of engineers decided to step in and make it easier for developers to create intelligent and adapting applications. **Spice AI** (`https://spiceai.io`) is, at the time of writing, a venture-capital-funded start-up that is working to create a platform to make it easier for developers to create AI-driven applications that can adapt and learn. They've open-sourced a product on GitHub called Spice.ai (`https://github.com/spiceai/spiceai`). It is currently in alpha development and utilizes Apache Arrow, Arrow Flight, as well as Dremio Sonar for its data processing and transport (`https://blog.spice.ai/announcing-spice-xyz-94323159cd2b`).

Generally, a traditional approach to integrating AI/ML into an application uses a completely separate service from the application. A dedicated team or pipeline, usually data scientists, acquires data from somewhere and trains a model on it. After a significant amount of time in a cycle of training the model on data, tweaking it based on the results, and then training it again, this model is deployed as a service. The application then interacts with that service to get answers or insights based on the model. In comparison, Spice.ai allows developers to incorporate the AI engine into the application directly instead of as a separate piece of infrastructure, as shown in *Figure 9.3*:

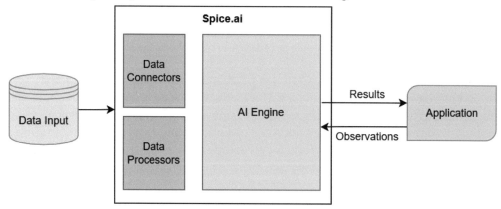

Figure 9.3 – The Spice.ai integration with an application

For the various levels of communication between data sources and data connectors/processors and those processors and the AI engine, Arrow is used for efficiency. Switching to using Arrow and Flight for communication and processing enabled Spice.ai to scale to datasets that were 10x–100x larger than it was previously able to. Also, it improved transport time for large datasets, just as we saw in *Chapter 8*, *Exploring Apache Arrow Flight RPC*. Integrating with Arrow also enabled them to connect with data sources such as InfluxDB, Snowflake, and Google BigQuery as input for the AI/ML engine. Essentially, they can integrate with anything that provides an Arrow Flight endpoint or an Arrow IPC record batch stream.

Bringing the AI engine to where the data lives

With any time-sensitive data, the best route for performance is to always bring your computation to where your data is. This is the premise behind Spice.ai's decision to provide a portable container runtime. Making it deployable using simple HTTP APIs allows it to be deployed alongside any application regardless of whether it is on-premises, part of a public cloud, or deployed on an edge device such as a cell phone. They are also keen into building a community by including a library of community-driven, reusable components for the Spice.ai runtime.

The next step for Spice AI is that they are targeting data scientists with blockchain and smart-contract data with the release of Spice.xyz (`https://spice.xyz`). Using an Arrow Flight API, Spice.xyz provides a SQL interface to a high-performance pipeline of blockchain data such as Ethereum gas fees or **Non-Fungible Token** (**NFT**) trading activity. By building on top of Arrow and Arrow Flight, they've created a unified and efficient platform across AI workflows and the data needed to train the ML models.

Now, let's take a more visual approach. Historically, trying to provide faster and more efficient processing of data inside web browsers has been extremely difficult to do. This tends to be the case due to the limitations of JavaScript, the primary language used for interactive websites. Being an interpreted language, with significant limitations on memory usage (for the user's protection), JavaScript is not exactly ideal for processing data. This sort of processing is critical for being able to create ways to easily interact with data. As a result, many projects have popped up to utilize Arrow in browsers to power these kinds of use cases, which we will discuss in the following section.

Arrow in the browser using JavaScript

One of the most common ways to currently deploy an application to consumers is by developing a web application. You can provide an application intended for mobile phones, tablets, or laptop/desktop browsers all in one location. When it comes to building modern interactive applications on the web, you can be sure that JavaScript and/or TypeScript are going to be involved somewhere. Now that we've covered some examples of services and systems utilizing Arrow, we'll cover a couple of projects that are leveraging Arrow front-and-center right in the browser.

Gaining a little perspective

In *Chapter 3*, *Data Science with Apache Arrow*, we briefly touched on a library named **Perspective** in the context of a widget for Jupyter notebooks. Perspective was originally developed at J.P. Morgan and was then open-sourced under the Apache Open Source License 2.0 through the **Fintech Open Source Foundation** (**FINOS**). Perspective is written in C++ and compiled for both WebAssembly and Python, with JavaScript components provided to wrap around the WebAssembly module. Two main modules are exported by the Perspective library: a data engine library and a user-configurable web component for visualization (which depends on the data engine).

> **Look It Up!**
>
> The home page for Perspective is `https://perspective.finos.org`. Here, you can find the documentation and a link to the GitHub repository. Additionally, it contains a variety of images and views showing what can be done with it.

In the browser, the Perspective engine runs as a web worker that runs as a separate process. When using Node.js, the engine runs in-process by default rather than as a separate process. In both cases, a `promise`-based interface is exported (`async/await` can be used with ES6). If the data is read-only, static, or provided by the user, then near-native performance can be achieved with the JavaScript client-only library running WebAssembly and a web worker for parallel rendering. The only drawback is that it requires the entire dataset to be downloaded to the client. Perspective is able to understand data in Arrow format, as raw CSV data, or as JSON (row-oriented objects) data.

When dealing with larger, real-time, or synchronized data being accessible by multiple users concurrently, one alternative is a client/server model. Servers are provided for either Node.js or Python, allowing JavaScript clients to replicate and synchronize the server-side data. By leveraging Arrow, data is able to be passed around extremely efficiently between the server and the client, while still allowing the browser's UI to render a variety of chart types ranging from simple bar charts to complex heatmaps or scatter plots. The rendering in the browser will dynamically and interactively update views as data, and updates are streamed from the server.

If you're ever working on an application that will be drawing visualizations of datasets, I highly recommend seeing whether you can leverage the perspective library and/or its components! For instance, this was done by the Visual Studio Code extension, **Data Preview** (`https://marketplace.visualstudio.com/items?itemName=RandomFractalsInc.vscode-data-preview`). This extension for the Visual Studio Code IDE utilizes the Perspective library to provide tools for importing, viewing, slicing, and charting a wide selection of objects or files and data formats, just as we saw previously with the Jupyter widget. What might you be able to build with it?

If Perspective isn't quite your speed, how about trying a different module called Falcon?

Taking flight with Falcon

Similar to Perspective, Falcon is a library for the interactive visual analysis of data in the browser. The module itself can be found at `https://github.com/vega/falcon` with a series of demos hosted to display its capabilities. What sets Falcon apart is its swappable engine to go along with the multitude of widgets and components it offers for cross-filtering between records.

For smaller datasets of up to 10 million rows, it has an engine built entirely on Arrow that operates completely in the browser. Alternately, even greater performance can be achieved using DuckDB's WebAssembly SQL database (`https://github.com/duckdb/duckdb-wasm`) for browsers (which is also built on top of Arrow!) as Falcon's query engine. Lastly, Falcon also can connect to the Heavy.AI (formula OmniSci) database to use as an engine (`https://www.heavy.ai/product/heavyidb`). And before you ask…yes, Heavy.AI also supports Arrow for data ingestion and uses libraries provided by Arrow to utilize GPUs for computation.

Remember, this chapter is just supplying brief snippets of information about projects that I think are utilizing Arrow in interesting ways. Go check some of them out if they catch your fancy!

Summary

It doesn't matter what the shape or form of your data is, if you're going to be doing any sort of processing or manipulation of the data, then it pays to see whether Arrow can enhance your workflows. In this chapter, we've seen relational databases, analytical engines, and visualization libraries all powered by Apache Arrow. In each case, Arrow was being leveraged for a smaller memory footprint and generally better resource utilization than what had previously been done.

Every industry has a need for processing large amounts of data extremely quickly, from brand new scientific research to manufacturing metrics. If you are doing work with data processing, you can probably leverage Arrow somewhere in your pipeline. If you don't believe me, have a gander at the projects listed on the official Apache Arrow website as *powered by Arrow*: `https://arrow.apache.org/powered_by/`. You'll find every project mentioned in this chapter on that list, along with many other interesting ones. I'm sure you'll be able to find something that's at least tangentially related to your particular use case; at a minimum, you'll pique your curiosity.

If you can't find something that already exists to leverage, maybe you'll build something and contribute to the Arrow project instead! That's the topic of our next chapter: *How to Leave Your Mark on Arrow*. Arrow has become what it is by nurturing a community and drawing people to it. Like any other open source project, it needs developers to contribute to it in order to grow. Maybe there's a feature you want or need that I haven't mentioned yet. Maybe there is a use case that no one has considered yet. If, like me, you enjoy diving into the meat of a library and building something that many others can use, then come contribute to the Arrow libraries. The next chapter will help you to get started!

10
How to Leave Your Mark on Arrow

So, you've got some ideas to make Arrow better, or maybe you've found a bug. Either way, you want to communicate your needs and ideas to the Arrow project and/or you want to contribute code changes upstream. Well, this chapter is a primer on how to go about doing so. Whether this is your first contribution to an open source project or you're a seasoned veteran, we're going to cover everything you'll need to know to make some contributions. Arrow, like any open source project, lives and dies through community involvement and developer usage. The more people that get involved, the better off the project will be.

Here's what we're going to cover in this chapter:

- How to interact and contribute to open source projects, specifically Apache projects
- The architecture of the Arrow repository, build scripts, and automation jobs
- Finding something you can contribute
- The life cycle of a pull request in an Arrow project

Much of the content for this chapter is my own spin on the information from the official Arrow documentation for contribution and development. If you find that you want additional information about any of the topics covered here, you can probably find it there: `https://arrow.apache.org/docs/developers/contributing.html`. Now, without further ado, let's get down to business.

Technical requirements

Here are the things you'll need for this chapter:

- An internet-connected computer and web browser.

- Python 3.6 or higher.

- Go 1.16 or higher.

- Access to the command line on your computer. On Windows, PowerShell is preferred and can be installed from `https://docs.microsoft.com/en-us/powershell/`.

All other necessary applications have instructions for installation at the time they are mentioned.

Contributing to open source projects

The world relies on open source software, full stop: Linux, Android, Mozilla Firefox, Chromium (the underlying code for Google Chrome and Microsoft Edge), Visual Studio Code, WordPress, Vue.js, React, and others. Everyone likely interacts with some sort of open source technology almost every day, even if they aren't aware of it. You can find a ton of really interesting open source code too! Even the original Apollo 11 guidance computer source code has been open sourced (`https://github.com/chrislgarry/Apollo-11/`)! But without people using and contributing to these projects, they wouldn't survive and propagate as they have.

Contributing to and participating in the open source community has changed a lot over the years, particularly with the advent of **GitHub**. In many ways, it's easier than it ever was before. GitHub has great search functionality, standardized source code management, and common terminology. Unfortunately, this has also resulted in a lot of participation in open source communities being just surface-level single contributions. Regardless, there are some things you need to keep in mind when contributing to any open source project.

Communication is key

Most open source communities have a code of conduct. All Apache Software Foundation projects follow the Apache code of conduct, which can be found on its website: `https://www.apache.org/foundation/policies/conduct.html`. The goal is collaboration, which means that people are going to have to interact with each other a lot. Make sure you're patient and friendly when interacting with the other members of a project. If you're trying to report a bug or error, give some context! Explain what you're trying to do and give steps that can be reproduced. If you're suggesting an enhancement, explain what the use case is and why it would be useful not just to you but also to others.

It's okay not to know things; no one knows everything. But make sure you show that you've at least done some leg work. Before you ask for help, make sure you've read the README.md file and documentation of a project. Do a quick Google search. People will appreciate that you're showing that you want to learn, not just have someone do your work for you. There's a difference between a request like *X is broken! Please fix it!* and *I'm not sure how to do X; I've checked the docs and can't find any references to it.* The latter is much more likely to be responded to than the former. Remember, it's very difficult to convey tone and mood through written text, particularly when collaborators on a project may be from different countries with different cultures. Assume good intentions in conversations until proven otherwise, respect community decisions, and be patient. Trust me – people will appreciate it.

You don't necessarily have to contribute code

Yes. That's right. You can contribute to and improve an open source project without ever writing a line of code. The non-code aspects are often the most overlooked or neglected portions of a project. Maybe you could improve or enhance some of the documentation (or write new documentation that was missing!). Maybe you have an eye for design and want to improve a project's usability and design. You could write a translation for the documentation in another language to increase adoption or curate a folder of examples, showing how to use a project. Just like a commercial project, open source projects often have a lot of needs above and beyond the source code itself. Starting by helping out with some of these areas is often easier and gets you acquainted very quickly with the other contributors of a project. Often, this ends up opening the door to other opportunities to contribute in different ways if you want to, including using code if that's your preference.

There are a lot of reasons why you should contribute!

If you're still not sold on the idea of contributing to open source projects in general, let's cover a few reasons why you absolutely should! Contributing to open source projects can be a rewarding method for learning, teaching, and/or building experience in just about any skill set you can think of:

- *You can improve the software you rely on!* If you find a bug in some software or library that you use, maybe you want to dig in and patch it yourself instead of waiting for someone else to do it. Not only do you potentially get a fix faster but now everyone else also gets to benefit.

- *If there's a skill you want to practice, there's a project that needs someone with that skill!* Whether you want to improve your UI design, writing, organizational skills, API design, or coding skills for a particular language, you can find a project that needs someone to do it. You just need to look for it.

- *Find people with shared interests!* Open source projects with welcoming, active communities can result in friendships that span around the world. You might form a friendship or just find someone interesting to talk to when collaborating on a project.

- *Work on your people skills!* Collaboration on open source projects offers many opportunities to practice leadership and interpersonal skills, such as prioritization of work, conflict resolution, and working as part of a team/organizing a team of people.

- *Find a mentor or teach other people!* Maybe you're a highly experienced engineer, or maybe you're new to coding. Either way, sharing work on a project and collaborating requires everyone to explain how they do things and potentially ask for help with concepts and implementation. Teaching can be worthwhile and fulfilling to all parties involved; don't knock it until you try it.

- *Build your reputation and (possibly) your career!* By definition, any work you contribute to an open source project is publicly available for anyone to see. Working with and contributing to multiple projects can build a significant public reputation for yourself, along with a portfolio of work and examples you can easily share. Over time, you might find opportunities to attend or present at conferences relating to the work and expand your professional network. It's literally how I ended up writing this book!

These aren't the only reasons why people contribute to open source projects; they are just a few that I was able to come up with. Ultimately, there's something very satisfying about having the ability and opportunity to spot a problem or have an idea and just fix it yourself. Maybe you'll want to contribute to the Arrow project; maybe you'll find an entirely different project that suits you better. Find what works for you!

For the rest of this chapter, we're going to focus on how you would specifically orient yourself within the Arrow code base and contribute to the project. But conceptually, many open source projects will be organized very similarly: **Continuous Integration (CI)** configurations, build and deploy scripts and tooling, issue tracking, mailing lists, and rules for how to contribute. Once you start contributing to open source projects, hopefully you'll enjoy it and keep doing so! Here we go!

Preparing your first pull request

Apache Arrow is a big project. Really big. It's a large-scale project that includes many different languages, build systems, concepts, and interactions. This means that everyone who contributes will eventually be faced with stuff they will need to learn. You might have been writing C++ code for 10 years, but you might still need to ask basic questions about R or Ruby. Among the contributors to Arrow, you'll find experts, engineers, and data scientists, but there are also users, new engineers, and enthusiasts learning too!

The primary method of communication for looking for help with Arrow is either subscribing to the `user` or `dev` mailing lists or creating a GitHub issue. For more information about the mailing lists and instructions to subscribe to them, you can go to the Arrow website here: `https://arrow.apache.org/community/`. When it comes to tracking bugs, feature requests, and other tasks that need to be done, Arrow utilizes **JIRA**. If you're reporting a bug, proposing a new feature, or proposing a large documentation change, you should likely file a JIRA issue.

Navigating JIRA

Since JIRA is the primary issue tracker that the project uses, you can easily sift through proposed and planned work by searching through the issues. Creating a JIRA issue will let you connect with other developers and discuss the context around your issue or how you plan on implementing a fix or enhancement. You don't want to spend a ton of time on something only to be told that the other developers don't think it's a good idea.

Creating a JIRA issue

The only thing you need to do to create a JIRA issue is make an account, which you can do at this URL: `https://issues.apache.org/jira/secure/Signup!default.jspa`. Once you log in, you can create an issue and just select the Apache Arrow project and the type of issue, as shown in *Figure 10.1*:

Figure 10.1 – Creating a JIRA issue

After you get more involved in the project and want to assign yourself to issues or simply get more involved with JIRA, you'll need *contributor* permissions. Just ask on the mailing lists or comment on the JIRA issue you created to get those permissions.

Whether you're creating a JIRA issue, GitHub issue, or emailing one of the mailing lists, make sure you use an appropriate title. What is an appropriate title? First and foremost, you need to prefix your title with the related components using brackets. For example, if you are referring to something about the Python libraries, you should include `[Python]` as the prefix of your title. When on JIRA, make sure the corresponding **Component/s** field of the issue is set for the prefixes you're using. *Figure 10.2* has an example of a properly titled and setup JIRA issue, with both a prefixed title and **Component/s** field set:

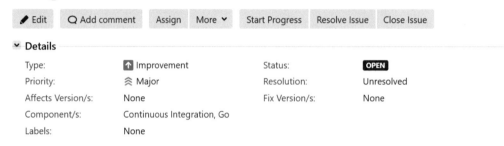

Figure 10.2 – A JIRA issue with the components set

Setting these components makes it easy for everyone to search through issues and have context regarding them. Before you go and create an issue, it's highly recommended that you first search through the existing issues so that you don't create a duplicate.

> **Finding Your First Issue**
>
> There are a few labels used on issues for new contributors, providing good starting issues to tackle. Look for issues labeled **beginner**, **beginner-friendly**, **good-first-issue**, **good-second-issue**, **newbie**, **easyfix**, or **GoodForNewContributors**. Typically, issues with these labels should take no more than a couple of days or a weekend at most to fix. That said, don't be afraid to ask questions in comments on an issue. After spending some time on it, you may find that the issue is more difficult than whomever originally filed the ticket thought it was. Make sure you add a comment to that effect! We're friendly!

So, let's assume that you've found an issue to work on. Maybe it's code, or maybe it's documentation. Either way, you've decided what you want to work on to contribute. What's the next step? Let's get set up!

Setting up Git

As you may have guessed by now, Git is used for version control of Arrow and is easily available on almost any operating system. You can go to GitHub's website and find easy instructions to install it if you don't already have it installed. Once you've got Git all set up, if you haven't already done so, don't forget to configure your name and email with these commands:

```
$ git config --global user.name "Your Name"
$ git config --global user.email your.email@example.com
```

> **Helpful Tip!**
> You can also follow the documentation on the GitHub site for how to authenticate your local Git installation with GitHub (https://docs.github.com/en/get-started/quickstart/set-up-git#next-steps-authenticating-with-github-from-git). That way, you don't need to retype your username and password with every Git command you run.

To contribute to the Arrow repository, you first need to create a fork of the repository under your own GitHub account. Fortunately, it's really easy to do this! Just go to the Arrow GitHub repository at https://github.com/apache/arrow and click the **Fork** button, as shown in *Figure 10.3*:

Figure 10.3 – How to fork the Arrow repository

The easiest route is to choose to fork it to your username, creating the forked copy of the repository with the https://github.com/<username>/arrow URL. Now you can clone the repository and set the upstream remote, referencing the official Apache Arrow repository. Assuming you've configured the authentication with GitHub from the documentation, there are two ways to clone the repository. You can clone it over HTTPS:

```
$ git clone https://github.com/<username>/arrow.git
```

Alternatively, you can clone it using **Secure Shell (SSH)**:

```
$ git clone git@github.com:<username>/arrow.git
```

By default, when you clone a repository, you refer to it by the name `origin`. The convention when developing Arrow is to reference the official Arrow repository as `upstream`. You can configure it with a simple command:

```
$ cd arrow # first enter the cloned directory
$ git remote add upstream https://github.com/apache/arrow
```

You can easily confirm that you have set it up correctly! Running this command should give you similar output to what you see here:

```
$ git remote -v
origin      https://github.com/<username>/arrow.git (fetch)
origin      https://github.com/<username>/arrow.git (push)
upstream    https://github.com/apache/arrow (fetch)
upstream    https://github.com/apache/arrow (push)
```

You should now have a copy of the Arrow source code locally on your machine in a directory named `arrow`, with two remotes referring to your own fork (named `origin`) and the official Arrow GitHub repository (named `upstream`). Now, you're all set up and ready to start poking around the code and documentation!

Orienting yourself in the code base

The implementations for most of the languages supported by Arrow are included in the `arrow` repository in their own corresponding subdirectories:

- `cpp` – C++
- `csharp` – C#
- `js` – JavaScript
- `c_glib` – GLib
- `go` – Golang
- `java` – Java
- `julia` – Julia
- `matlab` – MATLAB
- `python` – Python
- `r` – R
- `ruby` – Ruby

> **Note**
> The Rust implementation is in a separate GitHub repository located at
> `https://github.com/apache/arrow-rs`.

Automation and configuration scripts along with documentation are in the other subdirectories:

- `.github`: The definition files for the CI workflows of GitHub actions. These workflows are triggered by various actions, such as opening a **Pull Request** (**PR**) and filing an issue.

- `ci`: The scripts and configuration files used by the CI tasks. This includes Docker definition files and build and testing scripts.

- `dev`: Scripts for developers used for packaging, committing, deploying, and testing the Arrow packages. It also contains definitions for CI tasks that are run on demand rather than triggered by actions, such as fuzzing tests.

- `docs`: The documentation and scripts to build the code base.

- `format`: The FlatBuffer and Protocol Buffer files for the binary protocol definitions of the Arrow format itself, such as the **inter-process communication** (**IPC**) protocol and Arrow Flight RPC definitions.

- `experimental/computeir`: The FlatBuffer definitions for the experimental **intermediate representation** (**IR**) format that is being developed (more on that in the next chapter!).

For any issue that you've decided to work on (writing a test, adding a new feature, fixing a bug, and so on), the next step is going to be figuring out what files to start looking at. Knowing which directory to start in is one thing, but sometimes, you'll need some help figuring out exactly which files you need.

GitHub Search is very powerful, with a lot of special syntax that you can utilize to find precisely what you need. Make sure you're using the search while looking at the official Arrow repository (not a fork) and leverage the language-specific search features and more to find function definitions or specific references. You can also use it to find specific issues or commits that reference a particular keyword! It can be extremely helpful to look at other PRs, commits, or issues that reference a similar issue to what you're working on. Looking at existing unit tests for a particular feature is an invaluable resource for finding out how to use it.

Another alternative is to use extensions and search features in your IDE of choice. Since you have the code locally copied onto your machine, most IDEs have available extensions and functionality to make it very easy to search large code bases.

If you're making a code change, then the obvious important thing you need to do is know how to build the Arrow libraries!

Building the Arrow libraries

So far in this book, we've focused on three languages that Arrow has libraries for: C++, Python, and Golang. We're going to continue with that here by building the libraries and running the unit tests in these three languages. First up is going to be the C++ library!

Building the Arrow C++ libraries

Most of the Arrow libraries are distinct and separate implementations of Arrow. But for C (GLib), MATLAB, Python, R, and Ruby, the libraries are actually built on top of the C++ Arrow implementation with bindings for those languages. If you're looking to make a contribution or change in one of those languages, you might have to make C++ changes or at least locally compile the C++ code. So, regardless of whether or not you're looking to work on the C++ library directly, this section can still be important to what you're doing.

Arrow utilizes a tool called **CMake** for managing its C++ library builds. CMake is a build-system generator that exists on multiple platforms; it generates configurations and then defers to another program such as make or ninja to perform the building. If you're using CMake version 3.21.0 or higher, you can utilize provided preset build configurations. So, let's get started!

Technical requirements for building C++ libraries

Building the C++ libraries requires the following:

- A C++ compiler capable of C++11 or higher. Using a Linux/Unix-style system such as gcc version 4.8 and higher will work. If you're using Windows, you'll need at least Visual Studio 2017 or newer.

- CMake version 3.5 or higher:

  - Building the benchmarks requires version 3.6 or higher.

  - Building the zstd library requires version 3.7 or higher.

  - Building the Gandiva JNI bindings requires version 3.11 or higher.

- On Linux or macOS, you'll need either the make or ninja build utility.

- Performing a minimal build will need at least 1 GB of RAM. A minimal debug build along with the tests will require at least 4 GB of RAM. If you want to use Docker and perform a full build, you'll need at least 8 GB of RAM. Thankfully, most modern machines come with at least 8 GB or more RAM by default!

Installing these minimum requirements is pretty easy on most systems:

- For Ubuntu/Debian systems, you can install these minimum requirements with the following:

```
$ sudo apt-get install build-essential cmake
$ sudo apt-get install python3-dev autoconf flex bison #
if you want to build the Python pyarrow module
```

- For Alpine Linux, you'd use this command:

```
$ apk add autoconf \
          bash \
          cmake \
          g++ \
          gcc \
          make
```

- For CentOS/RHEL, use the following:

```
$ sudo yum install gcc gcc-c++ make cmake3
$ sudo yum install autoconf bison python39-devel # if you
want to build the Python module
```

- If you are using Fedora Linux, use the following:

```
$ sudo dnf install \
        cmake \
        gcc \
        gcc-c++ \
        make
$ sudo dnf install autoconf bison python39-devel #if
building pyarrow
```

- Using macOS? Not a problem! Use Homebrew (https://brew.sh/):

```
$ git clone https://github.com/apache/arrow.git
$ cd arrow
$ brew update && brew bundle --file=cpp/Brewfile
```

- If you are using vcpkg (https://github.com/Microsoft/vcpkg), use this:

```
> git clone https://github.com/apache/arrow.git
> cd arrow
> vcpkg install \
    --x-manifest-root cpp \
    --feature-flags=versions \
    --clean-after-build
```

- If you are using the conda utility, use the following:

```
$ conda create -y -n pyarrow-dev -c conda-forge \
    --file arrow/ci/conda_env_unix.txt \
    --file arrow/ci/conda_env_cpp.txt \
    --file arrow/ci/conda_env_python.txt \ # for building
pyarrow
    --file arrow/ci/conda_env_gandiva.txt \ # for gandiva
compilers \
    python=3.9 \ # for building pyarrow
    pandas # only needed for Python
$ conda activate pyarrow-dev
```

- And finally, if you're using MSYS2, here you go:

```
$ pacman --sync --refresh --noconfirm \
    ccache \
    git \
    mingw-w64-${MSYSTEM_CARCH}-boost \
    mingw-w64-${MSYSTEM_CARCH}-brotli \
    mingw-w64-${MSYSTEM_CARCH}-cmake \
    mingw-w64-${MSYSTEM_CARCH}-gcc \
    mingw-w64-${MSYSTEM_CARCH}-gflags \
    mingw-w64-${MSYSTEM_CARCH}-glog \
    mingw-w64-${MSYSTEM_CARCH}-gtest \
    mingw-w64-${MSYSTEM_CARCH}-lz4 \
    mingw-w64-${MSYSTEM_CARCH}-protobuf \
    mingw-w64-${MSYSTEM_CARCH}-python3-numpy \
    mingw-w64-${MSYSTEM_CARCH}-rapidjson \
    mingw-w64-${MSYSTEM_CARCH}-snappy \
```

```
mingw-w64-${MSYSTEM_CARCH}-thrift \
mingw-w64-${MSYSTEM_CARCH}-zlib \
mingw-w64-${MSYSTEM_CARCH}-zstd
```

Phew! Okay. Now that you've got your minimum requirements all set up, make sure you've cloned the Arrow Git repository and have navigated to the cpp directory. All set? Let's get building!

Let's build this thing!

Before we do anything else, let's take a look at the available CMake build presets!

> **Remember**
>
> CMake presets were a feature introduced in CMake version 3.20. While you can use an older version of CMake to build the Arrow libraries, you can only utilize the provided presets if you are using CMake version 3.20 or higher!

You can use the cmake --list-presets command to get the list of presets. It'll look a bit like this:

```
$ cmake --list-presets # make sure you're inside the 'cpp' dir
Available configure presets:

  "ninja-debug-minimal"      - Debug build without anything
enabled
  "ninja-debug-basic"        - Debug build with tests and
reduced dependencies
  "ninja-debug"              - Debug build with tests and more
optional components

  ...
```

If you want to look at the options that are being enabled by a particular preset, you can run the cmake -N --preset <preset name> command:

```
$ cmake -N --preset ninja-release-minimal
Preset CMake variables:
  ARROW_BUILD_STATIC="OFF"
  ARROW_WITH_RE2="OFF"
  ARROW_WITH_UTF8PROC="OFF"
  CMAKE_BUILD_TYPE="Release"
```

> **Note**
>
> These presets are all referencing the `ninja` build utility, rather than using `make`. While `make` is more readily available and standard, many developers will use `ninja` instead for faster builds. It is particularly effective at speeding up incremental builds. In most cases, you can just add `ninja` to the list of packages to install in the previous *Technical requirements for building C++ libraries* section to install it with everything else. To use `ninja` with CMake, pass the `-GNinja` option.

When you are building the C++ libraries with CMake, there are two primary types of builds with the following terms:

- **In-source build**: Running `cmake` directly in the `cpp` subdirectory. If you plan on maintaining more than one build environment (such as separate release and debug builds), then this can be more difficult and less flexible.

- **Out-of-source build**: Running `cmake` from a different directory to keep builds isolated from one another. The common method for this would be to create a subdirectory such as `cpp/debug-build` and run `cmake $ARGS ..` from that directory. This is the recommended approach and the one we're going to take.

Let's create a build from the `ninja-debug-minimal` preset:

```
$ mkdir debug-build # from the 'cpp' directory
$ cd debug-build
$ cmake .. --preset ninja-debug-minimal
Preset CMake variables:

  ARROW_BUILD_INTEGRATION="OFF"
  ARROW_BUILD_STATIC="OFF"
  ARROW_BUILD_TESTS="OFF"
  ARROW_EXTRA_ERROR_CONTEXT="ON"
  ARROW_WITH_RE2="OFF"
  ARROW_WITH_UTF8PROC="OFF"
  CMAKE_BUILD_TYPE="Debug"


 -- Building using CMake version: 3.22.1
...
 -- Configuring done
 -- Generating done
```

```
-- Build files have been written to: /home/matt/arrow/cpp/
debug-build
```

You can also pass custom options to be used in addition to the preset options:

```
$ cmake .. --preset ninja-debug-minimal -DCMAKE_INSTALL_
PREFIX=/usr/local
```

Assuming there are no errors or problems, you can then compile the libraries with a single command:

```
$ cmake --build . # inside the debug-build directory
[143/143] Creating library symlink debug/libarrow.so.800 debug/
libarrow.so
```

And voila! You've built the base Arrow C++ library!

While the presets are provided to help people get started and understand the most common build configurations and options, they aren't guaranteed to stay the same. Individual developer feedback might result in the presets changing over time. If you are preparing any sort of automated build, CI, or scripts, you should manually configure your build and explicitly specify the options you want instead of relying on a preset.

Configuring the build manually

There are three types of builds you can pass to the CMAKE_BUILD_TYPE option:

- Debug: No compiler optimizations and adds debugging information in the resulting binaries.
- RelWithDebInfo: Applies the compiler optimizations but still adds the debug information to the compiled binaries.
- Release: Applies the compiler optimizations but removes the debug information from the final binaries. This produces the smallest output.

There's also another option that you can set, -DARROW_EXTRA_ERROR_CONTEXT=ON, which will provide additional context and debugging output inside of the error checking code.

Developing on Windows?

If you're building the libraries on Windows using Visual Studio, there are more steps that you'll have to perform and more options that you will have to set. The best resource for this is the Arrow documentation itself: https://arrow.apache.org/docs/developers/cpp/windows.html#developers-cpp-windows.

For the most minimal release build, you can simply pass no options and let all the defaults get used:

```
$ mkdir build-release # in the cpp directory
$ cd build-release
$ cmake ..
$ make -j8 # for 8 CPU cores, otherwise swap out the 8
accordingly
```

The unit tests are not built by default but instead require a specific option to enable them. On some Linux distributions, you might run into locale-related errors when running the test suite. If you see any of these, try setting the `LC_ALL` environment variable like so (this requires the `locales` package or an equivalent):

```
$ export LC_ALL="en_US.UTF-8"
```

So, let's change our build options to build and run the unit tests:

```
$ git submodule update --init --recursive # pull down the test
data
$ export ARROW_TEST_DATA=$PWD/../testing/data
$ export PARQUET_TEST_DATA=$PWD/cpp/submodules/parquet-testing/
data
$ mkdir debug-build # only needed if you didn't already create
it
$ cd debug-build
$ cmake -DCMAKE_BUILD_TYPE=Debug -DARROW_BUILD_TESTS=ON ..
$ make -j8 # for 8 CPU cores, otherwise change 8 accordingly
$ make unittest # runs the unit tests
```

There are quite a large number of optional components in the Arrow project. By default, you'll get a minimal build, but you can pass a multitude of Boolean flags to the `cmake` command to enable the components you want. I'll cover a few here, but for the full list, you can check the Arrow documentation. Alternatively, the last portion of the output from `cmake` will contain a **build configuration summary**, listing all the options and what values you got from the `cmake` command. This makes it easy to double-check what options you've set before you start building.

Here's a small selection of component options that I think will be useful:

- `-DARROW_BUILD_UTILITIES=ON`: Build the Arrow command-line utilities.

- -DARROW_COMPUTE=ON: Build the Arrow compute library; we covered this in *Chapter 5, Crossing the Language Barrier with the Arrow C Data API*.

- -DARROW_CUDA=ON: Enable GPU development with CUDA integration. This depends on the NVIDIA CUDA Toolkit, customized by setting the $CUDA_HOME environment variable.

- -DARROW_DATASET=ON: Enables building the Datasets API we covered in *Chapter 7, Using the Arrow Datasets API*. This implies -DARROW_FILESYSTEM=ON, which builds the Filesystem APIs.

- -DARROW_FLIGHT=ON: Build the Arrow Flight libraries that we covered in *Chapter 8, Exploring Apache Arrow Flight RPC*, which depends on gRPC.

- -DARROW_GANDIVA=ON: Build the Gandiva expression compiler that we briefly touched on in *Chapter 9, Powered by Apache Arrow*, when discussing Dremio Sonar.

- -DARROW_ORC=ON: Build the Arrow integrations with the Apache ORC file format.

- -DARROW_PARQUET=ON: Build the Parquet libraries and the Arrow integration with Parquet.

- -DARROW_PYTHON=ON: Build the Python C++ library, required for building the Python pyarrow module. You need to build this against the same Python version that you want to build the pyarrow module for, which requires the NumPy module to also be installed. This also enables several other options that are required for Python bindings, such as ARROW_COMPUTE, ARROW_DATASET, ARROW_FILESYSTEM, ARROW_CSV, ARROW_HDFS, and ARROW_JSON.

- -DARROW_IPC=ON: Build the IPC extensions, which can be switched off to improve build times if you don't need them.

Nearly all of the other dependencies that Arrow has can be built from source as part of the C++ build, taken care of by CMake. For a full list of these dependencies, you can go to the Arrow C++ documentation located at https://arrow.apache.org/docs/developers/cpp/building.html#build-dependency-management. The important thing here is that you can control how CMake resolves the dependencies. To control the dependency resolution, you use the CMake ARROW_DEPENDENCY_SOURCE option. Here are the available options to resolve dependencies:

- AUTO: CMake will attempt to find the dependencies in the default system locations, building them from source if it cannot find them.

- BUNDLED: Ignore the system and only build all dependencies from source.

- SYSTEM: Use CMake's built-in find_package functionality to locate dependencies; use pkg-config for any that aren't supported by it.

- CONDA: Similar to SYSTEM, but use $CONDA_PREFIX instead of the SYSTEM path.

- VCPKG: Use VCPKG to find dependencies, or install them with vcpkg install if it can't find them.

- BREW: Similar to SYSTEM but using Homebrew's default paths as an alternative to the SYSTEM path.

By default, AUTO is used for the dependency resolution unless the $CONDA_PREFIX environment variable is detected by developing in an active conda environment. In that case, CONDA is the default. This option sets a global default for all packages, but you can override the resolution for individual dependencies too! Each package can be overridden by setting an option with the -D<package name>_SOURCE=<value> pattern.

> **Note**
>
> Unfortunately, the package names for setting individual resolution strategies are case-sensitive. You can find the up-to-date listing of package names with the proper casing in the file located at cpp/cmake_modules/ThirdpartyToolchain.cmake in the repository. For example, to override the Protocol Buffers library to force building from source, you'd set the -DProtobuf_SOURCE=BUNDLED option. But it won't recognize PROTOBUF_SOURCE or protobuf_source; you must use the right casing of Protobuf_SOURCE.

Now that we've got everything all configured and ready to build, you can run make or ninja to start the build. With the C++ libraries built and installed, as long as you passed the ARROW_PYTHON=ON option, we can go and build the Python library now! If you didn't use the ARROW_PYTHON=ON option, you can go back and rerun the cmake command with it, and then rebuild. It should only build what is required for the new options rather than rebuilding everything. You can even use the ninja-release-python preset if you like.

Building the Arrow Python module

If you've followed the previous section, you should have a local version of the Arrow C++ libraries that you've built. Huzzah! Now, we can set up our environment for building the pyarrow Python module. There are a couple of possibilities for what your environment might be like based on the toolchain you are using. For the example commands following this, we will assume that the $ARROW_DIR environment variable represents the path to where you cloned the Arrow repository. You can even set the environment variable accordingly to make it easy to copy and paste the code snippets!

> **Before You Go Any Further!**
>
> Make sure you added the packages that were marked as needed for `pyarrow` development for your environment in the previous *Building the Arrow C++ libraries* section. These dependencies are necessary for building the Python module. You may even have gotten errors if you tried building the C++ libraries with the `ARROW_PYTHON=ON` option without them.

Why all this talk about C++? I thought this was the Python module?, I hear you cry. Like several of the other Apache Arrow library implementations, the Python module is largely a wrapper around the C++ library itself, with bindings to Python classes and functions to provide the functionality.

pyarrow's Architecture – Cython is more than just a clever name

The `pyarrow` module mostly tries to take what is available in the C++ Arrow library and expose it as a Pythonic interface that is less complex to utilize. In some cases, it maps almost one to one between a Python class and a C++ class, but in other cases, the C++ classes and functions are used as a foundation for easier-to-use objects and structures. **Cython** (`https://cython.org`) can be used to make this easier to manage and is significantly easier to create.

For all intents and purposes, Cython is a programming language. Its goal is to essentially be a superset of the Python language while providing support for static type declarations. Simply put, it translates specialized Cython code into optimized C/C++ code and compiles it as a Python extension module. As a result, you can get the performance benefits of a compiled C/C++ program and tight integration with other libraries while still, for the most part, writing Python code. I'm not going to go into the nuances of the technical details for how it does this here, but it's really interesting, and I highly recommend reading up on it if that's the sort of thing you're interested in! You can find the documentation at `https://cython.readthedocs.io`. For now, you can easily install Cython using `pip` (which is included in the requirements files that we'll install packages from shortly).

What this means for the `pyarrow` module though is that the architecture of the code looks like *Figure 10.4*:

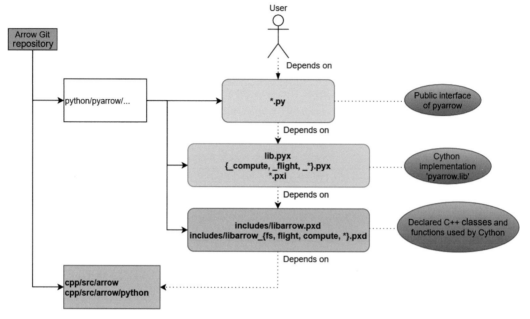

Figure 10.4 – pyarrow code architecture

As you can see, there are four layers to the design of the code (from top to bottom):

- The `*.py` files form the public Python interface of the `pyarrow` module. Everything below this should be considered "internal" to the `pyarrow` module.

- The `lib.pyx` file exposes most of the core C++ Arrow library functionality to Python. It includes the `*.pxi` files for specific implementations, and the `*.pyx` files contain the glue code to expose C++ functionality as Python classes and methods. The file is exposed to Python as `pyarrow.lib`.

- The `includes/*.pxd` files contain the declarations for the raw C++ APIs from the Arrow library. They are similar to C++ header files in this regard; they are included and used in other `*.pyx` files to implement classes, functions, and helpers.

- Finally, the C++ Arrow library itself and dedicated code in the `cpp/src/arrow/python` directory of the C++ source code. These provide lower-level capabilities such as converting to and from `numpy` or `pandas` objects, along with classes for using Python objects and callbacks in the C++ code. This is what is compiled by adding the `ARROW_PYTHON=ON` option with CMake, producing the `libarrow_python.dll/.so` library.

Now that we've finished our little side trip to explain Cython, we can get back to building.

Back to building the module...

For managing our Python environment, we're going to use a utility called `venv`. If you're using the `conda` utility, you should instead use `conda-activate` to activate the development environment instead. To set up our environment with `venv`, we can use the following commands:

```
$ python3 -m venv pyarrow-dev
$ source pyarrow-dev/bin/activate
$ pip install -r $ARROW_DIR/python/requirements-build.txt \
    -r $ARROW_DIR/python/requirements-test.txt
$ mkdir dist # this is where we are going to install our Arrow
libraries
```

If you're on an Ubuntu/Debian-based system, you may need to run the following command to install `venv` separately:

```
$ sudo apt-get install -y python3-venv
```

Now that we've installed the Python dependencies, let's set a couple of environment variables for Arrow's build toolchain. We have to tell the Python build where it can find the Arrow libraries:

```
$ export ARROW_HOME=$(pwd)/dist
$ export LD_LIBRARY_PATH=$(pwd)/dist/lib:$LD_LIBRARY_PATH
```

Now, go back to the directory you created and built the Arrow C++ libraries in. We need to tell it where we want to install those libraries; don't worry – it's not going to rebuild them. You just need to run `cmake` again, passing two new options:

```
$ cmake -DCMAKE_INSTALL_PREFIX=$ARROW_HOME \
    -DCMAKE_INSTALL_LIBDIR=lib \
    ..
```

Then, just run `make install` or `ninja install`, depending on which one you were using previously. Running the `install` command will now populate that `dist` directory we created with the Arrow headers and compiled libraries, making them available to the Python build. This is also a good time to ensure that any features you want to have available to you in the Python module have the corresponding feature flags set to ON in your C++ build. For instance, if you want to use Arrow Flight with the `pyarrow` build, you need to make sure you built the C++ libraries with the `-DARROW_FLIGHT=ON` option passed to `cmake`, and so on.

Dealing with Build Issues

If you run into any issues with the C++ build or the `install` command, refer to the previous *Building the C++ Arrow libraries* section or the official *Arrow C++ Development* documentation, which is located at `https://arrow.apache.org/docs/developers/cpp/index.html`. You will also find Windows-specific instructions there for necessary modifications to these instructions if building on Windows.

Assuming you now have the dependencies handled and the C++ libraries installed to the directory referred to by `ARROW_HOME`, you can finally run the Python build. If you built any of the optional C++ components such as Flight or Gandiva, you need to set a corresponding environment variable of `PYARROW_WITH_<COMPONENT>=1` for each to enable them in `pyarrow`. Let's build!

```
$ cd $ARROW_DIR/python
$ export PYARROW_WITH_PARQUET=1
$ python3 setup.py build_ext -inplace
```

If you want, you can also build a self-contained Python wheel that bundles the Arrow and Parquet C++ libraries into it for easy distribution. You just need to set the `--bundle-arrow-cpp` option like so:

```
$ pip install wheel # if you don't already have it installed
$ python3 setup.py build_ext --build-type=<release|debug>
--bundle-arrow-cpp bdist_wheel
```

If everything is built successfully, you should see the `pyarrow` whl file in the `dist` directory we created. You can install the wheel by running `pip install <whl file>`. If you're having difficulty with building the Python libraries, take a look at the Docker-based examples in the Arrow repository. The Docker files are located in the `$ARROW_DIR/python/examples/minimal_build` directory.

With the `pyarrow` module built, you can run the unit tests now. The `pytest` utility is used for running the unit tests, which can be run using `pytest $ARROW_DIR/python/pyarrow`. There's a variety of options that can be passed to control what tests are run and how to run them. You can see all of the options by running `pytest pyarrow --help`.

Only one build left to do! Let's build the Arrow Go modules.

Building the Arrow Go modules

Personally, I find that the module management of Go makes building the Go modules significantly simpler than the C++ and Python builds. At the time of writing, the minimum version of Go required is version 1.16. If you don't have Go installed, you can follow the instructions at `https://go.dev/doc/install` to do so.

Performing the minimal build of the Arrow Go modules is this simple:

```
$ cd $ARROW_DIR/go
$ go build ./...
```

It's that easy. Running the `go build` command will automatically download the dependencies before attempting to compile the modules. You can then run the unit tests with the `go test` utility:

```
$ git submodule update --init --recursive # if you haven't
already pulled the test data down
$ export PARQUET_TEST_DATA=$ARROW_DIR/cpp/submodules/parquet-
testing/data # if not already set
$ go test ./...
ok      github.com/apache/arrow/go/v8/arrow      0.015s
...
```

The Go modules also utilize a few different Go build tags to control some features, which can be enabled by adding `-tags "tag1,tag2,..."` to the `build` and `test` commands. The available tags are as follows:

- `assert`: Enable debug asserts in the libraries that can `panic` or otherwise print information in specific instances, such as calling `Release` on an `Array` too many times.

- `cdata_test`: Build/run the tests to use the C Data API in the `cdata/test` directory.

- `test`: Build and run additional tests requiring `cgo`.

- `ccalloc`: Build `CgoAllocator`, which requires having the C++ Arrow libraries accessible to link against.

- `noasm`: Disable the optimized assembly and force usage of pure Go implementations of several low-level modules.

Finally, to install the integration test command-line binaries, you can use the `go install` command:

```
$ go install ./...
```

This will install several command-line utilities such as `parquet_reader` and `parquet_schema`, along with the binaries used for running the integration tests.

Regardless of whether you want to make some changes in the C++ code, Python code, or Go code, we've covered how you can build your changes and test them using the unit tests. Once your changes are ready, there are just a couple of steps left involving using Git!

Creating the PR

If you haven't used Git before, it can be a lot to wrap your head around. Essentially, you have *your* copy of the repository (your fork that was created in the *Setting up with Git* section) and the official copy (we called it `upstream`). Within the repository, there are various **branches**, effectively a pointer to a snapshot of a set of changes. The "source of truth" as it were is the `main` or `master` branch. When you create a PR, you're requesting to merge your changes into the official repository's `master` branch. To encapsulate your changes and isolate workspaces, you should create branches in your own repository.

When you create branches, you obviously have to name them! When working on the Arrow libraries, the common convention is to name your branch after the JIRA card number. For example, if the JIRA card you've chosen to work on is `arrow-12345`, you can use the following command:

```
$ git checkout -b arrow-12345-<clever descriptive name>
```

Following this convention makes it easy to keep track of which of your working branches is associated with a specific issue in JIRA. Of course, over time, your local version will fall behind the official repository. As long as you've created branches on your fork to work in rather than making changes directly to the master branch, you can easily update your fork! On the GitHub page for your fork, there is a very convenient **Fetch upstream** button that you can press, as shown in *Figure 10.5*:

Figure 10.5 – GitHub with Fetch upstream

Clicking the **Fetch and merge** button that appears will automatically update your fork's master branch to the current commit of the official repository. After doing this, you'll be able to update your local version with `git`:

```
$ git checkout master
$ git fetch
$ git pull
```

Finally, you pull all those changes into your working branch using the `rebase` command – nice and simple:

```
$ git rebase master arrow-12345-<clever descriptive name>
```

If there aren't any conflicts, you're all set! Everything will be updated, and you can simply push the updated branch with `git push -f`. If there are conflicts, then you'll have to go to each file and manually fix the conflicts. Afterward, you re-add the fixed files with `git add` and continue your rebase with `git rebase --continue`. For more of the nuances of using `git` and other fancy stuff, you can likely find any help you need via `https://stackoverflow.com` or the `git` documentation.

Once you've committed some changes on a branch in your local `git` repository and pushed them to your fork, you can create a PR. When you do, a whole bunch of automated jobs will be triggered, performing builds in different environments, running tests, and checking the formatting of the code. If any of those jobs fail, you'll need to look into what happened. So, the next thing we're going to cover is the main components of the CI workflows and automated jobs.

Understanding the CI configuration

Arrow tries to be compatible with as wide a range of platforms, compilers, operating systems, and package managers as possible. As a result, the automated workflows are fairly complex to account for all of these variations.

Automated action-triggered jobs

Most of the automated jobs for Arrow are defined in the YAML files located in the `.github/workflows` folder. Most of the workflows are specific for particular Arrow implementations and only run on changes to the corresponding code, such as running C++ builds if C++ source files are in a PR. These are generally easy to find as they are named appropriately, based on the language they operate on. There are also a few other workflows to keep in mind:

- `archery.yml`: Validation checks to run for changes to the Archery utility or its tasks.

- `comment_bot.yml`: Allows the manual triggering of actions by making a comment on a PR. It listens for the following comment strings:

  - `@github-actions crossbow submit` ...: Crossbow is a utility for packaging and testing deployments of Arrow; a comment of this form will run the specified `crossbow` command.

  - `@github-actions autotune`: This will run a series of code stylers and formatting on a PR and commit them back to the branch. It will also build some of the documentation and commit those results back. This is useful, and necessary, when making any documentation changes.

  - `@github-actions rebase`: Automatically performs a rebase for the PR onto the master branch.

- `dev_pr.yml`: All PR have a series of checks run on them. The title of the PR should always be of the `ARROW-####: [Components] Title` form, where `ARROW-####` is the JIRA ticket that the PR is tied to. If the title is incorrectly formed, a comment is added to the PR, asking the user to fix the issues. It will also add relevant GitHub labels such as `lang-c++` or `lang-go`, based on which files have been modified in the PR.

- `dev.yml`: Whenever any activity happens on a PR, this job will run the linters and test whether the PR can be merged or not.

In the root folder of the Arrow repository, there are two more configuration files for automated jobs:

- `.travis.yml`: Uses `https://travis-ci.com` to run automated tests for Arm and **s390x** architectures
- `appveyor.yml`: Defines `appveyor` jobs to run Windows builds on Python and C++ commits

To make many development tasks easier to configure and perform, the Arrow repository is also home to a Python utility called **Archery**. Archery can be utilized to run the benchmarks, perform linting of Arrow source code, and build the various Docker images that are utilized in the CI tasks. If you want to run these jobs and checks locally before you submit your PR, you can use the Archery utility to do so, along with several other common development tasks.

Development using Archery

Archery requires Python 3.7 or higher to run, along with the Docker and Docker Compose utilities. You can find installation instructions for these at `https://docs.docker.com` and `https://docs.docker.com/compose`. To make sure that any changes to the Arrow repository (such as when you pull down the latest version of the repository) are reflected and automatically updated with your Archery installation, you should *install Archery in editable mode*. This will retain the reference to the working directory of your Arrow repository rather than copying everything into your Python installation. You can do this by running the following:

```
$ cd $ARROW_DIR
$ pip install -e "dev/archery[all]"
```

You can then run the `archery` command on your command line and pass the `--help` option to print the usage instructions. Each of the subcommands is independent and frequently has its own help output, so have a look around and explore the options, since we're only going to cover a subset of them here.

Running local builds with Archery and Docker

The Docker builds are designed to be reusable containers defined in a hierarchy of components. While this does make the Docker Compose configuration a bit complex, it reduces duplication by allowing the configuration of, for example, the C++ environment to be reused across the various language bindings that rely on it, rather than being duplicated in all of them. I'm not going to cover all of the build parameters and options here, but I'll cover enough to help you understand what's going on. As usual, if you want more detailed information, you can go to the Arrow documentation site, specifically this page: `https://arrow.apache.org/docs/developers/continuous_integration/docker.html`.

The basic commands for manipulating the Docker images using Archery are the following:

- List the available images – `archery docker images`.
- Execute a build – `archery docker run <build name>`:
  - An example is `archery docker run debian-go-cgo`.
  - Running a build will pull down all dependent images, with them being built locally if the build can't pull them down, and then run the requested build.
- Show the commands instead of executing – `archery docker run --dry-run <build name>`.
- Disable image pulling and only build locally – `archery docker run --no-cache <build name>`.
- Add environment variables to the build – `archery docker run --env VAR=value <build name>`:
  - An example is `archery docker run --env CMAKE_BUILD_TYPE=release ubuntu-cpp`, which forces a release build instead of debug.
- Run a custom command instead of the default – `archery docker run <build name> <command>`:
  - An example is `archery docker run ubuntu-cpp bash`, which will start an interactive Bash session, allowing you to debug the build interactively.

Most, if not all, of the Docker images will invoke build and test scripts. These scripts live in the `ci/scripts` directory and typically are appropriately named to encapsulate what they do. For example, `cpp_build.sh` builds the C++ libraries without running the tests, and `cpp_test.sh` will then get called to run those tests.

The scripts will leverage environment variables to ensure parameterization for easy configuration. All of the Docker images are defined in the `docker-compose.yml` file in the root of the repository. This file is extremely well commented on, describing how to add new images and where everything is defined. Looking in this file and seeing how the variables are passed is the quickest way to understand how the pieces fit together.

You are now armed with the knowledge of how to make changes, test them, and check the automated jobs. But what should you do if you want to contribute but don't know how or where to start? Well, I'm getting to that!

Find your interest and expand on it

In the first section of this chapter, *Contributing to open source projects*, we looked at a bunch of ideas about how and why you could, or should, contribute to an open source project. At this point, I'd like to provide just a bit of friendly advice about finding a good place to start if you want to contribute to the Arrow project specifically. Yes, there's the obvious case of looking at the implementation in your preferred programming language. But most of the code bases are still quite large, even when limited to only looking at code relevant to one language. My first piece of advice is to figure out what you are interested in. I've put a small flowchart together in *Figure 10.6* to help with some ideas:

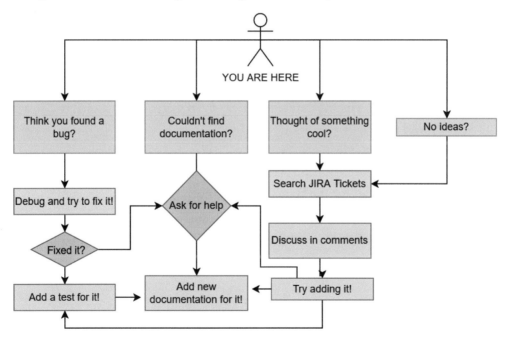

Figure 10.6 – A flowchart of ideas

Of course, it doesn't cover everything. It's not supposed to. The Arrow libraries house many different ideas and different ways of doing things. If you're interested in data transportation, look at the Flight RPC and IPC. If you're interested in performance, look at the benchmarks and read comments to find the code relevant to what you want to improve. Maybe the libraries for your preferred language are missing a feature? Well, the implementations for other languages are immensely helpful in figuring out how you might go about adding that functionality to the library you want.

Above all, subscribe to the mailing lists! There are always interesting discussions going on in the `arrow-dev` mailing list. It's a great place to form the kernel of an idea and expand on it before searching through the JIRA tickets. If you're unsure where to start or how to do something, just ask on the mailing list, and you'll likely get a helpful response. The next best place to look is the existing unit tests and examples, which are frequently great sources of how to utilize newer features that have yet to get updated documentation.

Just remember – I may not have met you, but I believe in you. You've got this! Come join the community of contributors!

Getting that sweet, sweet approval

So, you found the perfect issue to work on, made a PR, and got the CI tests to succeed. What next? How do you get your contribution to be accepted and merged?

Well, core Apache Arrow developers and possibly others who have a stake in the particular area of the Arrow libraries you're modifying will review your PR. To ensure a good review, keep the following in mind:

- Aside from passing existing unit tests, it's expected that new functionality also adds new unit tests to ensure that it is properly tested.

- As much as possible, break your work into smaller single-purpose patches. It's significantly more difficult to get a larger change with disjointed features merged.

- Follow the style guide for the library you're modifying (more on that in the *Finishing up with style!* section next).

Once any feedback has been addressed and the PR is approved, one of the committers will merge your PR. Congratulations! You've just contributed your first patch!

Finishing up with style!

Before we wrap this chapter up, I'd be remiss if I didn't broach one last topic – code style!

To avoid wars and arguments about most aspects of code style, most of the implementations of the Arrow library have very well-defined style checking and linting rules. These rules are checked using the automated CI checks that we covered and are required to pass, in order to merge a PR. We're not going to spend a ton of time on this, since this is enforced and automated with tooling, but it's good to know what tooling is in use.

C++ styling

Arrow follows Google's C++ style guide (`https://google.github.io/styleguide/cppguide.html`) with a few exceptions:

- Line length is relaxed to 90 characters.
- The `NULLPTR` macro is used in header files, rather than `nullptr`, for wider C++ version build support.
- There are relaxed rules regarding structs for convenience.

The style is enforced using the `clang-format` and `clang-tidy` utilities, which can be run using Archery with the following command:

```
$ archery lint --cpplint --clang-format --clang-tidy –fix
```

Source files and header files should use underscores for word separation while compiled executables will use hyphens. For more details specifically regarding the code styling for C++ along with comment style and so on, please read `https://arrow.apache.org/docs/developers/cpp/development.html#code-style-linting-and-ci` and `https://arrow.apache.org/docs/developers/cpp/conventions.html`.

Python code styling

Arrow's Python code follows a PEP 8-like coding style that is similar to the `pandas` project. Just like the C++ linting checks, Archery can also be used to run the local Python linting and style checks using the following command:

```
$ archery lint --python
```

If you add the `--fix` argument, some of the issues found will automatically be fixed – simple and straightforward.

Go code styling

The code for Arrow's Go modules is expected to be formatted using the standard `go fmt` utility. The Go code will be linted during the CI, using the `staticcheck` utility. You can install this tool locally with the command:

```
$ go install honnef.co/go/tools/cmd/staticcheck@latest
```

The `staticcheck` utility will get installed in `$GOPATH/bin`, with the easiest way to invoke it being to ensure that this path is added to your `PATH` environment variable. You can then run the tool on your local code by simply using the `staticcheck ./...` command from the `go/` subdirectory of the Arrow repository.

Summary

Contributing to any open source project can be an enriching experience. As long as a project can build up a community of its developers and users, it can continue to sustain itself indefinitely. These contributors and users are the lifeblood of any successful open source project, so if you have a stake in the continued existence of a project, contribute! The Apache Arrow project is a fairly active project currently, with a lively community of individuals who are passionate about data and analytics. The easiest way to see the features you want to get prioritized is to become part of the conversation or, better yet, contribute them yourself if you can! This community is how new features and releases happen. Votes are held publicly on the development mailing list by the Arrow Project Management Committee on whether new proposed features get accepted or new versions are released. Join the conversation!

Coming up to the end of our journey here, we've got one more chapter left – *Chapter 11, Future Development and Plans*. We've just finished looking at the process in which people contribute and expand the Arrow libraries. So, the last thing we're going to do is get you all excited about the upcoming features, discussions, and technologies. We're going to look at upcoming enhancements for Flight SQL, a distributed scheduler and query execution framework called **Ballista**, and work being done to create a cross-language specification for compute engines.

Welcome to the community, and enjoy your stay! Now, come help us grow!

11
Future Development and Plans

There is quite a lot of development still going on in the Arrow libraries and utilities. Aside from updating and improving the libraries as they currently stand, multiple efforts are operating simultaneously to build community tools utilizing **Apache Arrow**. Sometimes, this results in new protocols and technologies; other times, it results in entirely new libraries and software. Given the size of the developer community surrounding Arrow, it's no surprise that there's plenty of development with new things in the works.

This chapter's goal is to get you excited about the development plans and projects that are in the works as of the time of writing. Hopefully, the following will intrigue you:

- Flight SQL is still under heavy development, so we're going to cover it a bit more in-depth, and the future plans such as a generic ODBC driver.

- An extensible and distributed query execution framework called **DataFusion** and its associated distributed compute engine named **Ballista**.

- Arrow Compute **Intermediate Representation** (**IR**) and the related **Substrait** project.

So, without further ado, let's dive in. With any luck, by the time you are reading this book, some of these ideas will be closer to production already!

Examining Flight SQL (redux)

Way back in *Chapter 8, Exploring Apache Arrow Flight RPC*, we briefly touched on the topic of Arrow Flight SQL and why it was important. Very briefly. Flight SQL is still very new, and while the protocol has stabilized (for the most part), it's very much under development and there are only C++ and Java reference implementations so far. So, first, let's quickly cover the motivations for Flight SQL's development and what it is and isn't.

Why Flight SQL?

We first mentioned the **Java Database Connectivity** (**JDBC**) and **Open Database Connectivity** (**ODBC**) standards in *Chapter 3, Data Science with Apache Arrow*. While they have done well for decades, the standards simply don't handle columnar databases well at all. Both of these standards define APIs that are row-based. If the connected database uses a columnar representation of the data, using ODBC/JDBC will require transposing the data not once, but twice! Once for the database to provide row-oriented data to the ODBC/JDBC API for its driver, then a second time for the consumer to get it back into columns. This is depicted in *Figure 11.1*, showing the difference between a dedicated column-oriented API such as Arrow Flight, and row-oriented APIs such as ODBC/JDBC:

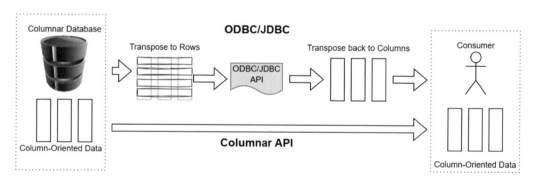

Figure 11.1 – Columnar API versus ODBC/JDBC API

Even when an ODBC API provides bulk access directly to the result buffers, the data still needs to be copied into Arrow arrays for use with any libraries or utilities that expect Arrow-formatted data. The goal of Flight SQL is to remove these intermediate steps and make it easier for database developers to develop a single standard interface designed around Apache Arrow and column-oriented data. Currently, any new database would need to design its own (or use an existing) wire protocol for communication between the database and the ODBC driver. For a database, *Figure 11.2* shows how Flight SQL could simplify things:

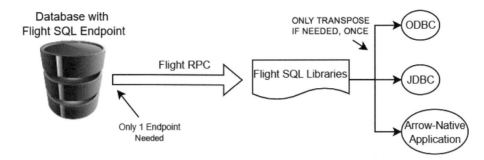

Figure 11.2 – Database with Flight SQL

Databases could use Flight directly, which already implements features such as encryption and authentication, without having to re-implement any of these features. Additionally, this would enable databases to easily benefit from the other features of Flight, such as the parallelization and horizontal scaling. While Flight defines operations such as DoGet and DoPut, it leaves the exact form of the commands used up to the application developer. Flight SQL takes this further and fully defines a SQL interface over the Flight wire protocol, complete with enumeration values, metadata structures, and operations. If you're building a database server, using Flight SQL gives you all the benefits of Arrow Flight, while still having a strongly defined universal interface to code against for you and your consumers.

Revisiting our comparison with ODBC, an important thing to note is that Flight SQL provides a unified driver and protocol, while ODBC only provides a unified API. The difference to highlight here is emphasized in *Figure 11.3*:

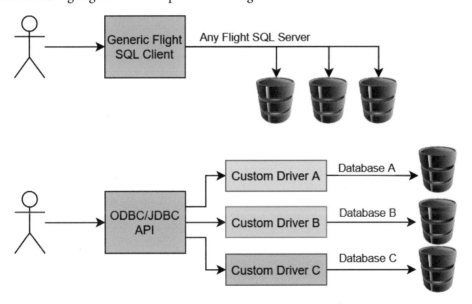

Figure 11.3 – Flight SQL versus ODBC/JDBC drivers

Using the generic Flight SQL client libraries allows you to connect to any server that uses Flight SQL. There's no additional work needed by a user or database vendor; just connect to the Flight SQL server and you're good to go. On the contrary, as *Figure 11.3* shows, ODBC may provide a generic API to write code against, but it requires a custom driver for a given database. Supporting multiple databases requires multiple, different drivers. To support ODBC/JDBC, database vendors have to create and distribute the specific drivers that facilitate connecting to their database. This difference in development burden is what's being referred to by saying that ODBC only provides a unified API while Flight SQL lifts the burden because it is a combined driver and protocol.

So, how does Flight SQL extend the regular Flight protocol?

Defining the Flight SQL protocol

The Flight SQL protocol defines new request and response message types using Protobuf to be used on top of the existing Arrow Flight RPC messages. While we'll briefly go over the new message types, we're not going to cover them as in-depth as we did for Flight. If you want to see the full definitions of the Flight SQL messages, you can look at the .proto file in the Arrow repository at https://github.com/apache/arrow/blob/release-7.0.0/format/FlightSql.proto.

The vast majority of requests for Flight SQL utilize this pattern:

1. The client uses one of the pre-defined Protobuf messages to construct a request.

2. The client sends the request using either the GetSchema method (to query what the schema of the response would be) or the GetFlightInfo method (to execute the request).

3. The client uses the endpoints returned from GetFlightInfo to request the response(s).

All the usual suspects appear as predefined messages in Flight SQL's protocol:

- **Requesting metadata**: The various message types for requesting metadata about the SQL database itself, including the available tables, keys, and SQL information:

  - CommandGetCatalogs – Get a list of catalogs from the database.

  - CommandGetCrossReference – Get a list of foreign key columns in one table referencing a specific table.

  - CommandGetDbSchemas – Get a list of schemas in a catalog.

  - CommandGetExportedKeys – Get a list of foreign keys referencing a table.

  - CommandGetImportedKeys – Get a list of foreign keys in a table.

- `CommandGetPrimaryKeys` – Get a list of primary keys from a table.

- `CommandGetSqlInfo` – Get database information and the dialect of SQL it supports.

- `CommandGetTables` – Get a list of tables in a catalog/schema.

- `CommandGetTableTypes` – Get a list of table types that are supported by the database, such as views and system tables.

- **Querying data**: The Protobuf messages for performing queries and creating prepared statements:

- `CommandStatementQuery` – Execute a SQL query.

- `CommandStatementUpdate` – Execute a SQL update query.

- Manipulating prepared statements:

  - `ActionCreatePreparedStatementRequest` – Create a new prepared statement.

  - `ActionClosePreparedStatementRequest` – Close a prepared statement handle.

  - `CommandPreparedStatementQuery` – Execute a prepared statement with the provided bound parameter values.

  - `CommandPreparedStatementUpdateQuery` – Execute a prepared statement that updates data with provided bound parameter values.

To utilize these message types, you simply serialize them to bytes and send them in the body of a `FlightDescriptor` or `DoAction` request to the Flight SQL server. In the Arrow GitHub repository, you can find the following examples:

- A C++ Flight SQL server implementation that wraps a SQLite instance: `https://github.com/apache/arrow/blob/release-7.0.0/cpp/src/arrow/flight/sql/example/sqlite_server.h`

- A Java Flight SQL server implementation that uses JDBC internally to bridge a connection to Apache Derby: `https://github.com/apache/arrow/blob/release-7.0.0/java/flight/flight-sql/src/test/java/org/apache/arrow/flight/sql/example/FlightSqlExample.java`

- A simple Flight SQL CLI client implementation: `https://github.com/apache/arrow/blob/release-7.0.0/cpp/src/arrow/flight/sql/test_app_cli.cc`

It's expected that there will be more refinements and extensions to this protocol as development continues and more individuals get involved, either as contributors or adopters of Flight SQL. Currently, the only engine I'm aware of that supports Flight SQL is Dremio Sonar. This makes sense given that engineers from Dremio were heavily involved in both the creation of Flight and Flight SQL in the first place! Other expected future improvements are Python bindings, Go bindings, and a generic ODBC/JDBC driver that communicates via Flight SQL. If this has piqued your interest and you want to get involved, reach out on the Arrow mailing lists or directly on the Arrow GitHub repository!

Up next, Arrow DataFusion and Ballista!

Firing a Ballista using Data(Fusion)

Started as a personal project, the distributed compute platform called **Ballista** was donated to the Arrow project. Ballista is implemented in **Rust** and powered by Arrow as its internal memory model. Underneath Ballista's scheduling and coordination infrastructure is Arrow **DataFusion**, a query planning and execution framework. What does all this mean? Well, I'm glad you asked!

Most large data computation is done using some sort of distributed cluster. Multiple machines work together in a coordinated fashion to complete complex tasks. A great example of a framework like this you might be familiar with is Apache Spark. Currently, the architecture of Ballista looks something like *Figure 11.4*. You'll note the usage of Arrow Flight as the communication protocol along with a client for Rust and Python:

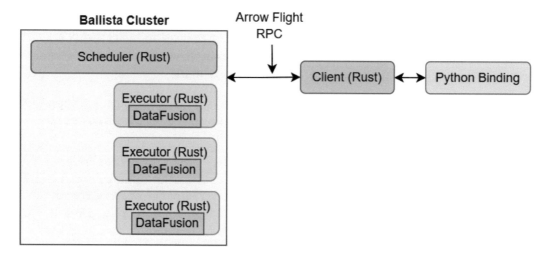

Figure 11.4 – Ballista cluster architecture (today)

The end goal of the project is to eventually have an architecture that looks like *Figure 11.5*. You can see integrated executors for user-defined functions in multiple programming languages, along with client connections for existing Spark pipelines and other utilities for ease of use. Using Arrow Flight as communication between executors allows for data to be passed between different languages with minimal overhead!

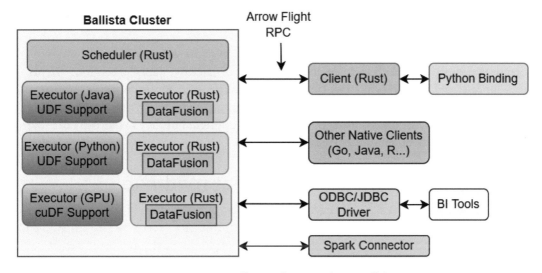

Figure 11.5 – Ballista architecture (eventually)

There's a long way to go with the development as it's still a fairly new project, but everything is looking extremely promising with it. As expected though, a large question that frequently comes up is how Ballista and DataFusion relate to Spark and why you'd want to use them instead of just using Spark. So, let's address that.

What about Spark?

Ballista's primary inspiration was, of course, Apache Spark. However, there are some significant differences between Spark and Ballista, which makes it a particularly interesting project:

- Ballista is written using the Rust language, which does not utilize a garbage collector or special runtime. As a result, Ballista's memory usage is much more deterministic than Spark's and does not have the overhead of pauses caused by a garbage collector.

- Although there is some column-oriented support in Spark, for the most part, it is still currently row-based. Instead, from the beginning, Ballista has been designed to be efficient with columnar data so that it can leverage the vectorized processing of **single instruction, multiple data (SIMD)**, and even utilize GPUs.

- Using Rust along with the Arrow libraries in it can result in some cases where Ballista requires 5x to 10x less memory than Spark. This means you can do more processing on a single node at a time and need fewer nodes to run your workloads.

- One of the largest restrictions on Apache Spark is how you can interface with it. Because of the usage of Arrow and Arrow Flight, executors for Ballista and DataFusion can be written in any language with very little overhead costs by being able to communicate by utilizing Arrow directly.

So far, DataFusion can be embedded and used as an in-process query executor and it can be combined with Ballista to create a cluster for distributed query execution. Clients exist in Rust and Python so far, but since it utilizes Flight RPC for its communication, it's possible to easily create clients in other programming languages. Ballista and DataFusion may be in the early stages of their development, but they are already capable of significantly performant query execution at scale.

Looking at Ballista's development roadmap

You can already deploy a Ballista cluster using Docker or Kubernetes if you want to test it out. You can find all the documentation, and more, at `https://arrow.apache.org/datafusion/index.html`. But, before we move on to the next topic, let me whet your appetite with the published roadmap containing the current priorities of contributors.

For Ballista, the current priorities are to evolve its architecture to allow for deployment in multi-tenant cloud-native environments, such as a cluster stretching across servers in both AWS and Microsoft Azure. First and foremost, ensuring that Ballista is scalable, elastic, and stable enough for production usage is the highest priority. After that, the next priority they have published is to develop more comprehensive distributed machine learning capabilities. If you're looking for something that can do any or all of this, you should probably watch the Ballista project for further updates and keep an eye out.

For DataFusion, aside from general enhancements and improvements to query optimization and execution, **interoperability** is a big priority. The addition of support for nested/complex structures (list and struct columns), along with better support and performance when reading data from remote locations such as S3, are both big priorities. Additionally, there is a desire to add DataFrame APIs, similar to Spark and pandas, to make it easier to integrate DataFusion and Ballista into existing computation pipelines.

DataFusion is already in use by several projects and its community continues to grow while still being intimately tied to the Arrow ecosystem. It's a worthwhile project to check out and worth your time to keep an eye on if you have any interest in distributed computation or something that could be faster and easier to use than Spark. I highly recommend checking out both the documentation and the GitHub repository at `https://github.com/apache/arrow-datafusion`. You won't be disappointed!

> **Note**
>
> Just to call attention to it, unlike the other Arrow library implementations, the Rust language Arrow implementation is not under the formal Apache Arrow repository at `https://github.com/apache/arrow`. Likewise, DataFusion is also in its own separate repository from the primary Arrow GitHub repository. The Rust library can instead be found at `https://github.com/apache/arrow-rs`.

Now for something very different: Substrait and Arrow Compute IR!

Building a cross-language compute serialization

It may surprise you to know that SQL execution engines don't actually execute SQL directly! (Or you may already know this, in which case, good job!) Under the hood of your favorite query engine, what happens is that it parses the query into some intermediate representation of the query and executes that. There are multiple reasons for this:

- It's really hard to optimize a SQL query directly and be sure that you haven't changed the semantics of what it is doing. Translating to an intermediate representation allows for easier, programmatic optimizations that are guaranteed to be equivalent to the original query.

- Abstracting the specific query language (ANSI SQL versus other dialects) from the execution reduces the impact that changes to the language have on the execution engine. As long as the same intermediate representation is created by the parser, it doesn't matter what changes in the query language.

- Representing a query as a logical or physical plan allows different optimizations to be made to improve performance based on deeper knowledge of the current resources available.

Figure 11.6 represents a simplified view of the flow of a query going through these steps:

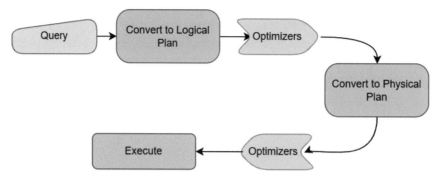

Figure 11.6 – Simplified query execution path

This approach is similarly taken by the LLVM compiler architecture that we mentioned when discussing Gandiva in the context of Dremio Sonar during *Chapter 9, Powered by Apache Arrow*. In that case, the compiler system is made up of several components, but I want to focus on three of them:

- Frontend modules that produce an intermediate representation for individual programming languages such as C/C++, Java, and Fortran

- A series of optimization modules that operate on the produced intermediate representation

- A code generator that can produce machine code from the intermediate representation for a variety of different processor architectures

Why should we architect the system like this, and what does this have to do with analytical computations with Arrow? Consider the life cycle of a query having three parts to it: the query itself, a parser/plan generator, and an execution engine for that plan. What if you could easily swap each of these pieces out for other modules without breaking your existing workflows? This would allow you to easily connect any plan generation you want to any execution engine you want, as shown in *Figure 11.7*. This is the goal of a project called **Substrait** (https://substrait.io):

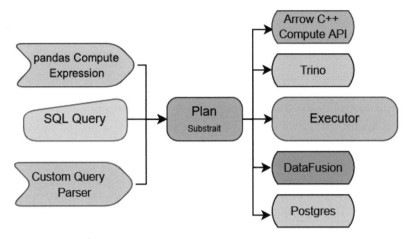

Figure 11.7 – Substrait's goal

As long as everyone can agree on what that intermediate representation looks like and how it should be built, both the producers and consumers of it can be swapped around. Consider taking an existing SQL parser and allowing it to communicate execution plans to an Arrow C++ computation kernel. Or, maybe allowing the execution of pandas expressions directly inside of a different execution engine without the overhead of passing the data to Python. While Arrow creates a standardized in-memory representation of columnar data, Substrait aims to create a standardized representation of the operations to be done on data. **Arrow Compute IR** is an implementation in the Arrow libraries of consuming that representation.

> **Keep in Mind**
>
> One thing to note is prototypes are being built to potentially include Substrait plans as a Flight SQL command type. Keep an eye out for more on this in the future!

Why Substrait?

Substrait is intended to be a cross-language specification for compute operations on data. The idea is to have a consistent way to describe common operations or custom operations, with the semantics strictly defined. Anything that can produce or consume the standard would then be able to interoperate with anything else that also does so. Many different projects and communities could benefit from this sort of a standardized effort, but they all have their own disparate existing systems. To resolve the competing priorities between various projects, one of the proposals for Substrait is to only incorporate something into the specification if it is supported by at least two of what they refer to as the *"top four OSS data technologies"*: *Arrow, Spark, Iceberg*, and *Trino*.

Because Substrait is not coupled to any individual technology that already exists, it should be easier to drive its adoption and get people involved. It's not driven by a single community but rather by many individuals involved in many different data communities all injecting their own ideas, pain points, and considerations. It is a new and independent community of individuals that work with data and want to see this new level of interoperability get achieved between projects. As such, in addition to a specification, Substrait will define a serialization format for these plans and representations.

Working with Substrait serialization

There are two defined serialization types for Substrait's specification: binary serialization using Protobuf and text serialization using JSON. Why these two?

Binary serialization is intended for *performance* and needs to be easy to work with in many languages. By defining the serialization using a binary definition language, someone can take just the binary format definition and build tools for any language without having to directly rely on the Substrait project itself. In this case, using Protobuf, the `.proto` definition files can be used to build libraries for any language to work with the specification. While many formats exist that can be used to provide a compact binary serialization with generators for most languages, the project chose Protobuf due to *"its clean typing system and large number of high-quality language bindings."*

Text serialization, on the other hand, is not designed for performance but for *readability*. By providing a text-based serialization format, it is much easier to bring new users into the project. Simple command-line utilities can be built for converting SQL queries to Substrait plans or vice versa, among other potential basic tooling. Hopefully, this will promote more experimentation and adoption among interested individuals, making it easier to jump right in and play with the specification.

Currently, there isn't much in the way of tooling for Substrait plans as it's still very much in the early stages, but a few examples of potential planned tools could be a pluggable query plan visualization tool or enabling query planning as a microservice.

Getting involved with Substrait development

Substrait is consensus-driven and released under the Apache 2.0 open source license, with development on GitHub. You can get in touch with the community via GitHub issues and pull requests, or via Twitter and Slack. All the information necessary to get involved can be found on the Substrait website: `https://substrait.io/community/`. There's much more work to be done with, in my opinion, an extremely great goal. If nothing else, you should definitely keep an eye on the progress of the project and how it ends up affecting other related projects such as Arrow, Apache Calcite, Iceberg, and Spark. It'll be interesting to see how widely adopted Substrait and Arrow's Compute IR can become, and how it potentially changes the shape of the data science tooling ecosystem. Go read about it! Go!

Final words

This brings us to the end of *this* journey. I've tried to pack lots of useful information, tips, tricks, and diagrams into this book, but there's also plenty of room for much more research and experimentation on your end! If you haven't done so already, go back and try the various exercises I've proposed in the chapters. Explore new things with the Arrow datasets and compute APIs, and try using Arrow Flight in your own work.

Across the various chapters in this book, we've covered a lot of stuff, such as the following:

- The Arrow format specification
- Using the Arrow libraries to improve many aspects of analytical computation and data science
- Inter-process communication and sharing memory
- Using Apache Spark, pandas, and Jupyter in conjunction with Arrow
- Utilizing existing tools for interactive visualizations
- The differences between data storage formats and in-memory runtime formats
- Passing data across the boundaries of programming languages without having to copy it
- Using gRPC and Arrow Flight RPC to build highly performant distributed data systems
- The impact that Arrow is having on the data science ecosystem by highlighting several projects that are using it

Hopefully, you can find a lot of use for the content we've covered here and this book can serve as a reference book of sorts for you. I expect that Arrow is only going to continue to get wider adoption among the data science and analytical ecosystems, and now you'll have a leg up on understanding it all.

It doesn't matter if you're a software engineer, data scientist, or someone else, don't stop at just *using* the Arrow libraries in your work. Learn from the concepts and ideas that were put into these projects and try to find new ways to apply them in your own projects, whether they are personal or professional. Like anything else, Arrow and its related technologies are the culmination of many individuals working together and building upon the ideas that came before them. Maybe you'll come up with something else new and different that you can contribute back to the community! Who knows?

Enjoy, take care, and above all else, have fun with this stuff!

Index

Packt.com

Subscribe to our online digital library for full access to over 7,000 books and videos, as well as industry leading tools to help you plan your personal development and advance your career. For more information, please visit our website.

Why subscribe?

- Spend less time learning and more time coding with practical eBooks and Videos from over 4,000 industry professionals

- Improve your learning with Skill Plans built especially for you

- Get a free eBook or video every month

- Fully searchable for easy access to vital information

- Copy and paste, print, and bookmark content

Did you know that Packt offers eBook versions of every book published, with PDF and ePub files available? You can upgrade to the eBook version at packt.com and as a print book customer, you are entitled to a discount on the eBook copy. Get in touch with us at customercare@packtpub.com for more details.

At www.packt.com, you can also read a collection of free technical articles, sign up for a range of free newsletters, and receive exclusive discounts and offers on Packt books and eBooks.

Other Books You May Enjoy

If you enjoyed this book, you may be interested in these other books by Packt:

Hands-On Data Analysis with Pandas - Second Edition

Stefanie Molin

ISBN: 9781800563452

- Understand how data analysts and scientists gather and analyze data
- Perform data analysis and data wrangling using Python
- Combine, group, and aggregate data from multiple sources
- Create data visualizations with pandas, matplotlib, and seaborn
- Apply machine learning algorithms to identify patterns and make predictions
- Use Python data science libraries to analyze real-world datasets
- Solve common data representation and analysis problems using pandas
- Build Python scripts, modules, and packages for reusable analysis code

Python Data Analysis - Third Edition

Avinash Navlani, Armando Fandango, Ivan Idris

ISBN: 9781789955248

- Explore data science and its various process models

- Perform data manipulation using NumPy and pandas for aggregating, cleaning, and handling missing values

- Create interactive visualizations using Matplotlib, Seaborn, and Bokeh

- Retrieve, process, and store data in a wide range of formats

- Understand data preprocessing and feature engineering using pandas and scikit-learn

- Perform time series analysis and signal processing using sunspot cycle data

- Analyze textual data and image data to perform advanced analysis

- Get up to speed with parallel computing using Dask

Packt is searching for authors like you

If you're interested in becoming an author for Packt, please visit `authors.packtpub.com` and apply today. We have worked with thousands of developers and tech professionals, just like you, to help them share their insight with the global tech community. You can make a general application, apply for a specific hot topic that we are recruiting an author for, or submit your own idea.

Share Your Thoughts

Now you've finished *In-Memory Analytics with Apache Arrow*, we'd love to hear your thoughts! Scan the QR code below to go straight to the Amazon review page for this book and share your feedback or leave a review on the site that you purchased it from.

https://packt.link/r/1-801-07103-9

Your review is important to us and the tech community and will help us make sure we're delivering excellent quality content.

Made in United States
Troutdale, OR
05/05/2024

19604503R10236